Rājadharma in Mahābhārata

Reconstructing Indian History and Culture, no. 37

Rājadharma in Mahābhārata

With Special Reference to Śānti-Parva

Priyanka Pandey

DK PRINTWORLD
Publishers of Indian Traditions

Cataloging in Publication Data — DK
[Courtesy: D.K. Agencies (P) Ltd. <docinfo@dkagencies.com>]
Pandey, Priyanka, 1986-
Rājadharma in Mahābhārata : in particular reference to Śānti-parva / Priyanka Pandey.
p. cm. (Reconstructing Indian history and culture; no. 37)
Includes bibliographical references (p.).
ISBN 13: 9788124608012

1. Mahābhārata. Śāntiparva – Criticism, interpretation, etc. 2. Hinduism and politics – India. 3. State, The, in literature. I. Title. II. Series: Reconstructing Indian history and culture; no. 37.

DDC 294.5923046 23

ISBN 13: 978-81-246-0801-2
First published in India in 2018

Printed and published by:
D.K. Printworld (P) Ltd.
Regd. Office: "Vedaśrī", F-395, Sudarshan Park
(Metro Station: ESI Hospital)
New Delhi - 110015
Phones: (011) 2545 3975; 2546 6019
e-mail: indology@dkprintworld.com
Website: www.dkprintworld.com

To
my dear
Father and Mother

नारायणं नमस्कृत्य नरं चैव नरोत्तमम्।
देवीं सरस्वतीं व्यासं ततो जयमुदीरयेत्॥

nārāyaṇaṁ namaskr̥tya naraṁ caiva narottamaṁ ।
devīṁ sarasvatīṁ vyāsaṁ tato jayamudīrayeta ॥

Mbh, Ādi-Parva I.1

Preface

What is here is found elsewhere.
What is not here is nowhere else.
— *Mahābhārata* I.62.53

Mahābhārata is a huge monument of Sanskrit literature. It is generally considered as a literary text and is one of the two great epics of India. It is the encyclopaedia of ancient India as it deals with different subjects in different contexts. It was enlarged at different periods by persons of different regions, time and mentalities. It occupies an important place in Indian tradition. Its importance lies in the fact that it has summarized the views of Indian political thinkers and further, its writers have discussed numerous political problems in detail and supplies various problems regarding the relation between man and state. Many scholars have tried to study the political ideas contained in *Mahābhārata*, many books have come to light dealing with the same subject. The idea of politics hardly finds an expression elsewhere as clearly as in *Mahābhārata*. The present work, in this regard is a modest attempt in the same direction. The purpose of the present work is to investigate the political thought in Śānti-Parva of *Mahābhārata*. The focus is to carve out the idea of the politics in the text. As we know in recent debates on the idea of the politics there are several positions like modernist and postmodernist.

One suggests that "political" defines the activities related to the statecraft, whereas the other proposes to take over personal as political. The main intention here is to make an intervention in the contemporary debate from the point of view of Sanskrit knowledge tradition. There are scholars in the West who have recently started exploring the political dimension of this knowledge system, however, their inability to comprehend the larger canvas of Sanskrit knowledge system fails them in such an endeavour. This book anchors itself in longer context of Indian philosophy and tries to read the political context of the text, which is considered merely as a religion or a literary text.

The aim of this work is show that *Mahābhārata*, apart from being an epic, is also a text in the study of politics. Whatever notion of politics we take, there is a possibility to find good amount of resources in *Mahābhārata* to articulate an Indian notion in this field. By comparing the notion of politics in the West, taking mainly the Greek tradition of thinking represented by Aristotle, and the Indian tradition represented by Śānti-Parva of *Mahābhārata*, I would like to argue that there are many similarities and dissimilarities between the two. Our central aim is to show that the idea of politics is not separated from the idea of ethics. The point perhaps will become clear if we explore the way these institutions are conceptualized. Therefore it is highly essential to study the notion of politics in *Mahābhārata* in the present context. The major focus areas of this work are:

1. Read *Mahābhārata* as a political text
2. Idea of political thoughts in Śānti-Parva
3. Constituting principles of politics in Śānti-Parva
4. Political institutions in Śānti-Parva
5. Relevance of these political thoughts in modern time.

The work has adopted the following methods in its course of delineation:

1. It has tried to interpret the original Sanskrit text, Śānti-Parva in relation to its political thinking.
2. Beside this, other writings on Indian political thoughts are also taken into account, via books, journals, articles, etc.
3. This work is focused on both the primary and secondary writings on *Mahābhārata*, by enquiring the basic political principles in Śānti-Parva.

4. It produces a comparative and critical study of the political thoughts in *Mahābhārata* with the modern politics, finding its place in the history of political thought.

Sources

For the present work, the following sources have been utilized.

1. *Mahābhārata* (Critical Edition), ed. V.S. Sukthankar, Poona, Bhandarakar Oriental Research Institute, 1933-66.

   (The complete edition of *Mahābhārata* (18 parvas, 89,000 verses in the constituent text and elaborate critical apparatus; 19 volumes; no. of pages: 13,000 + demi quarto size) was released on 22 September 1966. This edition was prepared with painstaking efforts of scholars for about five decades consulting 1,259 manuscripts.)
2. *Mahābhārata* (6 volumes in Hindi and Sanskrit), ed. Pandit Ramanarayana Dutt Shastri Pandey, Gita Press, Gorakhpur, 1980.

Other secondary sources consist of *Bhāratabhāva-Dīpīkā*, Nīlakaṇṭha's commentary on the epic, different translations of, and general works on *Mahābhārata*. Some other books like *Rāmāyaṇa*, *Manu-Smṛti*, *Kāmandakīya Nītisāra* and *Śukra-Nītisāra* have also been taken into account. Many books on political science have also been referred. And the writings of Indian and Western scholars have also been consulted. At some places archaeological, numismatic and epigraphic evidences have been used.

Beside the utilization of the secondary sources, attempt has been made to go through the reviews both of the occidentalists as well as of the orientalists. A glance at the reviews of the books has helped in two ways. One, it has given information about the limitations as pointed out by the reviewers in the scholarly works, and two, it also has made the researcher balanced in thought and meditation on the discussed problems. Hence the chapter-wise analysis of the topic has been made. The extant research is undertaken from the political point of view. The evidences of the epic have been collected as possible aid to research. They have also been used tentatively as historical material.

The topics, namely, *daṇḍanīti*, origin of state, the seven elements of state, functions of state, types of state, kingship, judiciary, administration, etc. have been discussed. The internal evidences from Śānti-Parva and also from other *parva*s of the epic have been collected, analysed and examined. The decisive conclusion made through introspection is tested on the objective data provided by the analytical chart. Thus, the work is the composite result of textual analysis, related literature and subjective contemplation.

Contents

List of Tables and Figures

Tables

Figures

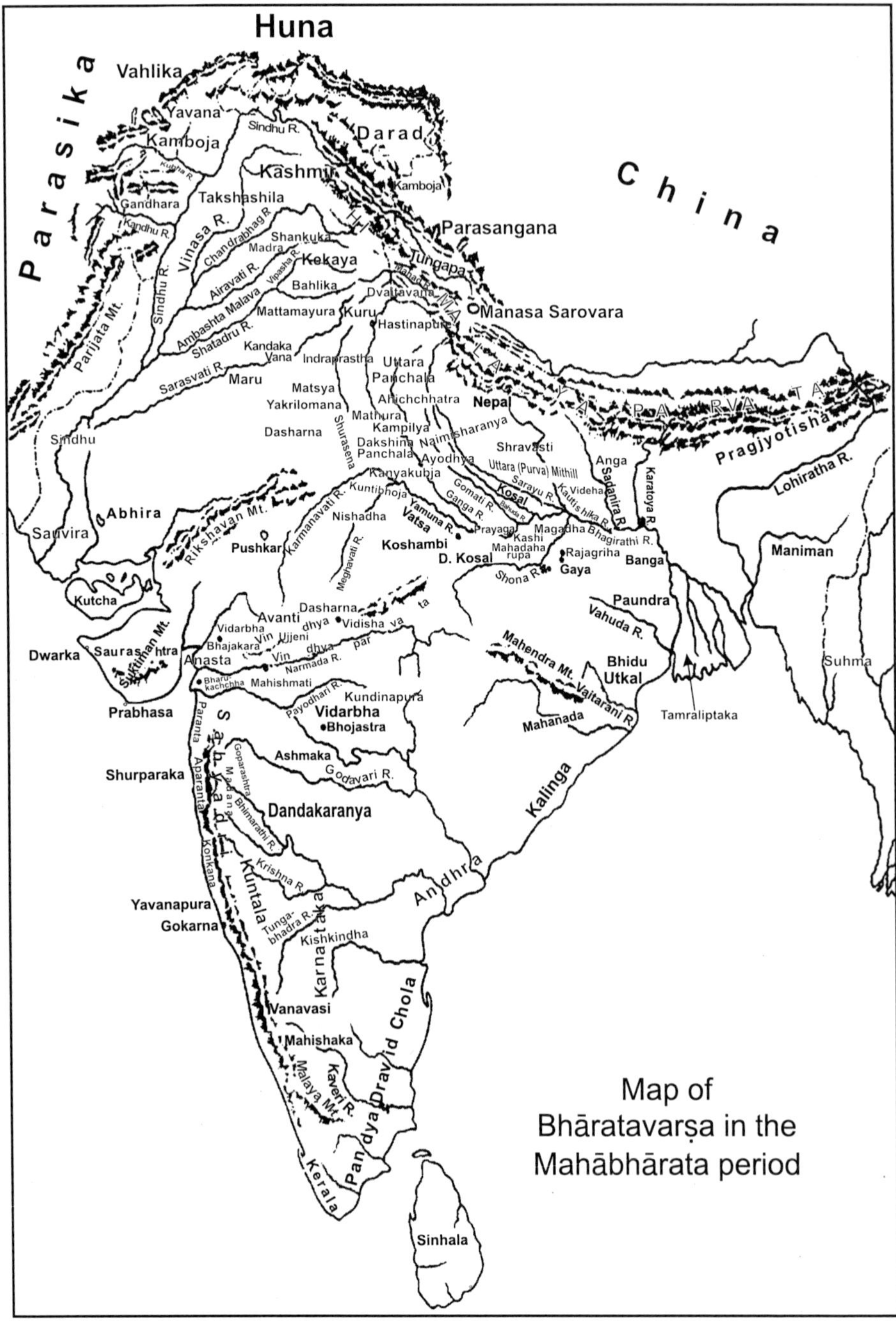

Map of Bhāratavarṣa in the Mahābhārata period

Abbreviations

ABORI	*Annals of Bhandarkar Oriental Research Institute*
AitBrā	*Aitareya Brāhmaṇa*
BhāgavataP	*Bhāgavata Purāṇa*
BṛUp	*Bṛhdāraṇyaka Upaniṣad*
BrSaṁ	*Bṛhat Saṁhitā*
Gītā	*Bhagavadgītā*
IHQ	*Indian Historical Quarterly*
JAOS	*Journal of the American Oriental Society*
JRAS	*Journal of the Royal Asiatic Society*
NK	*Nītisāra* of Kāmandaka
KA	*Kauṭilya Arthaśāstra*
Manu	*Manu-Smṛti*
Mbh	*Mahābhārata*
NŚ	*Nītisāra of Śukra*
ŚP	Śānti Parva
YS	*Yājñavalkya-Smṛti*

Transliteration Key

अ	=	a	ढ्	=	ḍh
आ	=	ā	ण्	=	ṇ
इ	=	i	त्	=	t
ई	=	ī	थ्	=	th
उ	=	u	द्	=	d
ऊ	=	ū	ध्	=	dh
ऋ	=	ṛ	न्	=	n
ॠ	=	ṝ	प्	=	p
ऌ	=	ḷ	फ्	=	ph
ए	=	e	ब्	=	b
ऐ	=	ai	भ्	=	bh
ओ	=	o	म्	=	m
औ	=	au	य्	=	y
क्	=	k	र्	=	r
ख्	=	kh	ल्	=	l
ग्	=	g	व्	=	v
घ्	=	gh	श्	=	ś
ङ्	=	ṅ	ष्	=	ṣ
च्	=	c	स्	=	s
छ्	=	ch	ह्	=	h
ज्	=	j	क्ष्	=	kṣ
झ्	=	jh	त्र्	=	tr
ञ्	=	ñ	ज्ञ्	=	jñ
ट्	=	ṭ	ऽ	=	’
ठ्	=	ṭh	ं (*Anusvāra*)	=	ṁ
ड्	=	ḍ	: (*visarga*)	=	ḥ

Acknowledgements

My efforts to accomplish this book would not have been possible, without the love, affection, help, guidance and encouragement of a number of people and institutions. Their altruistic contributions deserve to be recalled.

First and foremostly, I am grateful to my esteemed supervisor Dr Santosh Kumar Shukla, Associate Professor of Special Centre for Sanskrit Studies (SCSS), JNU, and to my respected co-supervisor Dr Manindra Nath Thakur, Associate Professor of CPS, JNU, for their perspective guidance, inspiration, encouragement, feedback and cooperation despite their busy schedule. Their gracious propositions have propelled me to academically explore whole new things. I am highly indebted to them.

I express my sincere gratitude and thanks to our Chairperson, Prof. Girish Nath Jha and other faculty members, namely, Dr Hari Ram Mishra, Dr Ram Nath Jha, Dr Rajnish Mishra, Dr Sudhir Kumar and to Dr Shashiprabha Kumar, SCSS, JNU, New Delhi for encouraging and allowing this work to come into fruition. I am thankful to the staff members of Jawaharlal Nehru University Library, University of Delhi Library and University of Allahabad Library for their timely assistance in finding out the right materials. I also express my sincere thanks to all the office staff of my centre and those who directly or indirectly helped me in completing this work.

I will be indebted forever to the unconditional and immutable love of my parents father Shri Pramod Chandra Pandey and mother Smt. Malti Pandey. I am delighted by recalling the adorable moral back-up that I have received from my elder sister Vandana and elder brothers

Bhupendra, Rajan and Pankaj. I am deeply indebted to my sister Monika and brother Rahul for their prayers, affection and immense support. Also it is hard to forget the lovely and unbreakable talks of Aditya and Gaargi. I owe my sincere gratitude to my *mamaji*, Shri Jaideva Mishra and to my *jijaji* Vashistha Narayana Shukla for their constant love and encouragement for completing this work.

I am very appreciative of unmatched help provided by my friends, classmates and seniors. They have been with me in each and every bit of my sufferings.

I also convey my gratitude and thanks to all the persons and institutions, those who have overtly or covertly propelled me miles towards this academic horizon. Without their cooperation this book could not have come out in its final form.

1

Mahābhārata : An Introduction

majjet trayī daṇḍanītau hatāyāṁ
sarve dharmāḥ prakṣayeyurvibuddhāḥ ।
sarve dharmāścāśramāṇāṁ hatāḥ syuḥ
kṣātre tyakte rājadharme purāṇe ॥

sarve tyāgā rājadharmeṣu dṛṣṭāḥ
sarvā dīkṣā rājadharmeṣu coktāḥ ।
sarvā vidyā rājadharmeṣu yuktāḥ
sarve lokā rājadharme praviṣṭāḥ ॥
— Śānti-Parva LXIII.28.29

In the history of literature, world literature in general and Sanskrit literature in particular, *Mahābhārata* occupies a central place. Perhaps after *Rāmāyaṇa* this great epic has deeply influenced the minds of scholars and researchers as well as of common people. So many of the scholars considered it as Itihāsa[1] (*itihās purṇābhyāṁ vedaṁ samupbṛhayet*), Purāṇa,[2] Ākhyāna,[3] Saṁhitā,[4] Kāvya[5] and the sources and basis of all the legends. It is the fifth Veda, namely, the Kārṣṇa Veda,[6] i.e. the Veda of Kṛṣṇa Dvaipāyana Vyāsa, being Kṛṣṇa Dvaipāyana Vyāsa its author. It is mentioned in the Svargārohaṇa-Parva that Vyāsa completed this work after working hard for three years:

---

1 Ādi-Parva I.19, 26, 54, 87, CCLXVI.67; II.36, 385.

2 Ibid. CCLXVI.67.

3 Ibid. II.33, 382, 384, 386, 390.

4 Ibid. I.21, 102.

5 Ibid. I.61, 72-73; II.390.

6 Ibid. I.268.

tribhirvarṣairidaṁ pūrṇaṁ kṛṣṇadvaipāyanaḥ prabhuḥ।
akhilaṁ bhārtaṁ cedaṁ cakāra bhagavān muniḥ॥

— Svargārohaṇa-Parva V.48

Mahābhārata is considered as the essence for all the Vedas. By itself it is equal to, nay, even greater than the remaining Vedas.[7] Hence one should study the Vedas with its help:

itihāsapurāṇābhyāṁ vedaṁ samupabṛṁhayet ॥

bibhetyalpaśrutād vedo māmayaṁ prahariṣyati ।

— Ibid. I.267-68

Besides these it is known as Dharmaśāstra, Arthaśāstra and Kāmaśāstra.[8] There is much truth in Vyāsa's challenge that:

dharme cārthe ca kāme ca mokṣe ca bharatarṣabha ।
yadihāsti tadanyatra yannehāsti na tat kvacit ॥

— Ibid. I.62.53

That which occurs here about *dharma, artha, kāma* and *mokṣa* (four ends of human life), occurs elsewhere and that which does not occur here, occurs nowhere else.

It is really an encyclopaedia of Indian intellectual tradition in which social, moral, ethical, economical and political conditions are described extensively. It removes ignorance the way sun removes darkness.[9] By its name, it is self-explanatory. In Svargārohaṇa-Parva, it has been stated that the significance of *Mahābhārata* lies in its greatness and weightiness. In Ādi-Parva, the meaning of the two compound words (*mahā-bhārata*) finds mention in more clear terms. Being a voluminous (*mahat*) work and heavy (*bhāravat*) to lift and carry, the great epic came to be called *Mahābhārata*. It contains a detail of life and death of Kuru *vaṁśa*, hence it is identified with *Mahābhārata*. As stated:

mahattvād bhāravattvācca mahābhāratamucyate ।

---

[7] Ādi-Parva I.271-72.

[8] Ibid. II.383.

[9] Ibid. II.84-87.

niruktamasya yo veda sarvapāpaiḥ pramucyate ||
— Ādi-Parva I.274

It is the longest poem known to the literary history with 100,000 verses (*śloka*s). So far as the prefix *mahā* is concerned, it is justified to add that *Mahābhārata* is larger than *Iliad* and *Odyssey* both in size and contents. Even the Vedas have a diminishing utility in comparison and contrast with *Mahābhārata*. The internal evidences of *Mahābhārata* refer to the utility of its study. Second, one should study the Vedas with its help. It is further stated that when one's knowledge of the Vedas is superfluous and useless, one delves into *Mahābhārata*. There is one more ground which adds a feather to its significance. It is open for both scholars and laymen. It will not be out of place to discuss its importance so far as its readers, reciters and listeners are concerned. Its study is fruitful for everyone irrespective of one's profession and caste (*varṇa*). It has been stated in Ādi-Parva that one gets emancipation and is free from all his committed sins, provided he reads the epic in the early morning.

Even a listener is bestowed with an equal merit if he listens to it. It holds great importance for warriors. One undoubtedly emerges victorious in the battlefield if one reads and listens to it. There is another significance of the epic as it has been interpreted in a different sense by the scholars. In the northern and southern recensions of the epic, it has been emphasized that its reading help to attain victory (*jaya*). R.C. Jain (1979) is desperately busy to prove that *jaya* was the nucleus of *Mahābhārata*. For the support of his statement, he has taken many references from *Ṛgveda* and the Brāhmaṇas.

It has been dwelling on that if the king wants to emerge victorious in the war, he must read the great epic. The advantage of its reading and listening is equal to the merit of Rājasūya and Aśvamedha Yajñas. As stated in Ādi-Parva LXII.21:

mahīṁ vijayate rājā śatrūṁścāpi parājayet |
idaṁ puṁsavanaṁ śreṣṭhamidaṁ svastyayanaṁ mahat ||

It is capable of liberating one from great sins, and of helping one in the attainment of long life, glory and heaven.[10] The merits of this "deathless poem" have been well recognized by many modern scholars also. To Winternitz (1927/1953), it is "in a poetic sense, not one poetic production at all, but rather a whole literature".[11] A.A. Macdonell (1928) calls it an "encyclopaedia of moral teaching".[12] R.C. Dutt (1944: 332) describes it as "an encyclopaedia of the life and knowledge of ancient India" and says "no single work except the Bible has such an influence in affording moral instructions in Christian lands as *Mahābhārata* and *Rāmāyaṇa* in India" (ibid.: 33). According to C. Rajagopalachari (1951) it is a "Veritable ocean, containing countless pearls and gems. It is, with *Rāmāyaṇa*, a living fountain of ethics and culture of our motherland."[13] P.C. Roy (1890) describes it as "pre-eminently the encyclopaedia of the heroic age of the Hindus…".[14]

The epic has several messages and the more one delves into it, the deeper one grasps its meaning. It is considered as the book of education not less significant than that of Plato's *Republic* which supplies information in connection with the education of the philosopher kings and communism of wives. So far as the impact of *Mahābhārata* is concerned; the poet Bāṇa was influenced by it.[15] It also has inspired the dramatists in the past. Ludwig, a Vedic scholar, was of the view that special attention should be paid to study the disjointed pieces of *Mahābhārata* (Sukthankar 1975: 29).

Similarly, Ācārya Śaṅkara and Kumārila, the celebrated Indian philosophers, as well as Jñānaeśvar and Rāmadāsa, the famous Indian

---

10 Ādi-Parva I.269-71.

11 *A History of Indian Literature*, vol. II, p. 316.

12 *A History of Sanskrit Literature*, p. 282.

13 *Mahabharata*, p. 3.

14 *Mbh*, tr. Śānti-Parva (1890), p. 2.

15 Bal Gangadhar Tilak (1965: 787) remarks: "Many of the dramas of Bhāsa have been written on the basis of certain chapters of *Mahābhārata*. It, therefore, follows that *Mahābhārata* was then available and was looked upon the authoritative."

saints, were influenced by its message.[16] Amartya Sen (2006: 3) has also written about it:

> With about one hundred thousand verses, long prose passages, or about 1.8 million words in total, the *Mahābhārata* is roughly seven times the length of *Iliad* and *Odyssey* combined or about the four times the length of *Rāmāyaṇa*.

W.J. Johnson (1998) has compared the importance of *Mahābhārata* to the world civilization to that of Bible, works of Homer and Quran. Though the *phalaśruti* (merit of regarding the people) has been questioned it is not an original part of *Mahābhārata*. But both the southern and northern recensions of *Mahābhārata* refer to its usefulness.

In Indian tradition *Mahābhārata* is considered as the great source of the best ideals (Sukthankar 1975: 30). In the vast parameters of the original narratives of Bharata-Vaṁśī heroes, the preachers of the Dharmārtha and Ākhyāyanas were included in this text. Because of these Ākhyānas, teachings and description on *dharma* and Nīti-Śāstric views, *Mahābhārata* is literally, historically and religiously considered a great and important text of Hindus. According to C.V. Vaidya (vs 1917: 26), *Mahābhārata* is not only a text of history and religion, but it is the best epic. In the starting of the text Veda Vyāsa himself called it poetry[17] and also there is an indication in *Mahābhārata* that this poetry will be *upajīvya* for all the major poets.

sarveṣāṁ kavimukhyānāmupjīvyo bhaviṣyati ||
— Ādi-Parva I.92

Mahābhārata is a great source of motivation for many epics and dramas of the Sanskrit language and also for the Kāvyas of Hindi poets (Sinha 1985: 20). It is the source of motivation for Sanskrit, Hindi and many other Indian languages texts.

---

16 Kumārila, *Tantra-Vārttika*, refers to ten *parva*s out of the eighteen *parva*s of *Mahābhārata*. Quoted by Macdonell 1928: 290-91.

17 *kr̥taṁ mayedaṁ bhagvān kāvya parampūjitaṁ* | — Ādi-Parva CLXI (Gita Press).

Beside these, *Mahābhārata* is also valuable from the political point of view. In *Mahābhārata* abundant materials are available on politics. In Śānti-Parva, a large part named "Rājadharma" is on politics. And many other *parva*s like Ādi, Sabhā, Āraṇyaka and Udyoga also have given valuable information on political ideas.

Many writers, who have written on "Ancient Indian Monarchy" or on the political field, have taken a great amount of valuable materials from *Mahābhārata*. D.R. Bhandarkar, N.C. Vandyopadhyaya, Beni Prasad, R.P. Giri, V.R.R. Dikshitar, T.V. Mahalingam, N.N. Law, P.C. Basu, A.K. Sen, R.C. Majumdar, R.K. Mukherjee, K.P. Jayaswal, J.J. Anjaria and H.N. Sinha are some of the great scholars, who have given their mature contribution to this field. The text *Government in Ancient India* of A.S. Altekar is quite well known. In these texts, the evidences are mainly taken from Śānti-Parva and one or two verses have also been taken from other *parva*s. U.N. Ghoshal in his *A History of Indian Political Ideas* has discussed about "Rājadharama", featured in Śānti-Parva, in four chapters, which is not available in such a form in any other text of political theory. Shyamlal's text, *Bhīṣma kā Rājadharma* is based on the Rājadharma section of *Mahābhārata*.[18] Due to the availability of abundant materials on politics, *Mahābhārata* is selected as the fundamental text for the present work.

Authorship of Mahābhārata

jayati parāśarasūnuḥ satyavatīhṛdayanandano vyāsaḥ ।
vyāsasyakamalagalitaṁ vāṅmayamamṛtaṁ jagat pibati ॥
— Harivaṁśa-Parva II.3

Traditionally, the authorship of *Mahābhārata* is attributed to Vyāsa. It is mentioned in Ādi-Parva that Kṛṣṇa Dvaipāyana Vyāsa was its author. And on the basis of Kṛṣṇa, which forms a part of its supposed author, it is called the Kārṣṇa Veda,[19] the Veda of Kṛṣṇa Dvaipāyana

[18] Mishra, 1972, *Mahābhārata Meiṅ Lokakalyāṇa kī Rājakīya Yojanāyeiṅ*, pp. 17-18.

[19] Ādi-Parva I.268.

Vyāsa. As said in Ādi-Parva I.10:

samīpe pārthivendrasya samyaka parikṣitasya ca ।
kṛṣṇadvaipāyanaproktāḥ supuṇyā vividhāḥ kathāḥ॥

Its critical survey reveals that it is not the composition by a single person, and was not composed within the period of three years but a large number of composers have contributed their shares to rise *Mahābhārata* from *Bhārata*. *Mahābhārata* has undergone many redactions. On the basis of internal evidence, we know with a certain degree of certainty, about its three composers, viz. Vyāsa, Vaiśampāyana and Sauti. The first began it with salutation to Nara, Nārāyaṇa and Sarasvatī, the second with "Sarpaśāstra", i.e. the beginning of the Āstika-Parva and third with the Aṁśāvataraṇa-Parva, whence starts the actual narrative of the Bhārata race.[20]

The epic itself informs that it was composed after the great battle by Vyāsa to spread the fame of the great Pāṇḍavas and other kṣatriyas in the world, and was known as Jaya Kāvya; it is corroborated by the fact that *Mahābhārata* calls itself the Itihāsa —*jaya nāmotihāsoayaṁ*,[21] as it narrates the events of the victory of the Pāṇḍavas over the Kauravas.[22] It is thus apparent that originally the present *Mahābhārata* was a war epic consisting of the heroic songs related to the great battle. This epic was known as Bhārata as it was composed on the theme of battle between Kauravas and Pāṇḍavas by Vyāsa and it consisted of only 24,000 *ślokas*.

---

20 ". . . the poem was recited on three different occasions; the first time by Vyāsa in the presence of his pupils; the second time by the brāhmaṇa Vaiśampāyana, Vyāsa's pupil, during a solemn sacrifice offered in the name of the Janamejaya; the third time by the Sūta Ugraśravā during a sacrifice by the Ṛṣi Śaunaka, a generation later". — G.J. Held, 1935, *The Mahābhārata*, Introduction, p. 3. Cf.

manvādi bhārataṁ kecitdāstīkādi tathā pare ।
tathoparicarādyanye viprāḥ samyagadhīyate ॥ — Ādi-Parva I.52

21 Svargārohaṇa-Parva V.51; see also V.41.

22 Ibid., LVI.19.

caturviṁśatiśāhastrīṁ cakre bhāratasaṁhitāṁ |
upākhyānairvinā tāvad bhārataṁ procyate budhaiḥ ||
— Ādi-Parva I.102

Finally, with the deliberate accession of considerable doses of fresh matter from time to time, aiming the work to be an encyclopaedia of Indian culture with all its components, it assumed the form of the compendium of all the existing knowledge called *Mahābhārata* with about 1,00,000 verses and was appropriately given the descriptive title *Śata-Śāhasrī Saṁhitā*.[23] This conjuncture is supported by *Āśvalāyana Gṛhyasūtra* III.4.4 referring to *Bhārata* and *Mahābhārata* both:

sumantujaiminīvaiśampāyanapailasūtrabhāṣyabhārata-dharmācāryā jānanti ||

Mahābhārata also calls itself by three names, viz. Jaya, Bhārata and Mahābhārata.[24]

Date of Mahābhārata

Dating of *Mahābhārata*, which has given rise to a heated controversy among the scholars, can be seen from the two standpoints: (1) the date of Kurukṣetra war, and (2) the date of the composition of *Mahābhārata*. And the latter issue is related with the question of its authorship. Since "there was no author of the great epic" (Hopkins 1901: 58), as we have already stated, no particular and exact date can be assigned to it, in its present form. Before reaching at the probable date of the composition of the epic, it is desirable to know the different views of the scholars for disagreement or concordance.

According to P.L. Vaidya (1937, vol. II: 56), the great epic in its present form is the outcome of a long and continuous literary activity. N. Jagannatha Rao (1931/1976) thinks that the war of Kurukṣetra was

23 The expression first occurs in the Kohl copper-plate charter of the Mahārāja Śarvanātha dated CE 534, vide Fleet, 1888, *Corpus Inscriptionum Indicarum* Vol. III; p. 137.

24 Ādi-Parva I.19, 77.

fought in 3139 BCE.[25] On the basis of the astronomy K.V. Abhayankar (1944) places the Great War in *c.* 3000 BCE.[26] The same view has been given by C.V. Vaidya (1907: 5)[27] and P.V. Kane (1965, vol. III: 896 and 923). 3102 BCE is the year from which Kaliyuga believed to be set in and according to Ādi-Parva, the war of Kurukṣetra was fought in the end of Dvāpara Age and it was the beginning of the Kaliyuga.

antare caiva samprāpte kalidvāparayorabhūta ।
samantapañcake yuddhaṁ kurupāṇḍavasenayoḥ ॥
— Ādi-Parva II.13

The traditional date for the Kali Age was first time given by the celebrated astronomer Āryabhaṭa (born 473 CE) and in Aihoḷe inscription (dated 634 CE) of the Cāḷukyan emperor Pulkeśin II of Bādāmī (Bījāpur district, Karnataka). However, there also exist some other almost equally early traditions dating this event a few centuries subsequent to the start of the Kali Age. According to a very persistent tradition, it occurred in 2449 (current) or 2448 (expired) BCE. This notion is first referred to by Varāhamihira (mid-sixth century CE) who in his *BṛhatSaṁhitā* gives the interval between the period of *Mahābhārata* hero Yudhiṣṭhira for his commencement of the Śaka era as 2526 years.[28]

The famous Kashmiri poet and historian Kalhaṇa (twelfth century CE) in his *Rājataraṅgiṇī* has quoted the statement of Varāhamihira and given the idea that the Bhārata war took place at the end of the Dvāpara Age and also assists that Kuru and Pāëḍavas flourished when 653 years of the Kali Age had elapsed:

śatesu ṣaṭsu śārdeṣu tryadhikeṣu ca bhūtale ।

---

25 *The Age of Mahābhārata War.*

26 "The Date and Time of the Bhārata War", *ABORI.*

27 According to C.V. Vaidya, "The epic period . . . extends roughly from 3000 to 300 BCE. As the Mahābhārata war was fought in 3101, the original Bhārata being composed not very long after that and *Mahābhārata* was last recast about 250 BCE at least unquestionably after Megasthenes and before Aśoka."

28 Shastri, 2004, *Mahābhārata*, Introduction, p. xxii.

kalergateṣu varṣāṇāmanubhvan kurupāṇḍavāḥ ||
— *Rājataraṅgiṇī* I.51

Some modern Indian astronomers have tried to show that even some astronomical references in *Mahābhārata* itself lend support to this date. What is interesting in the present context is the fact that this tradition is also sought to be buttressed by some scholars on the basis of a certain assertion met with in the copper-plate characters of the Prāgjyotiṣa monarch Bhāskarvarman (600-50 CE).[29] It is averred in his Nīdhānpura plates that Vajradatta, son of Bhagadatta who played an important role in the Bhārata war, was followed by his descendants who ruled for 3,000 years after which Puṣyavarman became a king.[30] P.C. Sengupta (1937) assigns 2449 BCE to the event (war).[31] Basing his investigation on the astronomical data J.S. Karindikar (1943: 749) suggests that 1931 BCE is the date of Kurukṣetra war*. According to K.P. Jayaswal (1967) it took place in 1424 BCE.[32] R.C. Datta (1910: 169, 323) assigns the thirteenth or fourteenth century BCE to the event. N.K. Siddhanta (1929: 33-42) tries to solve the problem in three ways.

On the basis of the gap between the birth of the Parīkṣita and the coronation of Mahāpadmananda, the founder of the Nanda dynasty, which was 1,050 and 1,015 years according to *Matsya Purāṇa* 272.36 and *Viṣṇu Purāṇa* IV.24.32 respectively, he regards 1472 and 1437 BCE as the date of birth of Parīkṣita, who was born immediately after the war of Kurukṣetra. By using the genealogical list, which is given

---

[29] Shastri, 2004, *Mahābhārata*, Introduction, p. xxiii.

[30] *vaṁśyeṣu tasya nṛpatiṣu varṣasahasratrayaṁ padmavāpya* |
yāteṣu devabhūyaṃ kṣītīśvaraḥ puṣyavermābhūta ||
— Sharma 1978: 41, verse 7

[31] "Some astronomical references from Mahābhārata and Their Significance", *Journal of Asiatic Society in Bengal*, 1937, III: 101-19.

[32] *Journal of Bihar and Orissa Research Society*, 1936, III: 246-62.

* *Proceedings and Transaction of All India Oriental Conference*, Twelfth Session, Banaras Hindu University, 1943-44, p. 479. According to him "the exact *tithi* (date) of the commencement of the War is Mārgaśīrṣa, kṛṣna, 11 and the *tithi* on which the war ended is Mārgaśīrṣa, śukla,14.

in the Purāṇas, he places the war in the eleventh century BCE. To K.G. Sankara (1930-31) war took place in 1183 BCE,[33] whereas K.L. Daftari favours 1197 BCE as its date.[34] The same differences of opinion are there about the composition of the epic. Regarding the period which the epic covers, A. Macdonell (1928: 241) and R.C. Majumdar[35] think that *Mahābhārata* in its present shape, existed in about 350 CE. According to George Bühler the epic took place during 300–500 CE.[36] In the words of E.W. Hopkins (1913: 397ff):

> As a whole poem dates from about the second century BCE extending to the second century CE or with the margin allowed by some scholars, its period extends from 400 BCE to CE 400, this representing the centuries during which the whole poem was developed into its present shape.

After making a comparative study of the geography of the Buddhist *Mahāvagga* with that of *Mahābhārata*, S. Levi concludes that the latter received its final redactions in the first three or four centuries CE.[37]

According to S. Paramavitana,

> This Epic may not have existed in its present form in the time of Aśoka but it is not impossible that the kernel of the epic is as old as, or older than, third century BCE. At any rate, the story of Pāṇḍavas and Kauravas must have been current in India in Aśoka's age or even earlier.[38]

So from the above account it is clear that the date of the "dateless"[39] *Mahābhārata* is obscure and concealed in mystery.

---

33 "Some Problems of Indian Chronology", *ABORI*, vol. XII: 301-61.

34 Daftari, 1946, "The Date of Mahābhārata War", pp. 481-89.

35 Majumdar, 1994, *Corporate Life in Ancient India*, Introduction, p. iv.

36 *Contributions to the History of Mahābhārata,* quoted in S.A.K. Dass, 1944, *The Economic History of Ancient India,* Preface, pp. iii-iv.

37 Winternitz, 1927/1953, *A History of Indian Literature*, vol. I, p. 465.

38 S. Paramavitana, 1955, "Some Aspects of Divinity of Kings in Ancient India", p. 227, fn 1.

39 Sukthankar, 1957, *On the Meaning of the Mahābhārata*, p. 32.

In *Baudhāyana Gṛhyasūtra* there is a clear description of "Viṣṇusahasranāma" and one verse of *Bhagavadgītā* IX.26[40] is quoted there as an evidence and it is known to all that *Gītā* is the part of *Mahābhārata*. Time period of Āśvalāyana and Baudhāyana was around fourth century BCE (Macdonell 1928: 287). It appears that the composition of *Mahābhārata* took place in 200 or 600 BCE, from the composition of these two Saṁhitās (Āśvalāyana and Baudhāyana). Based on these two quotes it can be said that *Mahābhārata* must have been composed before the spread of Buddhism (450-400). Time period of Āśvalāyana is considered around 400 BCE, and before *Āśvalāyana Gṛhyasūtra* there was no description of *Mahābhārata* in any available literature.

So from the above references it becomes clear that *Mahābhārata* was composed about fifth century BCE. Some German scholars have estimated that the present form of the epic must have got composed between ninth and tenth centuries BCE, but the great German scholar Winternitz did not agree with this because it has been proved from the evidences of literary inscriptions and description that the time period of *Mahābhārata* was about fifth century BCE. According to Winternitz, *Mahābhārata* covers a period ranging from fourth century BCE to fourth century CE.[41] Hence from the above reviews it becomes clear that it was composed not earlier than 400 BCE. Therefore, it is estimated that its composition may be occurred between fourth and fifth centuries BCE.

Contents in Mahābhārata

According to the nineteen voluminous parts of BORI's critical edition, the great epic *Mahābhārata* is divided into eighteen major sections known as *parvas* (books), namely, Ādi, Sabhā, Vana, Virāṭa, Udyoga, Bhīṣma, Droṇa, Karṇa, Śalya, Sauptika, Strī, Śānti, Anuśāsana, Āśvamedhika, Āśramavāsika, Mausala, Mahāprasthānika and Svargārohaṇa. Each *parva* is subdivided into chapters made up of verses composed in various metres, usually in *śloka* form, but also in

---

40 *patraṁ puṣpaṁ phalaṁ toyaṁ yo me bhaktyā prayacchati* |
tadahaṁ bhaktyupahṛtamaśnāmi prayatātmanaḥ ||

41 Winternitz, 1927/1953, *A History of Indian Literature*, vol. I, pp. 454-75.

triṣṭubhs and other less common metres as well as occasional prose passages. It contains an appendix (Khila-Parva) called Harivaṁśa which has 16,375 verses. All these eighteen *parvas* and one additional Harivaṁśa contain 100 sub-*parvas*. These *parvas* have been named after some important incidents of the main narrative of the epic, which is related with the Kuru dynasty and may be summarized as follows:

1. ***Ādi-Parva***: *Mahābhārata* begins with Ādi-Parva. Here the word *ādiḥ* means the beginning or the first. Its 225 chapters first present the cycle myths leading up to King Janamejaya's snake sacrifice at which *Mahābhārata* is first spoken by Vaiśampāyana, a disciple of Vyāsa. After this, it proceeds to tell the origin of the Pāṇḍava brothers and their cousins the Kauravas, the marriage of the Pāṇḍavas to Draupadī and the roots of the conflict between them, which is the main theme of the central narrative.

2. ***Sabhā-Parva***: Sabhā-Parva has 72 chapters and takes the narrative further by telling how the kingdom was divided between the two branches of the family and how the great Rājasūya sacrifice was performed by Yudhiṣṭhira and the Pāṇḍavas. It tells of the envy of Duryodhana and the Kauravas and finally of the gambling match at which Yudhiṣṭhira loses everything to the Kauravas, Draupadī is insulted and the Pāṇḍavas are exiled to the forest.

3. ***Vana-Parva***: Vana-Parva (229 chapters) describes Pāṇḍavas' life in different forests. It contains discourses of Dhaumya, Mārkaṇḍeya, Lomaśa and Ariṣṭisena to Yudhiṣṭhira, and many discussions on the moral virtues. Two famous episodes, the Nalopākhyāna and the Rāmopākhyāna, occur in this *parva*.

4. ***Virāṭa-Parva***: Virāṭa-Parva (67 chapters) describes how the Pāṇḍavas pass their final year of exile (*ajñātavāsa*) living incognito at the court of King Virāṭa. Here the drama is not punctuated by didactic passages as in the vane.

5. ***Udyoga-Parva***: From the Udyoga-Parva (197 chapters) we come to know after the expiry of the thirteen years of banishment,

Yudhiṣṭhira once more claimed the kingdom, but Duryodhana refused to give even an inch thereof to him. All attempts at negotiations proved futile and ultimately war was declared. Both the parties, that of the Kauravas and that of the Pāṇḍavas, began making preparation for the war.

6. ***Bhīṣma Parva***: The Bhīṣma-Parva (117 chapters) describes the initial drawing up of the armies at Kurukṣetra and contains *Bhagavadgītā*, in which Kṛṣna convinces Arjuna that it is right for him to wage war. The battle is then described up to the point at which Arjuna shoots down Bhīṣma, the Kaurava's general.
7. ***Droṇa-Parva***: The Droṇa-Parva (173 chapters) is the seventh *parva* among the eighteen *parva*s of *Mahābhārata*. This *parva* starts with the defeat of Bhīṣma in the battle of Kurukṣetra and with the taking over of the command of the entire Kuru army by Droṇācārya. A major part of this episode deals with the narration of the battle. In this *parva* there is a description of about most of the great warriors and their end while fighting in the battle of Kurukṣetra war.
8. ***Karṇa-Parva***: The Karṇa-Parva (69 chapters) concentrates specifically on the conflict between Arjuna and Karṇa. This *parva* starts with the birth of Karṇa and it ends with the death of Karṇa in the great battle of Kurukṣetra in the hands of Arjuna.
9. ***Śalya-Parva***: Śalya-Parva (64 chapters) is the ninth *parva* of the great epic. This *parva* describes the taking over of the charge of the commanding the Kuru army by Śalya, the king of Madra, after the death of Karṇa. And this *parva* also tells of the final stages of the battle in which Yudhiṣṭhira kills his uncle, Śalya, and Bhīma puts an end to Duryodhana in a single combat. This *parva* describes the last date of the battle at Kurukṣetra.
10. ***Sauptika-Parva***: The Sauptika-Parva (18 chapters) describes the massacre in the Pāṇḍava camp by three survivors from the Kaurava side.
11. ***Strī-Parva***: Strī-parva (27 chapters) has been devoted to the

vilāpa (lament) of the ladies, who lost their near and dear once in the war of Kurukṣetra. This is followed by a description of the performance of the funeral rites, viz. *dāha* and *śrāddha* of the deceased warriors.

12. ***Śānti-Parva*:** Śānti-parva (353 chapters) is the twelfth *parva* among the eighteen *parva*s of *Mahābhārata*. This *parva* comprises a sixth part of the total extent of *Mahābhārata* and this *parva* opens with the victorious Yudhiṣṭhira lamenting over the suffering he has caused and wishing to abandon the kingdom he has won to take up the life of an ascetic. There follows a great discussion on the proper duty of the king, before everybody returns to the battlefield where the fallen Bhīṣma gives more detailed instructions on this subject.
13. ***Anuśāsana-Parva*:** The Anuśāsana-Parva (154 chapters) consist of the final instruction or the *anuśāsana* from Bhīṣma to Yudhiṣṭhira. This episode is a long interval in the great epic of *Mahbhārata* and it explains in detail the instructions given by Bhīṣma while he was in deathbed of arrows in the battlefield. This *parva* is considered to be a very large treasure-trove of the Brāhmaṇic lore which is later added to the epic of *Mahābhārata*.
14. ***Āśvamedhika-Parva*:** The Āśvamedhika-Parva (96 chapters) then narrates how the Pāṇḍavas executed a horse sacrifice to atonc for the sins incurred by killing others in the battle. Much of the *parva*, however, consists of teachings from Kṛṣṇa to Arjuna.
15. ***Āśramavāsika-Parva*:** Āśramavāsika-Parva (47 chapters) deals with Dhṛtarāṣṭra's departure to the forest as a hermit.
16. ***Mausala-Parva*:** Mausala-Parva (9 chapters) gives an account of the destruction of the Yādavas with the *mūsala* (pestle) in accordance with the curse of Vālmīki.
17. ***Mahāprasthānika-Parva*:** The Mahāprasthānika-Parva (3 chapters) describes the death of the Pāṇḍavas and of Draupadī after they have given up their kingdom and journeyed to the Himalayas.

18. ***Svargārohaṇa-Parva*:** As indicated by its name Svargārohaṇa, the eighteen and the last *parva* with 5 chapters, describes the attainment of *svarga* (heaven) by the leading characters of the great epic.

Table 1.1: Parvas of Mahābhārata

Parva	*Sub-parvas*	*Adhyāyas*	*Ślokas*
Ādi-Parva	19	225	7,197
Sabhā-Parva	9	72	2,390
Vana-Parva	16	299	10,338
Virāṭa-Parva	4	67	1,824
Udyoga-Parva	11	197	6,063
Bhīṣma-Parva	5	117	5,406
Droṇa-Parva	8	173	8,192
Karṇa-Parva	1	69	3,871
Śalya-Parva	4	64	3,315
Sauptika-Parva	3	18	772
Strī-Parva	5	27	730
Śānti-Parva	3	353	12,902
Anuśāsana-Parva	2	154	6,439
Āśvamedhika-Parva	2	96	2,743
Āśramavāsika-Parva	3	47	1,062
Mausala-Parva	1	9	273
Mahāprasthānika-Parva	1	3	106
Svargārohaṇa-Parva	1	5	194
Total in 18 *parvas*	**98**	**1,995**	**73,817**
Harivaṁśa (Khila-Parva)	2	—	16,375
Total (including Khila-Parva)	**100**	**1,995**	**90,192**

Source: Mahābhārata (according to BORI's critical edition).

The division of eighteen *parva*s is given in Table 1.1.

Commentators on Mahābhārata

Mahābhārata has a long tradition of commentators under which great scholars, religious and wise (*adhyātmavettā*) hermits are counted. According to Sukthankar the name of the famous commentators of *Mahābhārata* are as follows: Anantabhaṭa, Arjuna Miśra, Ānanda, Devabodha, Nārāyaṇa, Nīlakaṇṭha, Caturbhuja Miśra, Jagadīśa, Rāmānuja, Lakṣmaṇa, Varad, Vādirāja, Vidyāsāgara, Vimalabodha, Śaṅkarācārya, Śrīnivāsa, Sarvajñanārāyaṇa and Sr̥ṣṭidhara. In addition to these commentators there are many other commentators also, such as, Gadānanda (has written commentary named *Bhāratajñānadīpikā*) which is available in the Vāṅgya Sāhitya Pariṣada, in handwritten form. Jagaddhar, Janārdana Muni and Vidyānidhibhaṭṭa (Ānandapūrṇa has given the indication of these four commentators in his commentary named *Bhārata-Ṭīkā*), Vaiśampāyana, Śāṇḍilya, Māghava, Ratnagarbha, Kavindra, Utkalakavi and Gadānanda.

The instruction of first one (Vaiśampāyana) is given by Vimalabodha and the description of the last two (Śāṇḍilya and Māghava) is given by Arjuna Miśra in his commentaries. *Virodhārthabhañjinī Vyākhyā* of Rāmakr̥ṣṇa and *Viṣamapāda-Vivaraṇa* of Ajñātanāma are also published on Virāṭa-Parva. Some commentaries on Vādirāja's *Lakṣābharaṇa* have been published on Virāṭa and Udyoga-Parva. Gujarati Printing Press has made a special contribution in the simulation of *Mahābhārata* by publishing Virāṭa-Parva (with eight commentaries) in 1950 and Udyoga-Parva (with five commentaries) in 1920.[42]

In addition to these, *Bhāratavyākhyā* of Kavīndra is also available. The name of the Vādirāja's commentary is *Lakṣaślokālaṁkāra*. Śrīdharācārya has also written his commentary on Mokṣadharma of *Mahābhārata*. Thus we have information on thirty-six commentators of *Mahābhārata*. Description of some famous commentators is as follows.

---

42 Upadhyaya 1953: 66-70.

DEVABODHA

He is one of the most ancient commentators of *Mahābhārata*. The name of his commentary is *Jñānadīpikā*. He is mentioned by later commentators with honour and respect. He is also called Devaswāmi. His commentary is accepted as a standard commentary. His text will not have original verses of *Mahābhārata* but contains chapter numbers, verse numbers, etc. He has given the meaning with very difficult expressions. He precedes Vimalabodha, Sarvajñanārāyaṇa and Vādirāja. Arjuna Miśra bases his commentary[43] on *Jñānadīpikā*. Devabodha commented on Ādi, Sabhā, Udyoga, Virāṭa and Bhīṣma-Parva. Time period of Devabodha should be just before 1766 CE.

VAIŚAMPĀYANA

Vimalabodha in his *Viṣam Ślokī* (known as *Mahābhārata-Vyākhya*) has mentioned the name of Vaiśampāyana.

> *vaiśampāyana ṭīkādidevasvāmimatāni ca* ।
> *vīkṣya vyākhyā viracitā durghaṭārthaprakāśinī* ॥

VIMALABODHA

The name of his commentary is *Durghaṭārtha-Prakāśinī*, also known as *Viṣamaślokī*. He commented on all the eighteen *parva*s of *Mahābhārata*. His time is considered as around 1802 CE. Gujarati Printing Press published his works on Virāṭa and Udyoga-Parva.

SARVAJÑANĀRĀYAṆA

The name of his commentary is *Bhāratārtha-Prakāśikā*. He was expected to have lived between the period 1110–1300 CE. According to P.V. Kane, Arjuna Miśra quotes him in his work.

CATURBHUJA MIŚRA

His commentary *Bhārata-Upāya-Prakāśa* is on Virāṭa-Parva. In his

---

43 *vedavyāsamukhāmbhojagalitaṁ vāṅmyāmṛtam* ।
saṁbhojayantaṁ bhuvanaṁ devabodhaṁ bhajāmahe ॥
— Upadhyaya, 2001, *Saṁskṛta Sāhitya kā Itihasa*, p. 67

commentary he presented *Medinī Koṣa* as an evidence. Time of the *Medinī Koṣa* is considered between CE 1200 and 1275. Ānanda-pūrṇa Vidyāsāgara has mentioned Caturbhuja Miśra in his commentary named *Vidyāsāgarī*. So from this, the time of the Caturbhuja can be made out as the end of the thirteenth century.

ĀNANDAPŪRṆA VIDYĀSĀGARA

The name of his famous commentary is *Vidyāsāgarī*. In the history of Advaita Vedānta he is famous as a great writer. His commentary on *Mahābhārata* is so vast and erudite, in which we find ancient commentators' name in a large number. His commentaries are available on the five *parva*s, namely, Ādi, Sabhā, Bhīṣma, Śānti and Anuśāsana-Parva. His time has been considered as the fourteenth century CE.

ARJUNA MIŚRA

He is also a great commentator on *Mahābhārata*. The name of his commentary is *Bhāratārtha-Dīpikā*. He commented on the whole text of *Mahābhārata*. According to Kane, he belonged to 1620 CE.

NĀRĀYAṆA

His commentary is *Nigūḍhārtha-Pāda-Bodhinī*. His time is considerd to be the closing period of the fourteenth century.

VĀDIRĀJA

Lakṣābharaṇa or *Lakṣālaṁkāra* is his famous commentary on *Mahābhārata*. He was a south Indian "Naiyāyika" (Indian logician), of Mādhava following lived during 1525-75 CE. This text neither follows the southern manuscript nor the northern. Gujarati Printing Press has published his works on Virāṭa and Udyoga-Parva.

NĪLAKAṆṬHA

Nīlakaṇṭha Caturdhara, the best known commentator on *Mahābhārata,* lived in Banāras in the second half of the seventeenth century. His commentary *Bhāratabhāvadīpa* is the only one that is widely used in Sanskrit studies today.[44] This is available on the whole eighteen *parvas* of *Mahābhārata*. He quotes Devabodha, Vimalabodha, Arjuna Miśra and Sarvajñanārāyaṇa. He wrote commentary for *Śivatāṇḍava* in 1680 and commentary on *Gaṇeśa Gītā* in 1693. The time period of the different handwritten form of *Bhāratabhāvadīpa* was 1687-95; so from this, one can estimate the time period of Nīlakaṇṭha as CE 1650–1700.[45]

Table 1.2 Lists the commentators of *Mahābhārata* and their commentaries.[46]

Important Sanskrit Recensions and Editions of Mahābhārata

1. The Calcutta edition, Asiatic Society; the Editio Princeps, in Nāgarī character (quarto); 4 volumes, 1834-39.
2. The Bombay edition, 1863.
3. The Madras edition, re-edited with *ṭīkā* by Nīlakaṇṭha Govinda, 1890.
4. The Southern Recension, 18 volumes, critically edited by P.P.S. Shastri, and published by Ramaswamy Sastrulu & Sons, Madras, 1932.
5. The Poona Recension (popularly called the "Bhandarkar edition") 1933-66, the most authoritative, a painstaking labour of scholarly love; the first critical edition, completed in 1966.
6. Complete *Mahābhārata*, with Hindi translation, Gita Press, Gorakhpur, 8 volumes.

Table 1.3 details the major editions of *Mahābhārata*.

---

44 *vādī madhye yathā rāja so'haṁ tasya kṛpābalāta* I
vādirājena svasaktyā vrīṇe varaṇayāmitat II
— *Bhāvaprakāśikā* I

45 Gode, 1953, *Studies in Indian Literary History*, vol. I, pp. 413-22.

46 *Note*: *Mahābhārata* has about thirty-two commentators as we come to know from the literary sources. But we have received information on some of them, so I have given information about some major commentators as much as possible.

Table 1.2: List of Commentators of Mahābhārata with Their Commentaries

Commentators	*Time Period*	*Commentary*	*Parva*
Devabodha	1766 CE	*Jñādīpikā*	Sabhā,Bhīṣma, Udyoga and Virāṭa
Vimalabodha	1050 CE	*Durghaṭārtha-Prakāśinī*	18 *parvas*
Nārāyaṇasarvajña	Sometime between 1110–1300 CE	*Bhāratārtha-Prakāśikā*	Virāṭa and Udyoga
Caturbhuja Miśra	1300 CE	*Bhārata-Upāya-Prakāśa*	Virāṭa
Ānandapūrṇa	1350 CE	*Vidyāsāgarī*	Ādi, Bhīṣma and Śānti
Arjuna Miśra	1534 CE	*Bhārtārtha-Dīpikā*	Virāṭa, Sabhā, and Anuśāsana
Nārāyaṇa	After fourteenth century	*Nigūḍhārtha-Pāda-Bodhinī*	Ādi, Sabhā, Bhīṣma, Śānti and Anuśāsana
Vādirāja	1525-75 CE	*Lakṣābharaṇa* or *Lakṣālaṁkāra*	Virāṭa, Udyoga and Śānti
Nīlakaṇṭha Caturdhara	1650–1700 CE	*Bhāratabhāvadīpa*	18 *parvas*
Mādhavācārya	1197–1276 CE	*Mahābhārata Tātparya Nirṇaya*	—

Mahābhārata in Other Indian Languages

For centuries together *Mahābhārata* has been popular not only in India but also in several parts of the world. From the fifth century BCE, saints, scholars, poets and dramatists have quoted copiously from it. In the second century BCE a Greek envoy referred to precepts called from this epic. In the second century BCE the whole poem was recited in temples in Cambodia. It has attracted the notice of the international community, because of its largest volume, with 100,000 stanzas, which is totally full of inordinate depth. So many works have been done based on *Mahābhārata*. It is a treasure house of the Indian culture, both secular and sacred. This epic provided the material and ideas for the numerous

Table 1.3: Important Information about Major Editions of Mahābhārata*

Edition	*No. of Vols*	*No. of Verses*	*Year of Publishing*
Bhandarkar edn (Poona edn) ed. V.S. Sukthankar	19	89,000	1933-66
Complete *Mahābhārata* (with Hindi tr.), Gita Press, Gorakhpur	6	100,217	1980
The Calcutta edn, Asiatic Society	4	—	1834-39
The Southern edn, ed. P.P.S. Shastri	18	100,217 more or less than this	1932

* *Note*: The number of *ślokas* is not confirmed, but information on them is given as it may be possible from literary sources.

works on Sanskrit literature. Its translation became the foundation for many of the Indian languages to generate once again a vast body of narrative poems and other poems in these languages.[47] Based on the original text of *Mahābhārata* many versions of it have been written in different Indian languages, the description of which is as follows:

1. ***Assamese:*** *Mahābhārata*, translated into Assamese by Mahindra Bora, Guwahati: Students Stores, 1988.
2. ***Bengali:*** Basu, Rajasekhara, *Mahābhārata*, Calcutta: M.C. Sarkar & Sons, 1955.
3. ***Gujarati:*** *Śrī Mahābhārata*, tr. Shankaradutt Shastri, Parvati Shankara; ed. Bhikshu Akhanadananda, 3rd edn, Ahmedabad.
4. ***Kannada:*** H.N. Rangaswami, *Śrīmadmahābhārata*, tr. and ed. Rangaswami et al., Bangalore: Bharata Darshan Prakashan.
5. ***Malayalam:*** *Bhāṣābhāratam*, tr. Kodungallur Kunjikkuttan Thampuran, Irinjalakuda: T.N. Namputiri, 1952-56, 7 vols.
6. ***Manipuri:*** *Mahābhāratam*, tr. Kallachand Shastri, Imphal: Manipuri Mahābhārata Committee, 1956-63.
7. ***Marathi:*** *Srimanmahābhāratache Marathi suras Bhāṣāntara*, tr.

47 Mishra 1987.

Narhar Raghunath Pathak, Bombay: Surekha Prakashan, 1967, 10 vols.

8. ***Oriya:*** *Mahābhārata*, tr. Gobinda Chandra Mahapatra, Bhubaneswar: Oriya Sahitya Academy.
9. ***Punjabi:*** *Mahābhārata*, ed. Swami Shabdanandaji, Amritsar: Bhai Jawaher Kripal Singh.
10. ***Konkani:*** Kelekar Ravindra, *Mahābhārata: A Trans-creation*, Goa: Jag Prakashan, 1987.
11. ***Maithili:*** Upendra Jha "Vyāsa", *Maithilī Mahābhārata*: *Ādi-Parva*, Patna: Dhirendra Kumar Jha, 1994.
12. ***Marathi:*** Chintamani Vinayak, Vaidya, *Mahābhārata*, Pune: Manak G.V. Chiplunkarni Mandali.
13. ***Sindhi:*** C. Rajagopalachari, *Mahābhārata*, tr. Tarachand Gajra, Bombay: Lok Seva Mandala, 1963.
14. ***Tamil:*** Cho Ramaswamy, *Mahābhārataṁ Pesugiradu*, Chennai: Alliance, 1998.

EARLIER WORKS ON MAHĀBHĀRATA

Mahābhārata has been studied by numerous celebrated scholars. Voluminous literature has come down to the readers from famous scholars both from native as well as foreign lands. They have delved into the epic from different angles. Although, the scope of the epic, no doubt, has been widened by the investigations made by Lasson, Ludwig Sorenson, Hermann Oldenberg, Matt Holzman, Ulrike Schröder, Joseph Dahlmann, Von Hermann Jacobi, etc. their inquiries were mainly concerned with the problems of the epic such as its authorship, date, text-criticism, origin and development. They have generally neglected the political and institutional aspects of life.

It is now proposed to attempt a survey of the important writings dealing with the politics, political ideas and other institutional aspects as delineated in the epic. This type of survey is necessary for the proper appreciation of the present study which is concerned with the politics in Śānti-Parva.

Edward Washburn Hopkins has been a pioneer and has made an intensive study of the epic. Though his work deals with the social, military, historical and political aspects of *Mahābhārata*, it is less informative as far as the political relevance of the epic is concerned. His work is based on the copious utilization of the contents of the epic.[48] Hopkins's work is valuable on the following grounds to the researchers and scholars. He has given the name pseudo-epic to the twelfth-thirteenth and subsequent *parvas* of *Mahābhārata*. To him, the narrative accounts of the epic are earlier than that of the didactic sections. Here the view of the scholar is in agreement that in an average chapter of the extant epic, one may read a stanza of the second century BCE followed by one written in the second century CE; sometimes, this gap is traceable in the middle of the lines. He has tried his best to distinguish by circumspection between the old and new epic tradition. He has taken into account the parallel literatures also. But Hopkins's view is not correct that, "The kingdom descended directly to the king's eldest son without any question". Hopkins has discussed the social and military positions of the ruling caste, in general, and that of the royalty, in particular.

N.K. Siddhanta's work is also valuable but he is primarily interested in a comparative estimate of Indian heroic poetry with that of the European lands and hence he lays stress on those features which are prominent in the latter. The writer considers the epic as the main source of information in connection with the Heroic Age of India (Siddhanta 1929: 139-40). His study is more literary than that of Hopkins. Nevertheless, he has discussed the nature of kingship. In this book, he has examined the royal succession, royal duties, taxation and king's ownership of the land as well as his relations with the council of ministers. He reckons that the king in the epic age behaved irresponsibly.

Siddhanta has also discussed in a passing way the relevance of interstate relations. He finds a considerable similarity between the Homeric poems and the Indian epic. There are stray references to the

48 Hopkins, 1899, *The Social and Military Position of the Ruling Caste in Ancient India*, pp. 8-9.

strength of the standing army in the epic. To him, the number of seven divisions with the Pāṇḍavas and eleven with the Kauravas is not correct. He is of the view that distinguished heroes in the *Iliad* generally used chariots as the Indian heroes did. Since more than half of the space in his work is devoted to various heroic epics of the European countries, the evidences of the epic *Mahābhārata* have received only criptive and selective treatment.

It is not an exaggeration to say that there is hardly any work since its publication which does not quote Jayaswal either in agreement or for the purpose of refutation. Jayaswal's (1967) work is, no doubt, a pioneer in the field, though the title of the book has been questioned by the scholars in a political science seminar and the word, "Hindu" is not generally favoured. He has taken extracts mostly from Śānti-Parva. He has tried to prove that there was the existence of republics during the epic days.[49] For sustaining his argument, he refers to (the republic) the chapters of Śānti-Parva. Actually the entire work of Jayaswal is devoted to proving the thesis of blue blood in political and constitutional evolution. Even in connection with monarchy, he has tried to prove it as the hedge with several constitutional checks. To him, the epic draws material generally old. He refers to its date as late as the fifth century after Christ, with a earlier systematization *c.*150 BCE.

He also traces that the epic records the existence of Hindu political science. He attaches great importance to the discourse of Bhīṣma as a part and parcel in political science. He has also defined *daṇḍanīti*. He is of the view that the treatise on political theories and practical governance was originally called *daṇḍanīti*, or the principles of government. His analysis of the coronation oath implies that the kingdom is a trust in the hands of a king. For this, he has relied on the authority of the chapters of Śānti-Parva 59.67. He has discussed the topic such as taxation, the council of ministers as well as law and administration. He deduces quite radical conclusions which

49 The majority of writers on the history of India have been obsessed with the idea of an "epic age" following the "later Vedic age". It is now quite clear that there was no epic age proper in India.

characterize the democratic welfare state of the present time. It appears from the above survey that Jayaswal has constructed the epic evidences generally as facts of history. He has made a selective use of data.

N.N. Law's (1960) publication has also focused lightly on the relevance of the institutional aspect of polity in Indian tradition. He has cited the evidences from *Agni, Skanda* and *Mārkaṇḍeya Purāṇa* on the royal duties and has made a comparative study of the epic. His work discusses the forms and types of government, the royal priest, regal succession and education of the prince. His book is valuable from the historical perspective, too. He has also relied upon the didactic portion of the epic.

Beni Prasad's contribution is not less important than that of Jayaswal. His work deals with the characteristics of ancient Indian polity, and has devoted some chapters to the study of epic. But in his opinion, the treatment of judicial administration is better in Manu than in the epic. Most of the evidences cited by him refer to Śānti-Parva, through he has tapped from Sabhā and other *parvas* too. He has discussed the standard of a good government in the light of king's performance established by law (*dharma*). He, like Jayaswal, is of the view that the epic tradition always welcomed the growth and development of republics. But his conclusion is based on the didactic portions of the epic.

The work of J.J. Anjaria (1935: XV) is a valuable dissertation submitted for a masters degree. In the Preface, he has acknowledged the importance of studying the institutional aspects in ancient India. He has tapped the evidence from the Vedas and Brāhmaṇas besides the epic. In the context of exploitation of the epic evidences, he parodies it mostly from Śānti-Parva. In the ninth chapter, he says that in ancient India, there was enough scope for studying the political thought. He refers to the profound sayings of Bhīṣma. He has discussed *daṇḍanīti*, the contractual origin of state, etc. He also refers to the Western political thought.

The work of A.S. Altekar (1977) is something different from others. He is in favour of a chronological study of ancient Indian political thought. He avoids any comparison and contrast with the modern times in the context of ideas in ancient tradition. He favours comparison and shows contrast with Greek political thought instead of seventeenth century's political thought. He holds the view that classical Indian tradition and writers often preferred to remain incognito. He has discussed the topics, sources and methods to study political ideas and institutions in ancient India, origin of state, *saptāṅga* theory of state, problem of stratification, kingship, taxation, etc. He does not supply systematic information in the context of the epic, though in the connection with origin of state, he has cited extracts from Śānti-Parva. He has discussed the polity on the pattern of the *saptāṅga* theory of state. His work is not very important from the epic point of view, because he has used references mostly from *Arthaśāstra* and from other literary sources and *Mahābhārata* has been neglected.

Ram Sharan Sharma (1959) deals with the historical and political problems as recorded in the early Indian literary sources since the Vedic times. He is of the view that the narrative portions of the epic go back to the tenth century BCE, as to him the didactic portions of the epic reflect an advanced society. Regarding the non-didactic sections of the epic, the author holds the view that it depicts a tribal and stateless society. For sustaining his argument, he refers to some archaic practices as noticeable in the internal evidences of the epic. Here the writer considers the evidences of the epic not as "pseudo-history" but as a fact of history.[50] The discussion on the *saptāṅga* theory of state is adequate from the epic point of view. Description of the elements is based more on the historical interpretation rather than on political consistency. He has taken references mostly from the *Arthaśāstra* of Kauṭilya.

U.N. Ghoshal's (1923a) book is valuable both for the study of historical and political aspects in ancient India since the Vedic times. In fact, any survey of the secondary sources on the political ideas would be incomplete without the examination of Ghoshal's work. His work is based on the material in a chronological order. He has not only discussed the works of Brāhmanical, Buddhist and Jaina sacred literature but his book also informs about the works in classical Sanskrit. He has devoted four chapters for the political ideas in the

---

[50] Sharma, 1985, *Material Culture and Social Formation in Ancient India*, pp. 135-57.

epic. He has put his focus on three chapters to discuss the ideas in the major didactic extracts. And the last one deals with minor didactic evidences. In the first three chapters he has concentrated on the Rājadharma section of Śānti-Parva. It is not erroneous to say that Ghoshal speaks on the political ideas of the epic, those of Bhīṣma. He has utilized the other *parva*s of the epic, narrative as well as didactic. But he fails to make a fruitful theorization.

He is of the view that *Mahābhārata* belongs to the period of the Mauryan empire and its succession states (325 BCE – 320 CE). To Ghoshal *Mahābhārata* represents the advent of a Brāhmanical renaissance. To sustain his argument, he places Smr̥tis of Manu and Yājñavalkya as products of the Brāhamanical renaissance. Ghoshal has examined the political ideas of the epic. He has discussed *rājadharma* and *daṇḍanīti*. To Ghoshal, these two concepts are combined in the epic tradition though they belong to the Smr̥tis and *Arthaśāstra*.

Ghoshal (1923a: 256) has discussed the characteristics of the clan republics. He has quoted extracts from Śānti-Parva. He has discussed the merits and demerits of *gaṇa*s as depicted in the epic tradition. But his conclusion is not convincing. In *Arthaśāstra* tradition, Kauṭilya is not keenly interested in the survival of republics while in the epic tradition an idea of peaceful coexistence both of monarchical and non-monarchical form of government is noticeable.

It is not erroneous to say that Ghoshal extensively drew his material from *Arthaśāstra*. He has made a theorization from the historical perspective. It has no political significance, though he stresses that ancient India had a political thought. He has made this assertion in the context of exaltation of the kingship. He considers the narrative accounts as a fact of history. He has an empirical approach because he concentrates on the behaviour of the king.[51]

Similarly, the works of B.K. Sarkar, P.V. Kane, B.K. Majumdar, J.N. Gupta, B.A. Saletore, Girija K. Mookerjee and Somnath Dhar are also valuable. But only some of them devoted a few chapters

---

51 ŚP CXXXIX.10.

to the studies of ideas in *Mahābhārata*. The rest are not so helpful for the present study. The works of B.K. Sarkar and P.V. Kane deal with the political as well as historical-cum-sociological aspects of ancient traditions. Kane has cited other *parva*s except Śānti-Parva. He has discussed the organism, origin of state and the uses of war instruments in *Mahābhārata*. To him, *Mahābhārata* has been the sourcebook for every kind of people. However his study is not a systematic one regarding the administration, interstate relations in the epic tradition.

There are many other scholars like Upendra J. Sandesara, M.A. Buch, P.N. Benerjee, H.C. Raychaudhary and Upendra Nath Thakur, who have also discussed the administrative aspects in *Mahābhārata*. There are also other erudite scholars who have studied this epic from different angles like Arthur A. Macdonell,[52] Moriz Winternitz, Monier-Williams and F. Max Müller. Their works deal polity in general, but this research proposal is different from them because here, our focus is to carve out the political aspects particularly and specifically in Śānti-Parva.

Śānti-Parva of Mahābhārata

Mahābhārata is considered as a main source of politics, because herein we get a comprehensive account of Indian political thought, the highest watermark being reached in Śānti-Parva, the Rājadharmānuśāsana chapters of which present a synthetic and systematic view of political thought of India. The primary source of present investigation is Śānti-Parva. Śānti-Parva is the repository of traditional knowledge and deals extensively with the political, social, moral, religious, philosophical and cultural aspects of ancient Indian society. Śānti-Parva is the twelfth *parva* among the eighteen *parva*s of *Mahābhārata*, which comprises of the total extent of *Mahābhārata* and is divided into three sections, namely, (1) Rājadharmānuśāsana, (2) Āpaddharma, and (3) Mokṣadharma.

---

52 Macdonell, 1928, *A History of Sanskrit Literature*, pp. 245-46. According to him "*Mahābhārata* is not only an epic but an encyclopaedia of moral teachings".

The first of these mainly deals with politics, the second with ethics and the third with *dharma* in the time of distress. This *parva* of *Mahābhārata* starts with the narration of crowning of Yudhiṣṭhira as the king of Hastināpura after the Pāṇḍavas defeated the Kauravas in the great battle of Kurukṣetra. This *parva* deals mainly with the aftermath of the great battle and it also gives an account of the instructions given by Bhīṣma to the newly-anointed king Yudhiṣṭhira. Bhīṣma spoke on economics, society and politics, and also gives more detailed instructions on the subject and the duty of the king. This section is known as Rājadharma. Bhīṣma then presents Mokṣadharma, teachings on the subject of salvation in the form of various loosely connected treatise based mainly on the ideas of Sāṁkhya and Yoga. The *parva* concludes with an exposition on devotion to the deity Nārāyaṇa known as the Nārāyaṇīya-Parva.

Among the three sections of Śānti-Parva, "Rājadharma" has special importance, inasmuch as it perhaps embodies the earliest systematic thought on the science of polity (*rājanīti*) in Indian literature. In fact, in the opinion of scholars like D.R. Bhandarkar, *Mahābhārata* thought on polity is prior even to that of Kauṭilya's *Arthaśāstra*. In spite of this relative antiquity, the political concepts presented here have depth and comprehensiveness which are really surprising. They deal with some fundamental aspects of polity such as the origin of state, the importance of punishment (*daṇḍa*) and the importance and duties of the kings. There are details about the duties of *varṇa*s and *āśrama*s, the seven constituents of state (*prakṛti*s) and their significance, foreign policy, taxation, the importance of *vārttā* (agriculture) and commercial activities, the various tactics of war, battle formations, etc. A very refreshing discussion is also found about republics and their functioning.

Śānti-Parva is regarded as one of the most timely and unforgettable chapters. It provides a glimpse into the trauma of the war and also narrates a long and the winding recapitulation of the Brāhmaṇic lore. It is said that Śānti-Parva was added to *Mahābhārata* at a later time as the main body of the epic. This *parva* brings together 100 messages of peace, from four interrelated sources, including the Upaniṣads, Vedas, *Bhagavadgītā* and *Mahābhārata*. By its name it is self-explanatory. In general the word *śānti* means peace. So in this *parva* Bhīṣma preaches about political ideas (*rājadharma*). Due to its richness in political thoughts and principles, I got inspired to work on this topic.

CONTENTS IN ŚĀNTI-PARVA

Śānti-Parva is divided into 353 chapters with 12,902 verses.[53] This whole *parva* is composed in *anuṣṭubh* metre. Somewhere in the middle we also find the use of *upendravajrā* metre. The descriptions of these 353 chapters are presented here in a very subtle form, because they are large in size and it is not possible to describe them in their original form.

In the starting, in chapters 1-7, there is a discussion on the Karṇa's life as how he gets cursed and how Duryodhana helps him, description of his bravery, relations of Karṇa with Yudhiṣṭhira, curse of Yudhiṣṭhira on women and prostration of Yudhiṣṭhira are discussed. In chapters 8-22, we see the family members of Yudhiṣṭhira are trying to console him. In chapters 23-28, Maharṣi Vyāsa preaches to Yudhiṣṭhira and suggests him not to get rid of his duty and kingdom. In chapters 29-37 Śrī Kṛṣṇa also tries to make Yudhiṣṭhira pain free. In chapter 38, on the insistence of both Śrī Kṛṣṇa and Vyāsa, Yudhiṣṭhira enters the city. In chapters 39-40 the death of Cārvāka and the crowning of Yudhiṣṭhira are discussed, and in chapter 41 Yudhiṣṭhira requests all to treat Dhṛtarāṣṭra as a king and the distribution of offices are done. In chapter 42 memorial and funeral services of the dead are mentioned. In chapters 43-44 Yudhiṣṭhira describes the various manifestations of Kṛṣṇa, and in chapter 45 he eulogizes Kṛṣṇa. In chapter 46 Vāsudeva asks Yudhiṣṭhira to receive instructions from Bhīṣma, who describes the prowess of Kṛṣṇa. In chapters 48-49 the episode (legend) of Paraśurāma is discussed; in chapter 50 Bhīṣma is praised by Kṛṣṇa. In chapter 51 Kṛṣṇa and Bhīṣma praise each other and Bhīṣma requests Kṛṣṇa to speak on *dharma*. In chapter 52 Bhīṣma orders Yudhiṣṭhira to come next day. In chapter 53 re-entrance of all in Kurukṣetra is

---

53 Sinha, 1985, *Śānti Parva Mein Viśleṣita Naitika Vicāra*, p. 26.

discussed. In chapters 54-55 there is a dialogue between Bhīṣma and Kṛṣṇa, and Yudhiṣṭhira goes again to Bhīṣma. From chapter 56 the description of *rājadharma* starts, discussion on which goes on to chapters 57 and 58. Chapter 59 describes the *varṇa-dharma*. In chapter 60, the duties of four orders are described and chapter 61 explains the four modes of life along with the duties of the brāhamaṇas. In chapter 62 the duties of brāhmaṇas are discussed; in chapters 63-64 the superiority of *rājadharma* is established over *varṇāśrama-dharma*. In chapters 65-66 it is clarified that by following *rājadharma* all the four *āśrama*s and *dharma*s can be protected. In chapters 67-68, the importance of the king is described, and the description of loss in the absence of king is also found in this chapter.

In chapters 69-72, duties of the king, his properties and his works to his subjects are discussed, and in chapters 73-75 the necessity of the priest to the king and discourse between Aila's son and Mucukunda are discussed. In chapter 76 the importance of the state is described. In chapters 77-79 the relations and cooperations between the king and brāhmaṇas are described. In chapter 80 the characteristics of *ṛtvij*, in chapter 81 the characteristics of ministers and in chapter 82 dialogue of Kṛṣṇa and Nārada are presented. In chapters 83-84, the characteristics and appointments of *sabhāsada*s, ministers of wars, law makers, commanders and counsellors and place for the secret meetings are discussed. In chapter 85 the importance of soft words, and in chapter 86 the purpose of *daṇḍa* and the properties of the officers are described. In chapter 87 the description of the city in which king should live, in chapter 88 how kingdom should be protected and in chapter 89 the procedure, how the king should collect money from his subjects are described. Chapter 90 details the duties of a king and in chapter 91 we see how the king should follow *dharma* and the necessity of *dharma* for the society. Chapters 92-95 contain preaching on *rājadharma* through many recitals. Chapters 96-100 discuss the tactis of war, the guileless demeanour of king, the duties of kṣatriyas, the regions which a hero aquires by blessed regions, and the attainment of heaven and hell respectively.

In chapters 101-04 the policies of military operations to subdue the enemy, in chapters 105-07 the preaching's of the Kālakvr̥kṣīya Muni on the political science are presented. In chapter 108 description of republican state and its policies, in chapter 109 the importance of services which are done to the parents and teachers are given. In chapters 110-13 practical policies are discussed with many examples. In chapter 114 the duties of king towards his enemies are elaborated. In chapters 115-19 properties and duties of the king and his ministers are described. Chapter 120 again describes *rājadharma* in short. Chapters 121-22 talk's about a true account of punishment, i.e. *daṇḍanīti* and the story Vasuhome. Chapter 123 describes the virtue, profit and pleasure. Chapter 124 gives the characterstics of virtuous conduct and also the tricks and methods to acquire them. In chapters 125-126, an account of hope is mentioned. Chapter 127 narrates the story of Riṣav and chapter 128 is on the discourse on hope. Chapter 129 describes the discourse on morality between Gotama and Yama. Chapter 130 explains the conduct of a king when he has no friends or when he is surrounded by wicked ministers. Chapter 131 also tells about the conduct of a king who is weak and whose kingdom is divided. In chapter 132 we get the descriptions about duties of brāhmaṇas and kings at the time of distress. Chapter 133 describes how should a king replenish his treasury in an emergency situation. In chapter 134, the acquisition of power by a kṣatriya is given and chapter 135 tells the story of a robber. Chapter 136 narrates the methods by which a king can fill his treasury and chapter 137 tells the excellent story of an idle man. Chapters 138-43 deal with the king's acts in different situations and his conducts when attacked by an enemy, robbers and his duties when sin prevails in his kingdom. Chapters 144-49 describe the story of a pigeon. Chapters 150-59 elucidate the duties of a king when a neighbouring and powerful enemy is offended by him. And chapter 160 describes the story of origin of sword and its importance. In chapter 161 the description of *trivarga*, in chapter 162 the characteristics of the friends and non-friends are described. In chapters 163-67 the discourse of *rājadharma* by Gautama is presented. In chapters 175-81 the origin of the world, *pañcamahābhūta* (earth, water, fire, sky and air), creation of the animals and caste system are described, and in chapters 182-85 the duties of all the *varṇa*s, importance of truth and *dharma* of all the four *āśrama*s are described. In chapter 186 the spiritual science and in chapter 188 rules of the silent recitation, in chapter 189 the kinds and importance of *yoga*, merit and demerits of *yoga* are given. In chapters 194-99 the elements *ātmā* and *paramātmā* are described. In chapters 200-02 the origin of five elements and description of Varāhāvatāra are also found. In chapters 203-10 life cycle of the world and soul (*jīvātmā*) as means of salvation are discussed. In chapters 211-17 the spiritual elements are discussed and in chapters 218-21 the place of Lakṣmī is fixed by the discourses of Indra. In chapter 222 *samatva buddhi* is described; in chapter 223 essential properties to get fame are described, and in chapter 224 the nature of Kāla and in chapter 225 the creation and devastation of the world are discussed. In chapters 226-27 the duties of the brāhmaṇas and in chapters 228-37 *karma*, *buddhi* and means of knowledge are described. In chapters 238-45 all the four *āśrama*s and their duties, *mahābhūta*, *buddhi*, knowledge and realization of *Parama-Brahma* are described. In chapter 246 ways to achieve salvation are presented; in chapter 247 again the description of the properties of *pañcamahābhūta* (five elements), man and *buddhi* is found. In chapters 248-50 the different forms of death are described; in chapters 251-66 diverse forms of *dharma*, *adharma*, *vairāgya* and means of salvation with many recitals have been presented in a very good manner.

Chapters 267-73 describe the fight between Indra and Vr̥trāsura and how the latter got defeated and died. In chapter 274, the destruction of the sacrifice of the Dakṣa by Mahādeva, and in chapters 275-78 the characteristics of Uśanā (Śukra) are described. And it also discusses the means by which one can acquire the greatest goals both in this world and in the next. Duties of the four *varṇa*s are also given. In chapters 279-87 *Parāśara-Gītā* is presented and in chapter 288 *Haṁsa-Gītā* is described. In chapters 289-90 Sāṁkhya-

Yoga is described; in chapters 291-97 Upaniṣadic *kṣara–akṣara*, *vidyā–avidyā*, *prakṛti–puruṣa* are described. In chapters 298-304 the elements of Sāṁkhya-Yoga are discussed. In chapter 305 measures of death are told. In chapter 306, the spiritual discourses between Yājñavalkya and Janaka are described, and in chapter 307 how can a man avoid death and decrepitude and the narrative of Pañcaśikha are also described. In chapter 308, the excellence of liberation is discussed. And said that one can acquire it in domestic mode of life. The discourse between Janaka and Sulabh is also found. In chapters 309-10 the penance of Vyāsa, his preachings on asceticism to Śukhadeva are described. In chapter 311 the birth of Śukhadeva and description of his childhood are found; in chapter 312 the Śukhadeva's departure to Mithilā and in chapter 313 regret of Śukhadeva by Janaka are mentioned. In chapters 314-17 meeting of Nārada with Śukhadeva and Nārada's instruction to Śukhadeva are described. In these chapters Nārada preaches the importance of *yoga* and knowledge of self. In chapters 318-20 the eternal situations are free from sorrows, Suka leaves his house and practice of *yoga* by Śukhadeva are described. In chapters 321-27 many discourses related with Nārada are given. In chapter 328 the role and importance of Kṛṣṇa are detailed. In chapters 329-30 war between Rudra and Nārāyaṇa is described. Chapter 331 is a dialogue between Nārada and Janmejaya. Chapter 332 speaks of the eminence of Vāsudeva. In chapters 333-34 the recitals of Nārada are presented. In chapter 335 the slaughter of Hayagrīva and Madhu–Kaiṭabha; in chapter 336 the *dharma* and in chapters 337-39 the description of the magnificence and glory of Nārāyaṇa are found. In chapters 340-50 the virtues of brāhmaṇas and honour of the guests, certified by the stories of Nāga king Padma and in the last three chapters the description of Uccha and Śīlavatī are found.

To conclude, this chapter provides general information on *Mahābhārata* such as its authorship and date. Here, the importance of *Mahābhārata* is also established highlighting by its contribution to Indian polity and political thought, as a pioneer text for the researchers of the political science and also for the students of other streams. Major works such as recension, editions, and valuable information about commentators and commentaries are also examined.

2

Politics in Western Tradition

> He who is unable to live in society, or who has no need because he is sufficient for himself, must be either a beast or God.
>
> — Aristotle, *Politics*, Bk. III

THE life of living together and cooperation with one another requires adjustment of behaviour, according to rules. These rules prescribe a course of conduct based on man's need for one another. The first and the most important rule of the social conduct is, "do unto others as you would have others do unto you". It means that one should provide for others the same condition of life as he wishes for himself. So the realization of this fact is a way of regulating human conduct. But all conducts in the society must confirm to certain uniform rules of the behaviour, and for this it needs a proper organization of society, and the organized society must be territorially settled. People cannot become a community of interests unless they live a settled life, occupying a definite territory.

Then it seems that an organized society requires the presence of some individuals who can make and enforce rules of universal application for universal behaviour. Such an organized society is called the state. And the rules by which the social behaviour is determined are known as the laws of the state and the individuals who make and enforce these rules are termed as the government. So the subject which deals with the state and government is called political science. Political science may be defined as the study of man in the process of governing himself.

Man is a social animal, and so being he lives in the society and practises for the society's *yogakṣema*. His personal growth depends on the social life. So, there is no such an importance of man without society and has no significance as an individual which he acquires being a part of the society. Therefore, it is the concern of all the sciences which relate man with the society. In this context man has a different type of mutual relationship. And based on such relationships many social sciences were developed. By economic relations of man economics and by the moral relations ethics were developed. While living in the society man is bound by many political relations, so by those relations the science that is developed is known as political science. Political relations of man are properly operated by the state, so the state is the main or basic theme of political science.

There is a difference of opinion on the subject matter of political science. Some writers restrict the scope of political science to the study of the state alone. For instance, Johann Kaspar Bluntschli, the renowned Swish jurist and politician, defines it "as the science which is concerned with the state, which endeavours to understand and comprehend the state in its fundamental conditions, in its essential nature, its various forms of manifestation, its development".

There are many others, like Stephen Leacock; according to him political science deals only with the government, the word state nowhere occurs in the definition.[1] But Laski,[2] Gettell[3] and Gilchrist[4] have more realistic view and emphasize that the scope of political science covers the study of both the state and the government. And it is also agreeing with this accepted view. There can be no state without government. The state is the organization of the people for law within a defined territory. It issues orders and punishes those who violate them. But no state acts by itself. The agency which acts on behalf of the state is called the government; so it becomes clear that the government is an integral part of the state. Without a government, there can be no state; therefore a description of the state must include

1 Stephen, Leacock, 1912, *Elements of the Political Science*, p. 3.

2 Laski, 1940, *The Danger of Being a Gentleman*, pp. 33-44.

3 Gettell, 1910, *Introduction to Political Science*, p. 4.

4 Gilchrist, 1921, *Principles of Political Science*, p. 2.

the study of the structure and function of the government, its forms and other institutions connected with it.

The state remains however the central subject of our study. The whole mechanism of government revolves around it. The necessity of government arises because there has been the need for the state and this need is deeply embedded in the nature and needs of man. Without the state life could not be sustained itself; but this is not the only object of the state. "The state comes into existence," as Aristotle says, "originating in the bare needs of life and continuing in existence for the sake of good life." The desires of man cannot be possible without the state; it is most important for his existence and development. As we know that state plays an important role in the life of man, so it becomes necessary to know it in its entirity: what it has been, what it is and what it ought to be?

To better understand the meaning and nature of the state, it is necessary to understand the past; without the proper knowledge of the past, one cannot understand its basic concepts in the present context. Without knowing the past we cannot understand the present fully. The historical perspectives involve the study of the origin and evolution of the state and the development of the mechanism through which it functions. We must also see how far the existing structure of the state responds to the need of the man and caters to his well-being; the intimate knowledge of the past and present makes us wiser for the future; and how the lessons we gain from there enable us to reform our political institutions according to our aspirations. It means, to discover the principles that should be adhered to in operating the machinery of the state, to criticize what is bad or inefficient and to suggest improvements, so that the state serves its purpose optimally in achieving social welfare.

It is the dream of an ideal state to provide the basic facilities for the fulfilment of man's desires which he has ever yearned for. Though every state strives to achieve this goal in different ways and scale, what an ideal state is and how can it be achieved have been a subject of great controversy throughout the human history.

All relates to the study of the state as it ought to be. Here political science becomes speculative in character, and we consider to evaluate the theories of the state and government which are created by the political philosophers, the problems of the social welfare, governmental economic programmes, international cooperation and amity, and a wide range of other matters that can confront mankind. It is clear that political science is a "historical investigation of what the state has been, an analytical study of what the state is and politico-ethical discussion of what the state should be".

The term "politics" was first employed by Aristotle and he used it as a title for his famous book dealing with the phenomenon of the state. The word politics is derived from the Greek word *politique* which comes from *polis,* meaning a city.[5] It is considered both as an art and a science of running the governmental, state affairs. The fundamental idea of the study of politics is concerned with the state in its theoretical as well as practical aspect, in the later capacity it deals with the government and its relation with the people and their social units.[6] To the Greeks the city was the state and the subject which dealt with the city state and its problems was named as politics. Political science is defined by many other scholars. For instance, according to Brewer,

> Political science considers the state, as an institution of the power, in the totality of its relations, its origin, its setting, its object, its ethical signification, its economic problems, its life condition, its financial side, its end, etc.[7]

J.W. Garner defines it in these words, "Political science begins and ends with the state". According to Paul Janet:

> The political science is that part of the social science which treats of the foundations of the state and principles of the government.

According to the R.G. Gettell:

5 *Webster's Dictionary*, S.V., Politics, p. 1304.

6 Vide Garner, 1928, *Political Science and Government*, pp. 11-14.

7 Sharma and Sharma, 2007, *Principles and Theory in Political Science,* vol. I, p. 5.

> It is thus the study of the state in the past, present, and future, and of political organization and political theories.

The statement of the Fareed Zakaria (2007) about political science is that:

> Political science sets forth in the systematic order and the fundamental principles according to which the state as a whole is to be organized and the sovereign power exercised.

From all the above definitions it becomes clear that political science is focused on the state and it is the subject of the study of political science. And it is the memorable point that state is the special organization of the human bodies and its all functional activities are done by the government. In this context the existence of the state cannot be possible without man and the government; both are essential for its entity and cannot be ignored.

According to H.J. Laski,

> The study of the politics concerns itself with the life of the men in relation to organize a state.[8]

Establishing the importance of men in the context of political science Hermann Heller in *Encyclopedia of Social Sciences* says that "it may be said that the character of the political science, in all of its parts, is determined by its basic pre-suppositions regarding man". So it becomes necessary that state and government, are the fundamental elements to define political science, and in the absence of these two, the value and existence of the state cannot be possible. So it can be said that political science is the study of both the state and the government.

The modern usage of the term politics gives entirely a different meaning. It is now commonly used to mean current political problems that face a country and its government. Gilchrist says:

> The term politics nowadays refers to the current problems of the government, which as often as not are more economic in character than the political in the scientific sense, when we speak that man is

[8] Laski, 1961, *An Introduction to Politics,* p. 34.

> interested in the politics, we mean that he is interested in the current problems of the day, in tariff questions, in labour questions, in the relation of the executive to legislature, in any question, in fact, which requires or is supposed to require the attention of the law-makers of the country.[9]

In the context of this explanation politics of one country differs from the politics of the other country. Indian politics and British politics are not identical. Even within the same country the politics of one party differs from the politics of another party, as each party offers its own solution to the problems which concern the country. For example, Conservative and Labour parties in England fundamentally differ from one another in their approach to the solution of the political and economic problems of their country; similarly the politics of the Indian National Congress differs from the politics of the Bharatiya Janata Party or the Communist Party of India.[10]

It follows, then, that a politician is a person who interests himself in the politics of his country and that of a particular political party which confirms to his political views. Political science enquires into the nature, conditions, origin and development of the state and government. It is the scientific study of the state as it has been, as it is and the state as it ought to be. A politician has nothing to do with all this. He uses the term politics, as the designation of the subject of our study, therefore highly ambiguous and confusing.

The science of the state and government is designated by different names, although we prefer to call it political science. Some call it as politics, others name it as political theory and many designate it as political philosophy. The absence of a commonly accepted term causes a good deal of confusion in understanding precisely what it concerns the state and government. For the proper appreciation of the subject matter of this study, it is necessary to know the concept of the meaning of each term with which it is designated and, then, how it got a correct name.

---

[9] Cited in A.C. Kapur, 1950, *Principles of Political Science*, pp. 3-4.

[10] Kapur, 1950, Ibid.

Some modern scholars/writers like George Jellinek, Peter Sedgwick and Sir Frederick Pollock, still prefer to use the term politics to political science, although they divided it into two parts: (1) theoretical politics, and (2) practical politics or applied politics.

In the former, they include the study of the fundamental characteristics of the state without reference to its activities or the means by which its end is attained. Theoretical politics as such relate to the origin, nature, attributes and the ends of the state, including the principles of political organization and administration. Applied or practical politics, on the other hand, embraces the study of the actual working of the government as we may say, the state in action; and a state in action is a dynamic institution adjusting itself to the needs of times. This is how Sir Frederick Pollock makes his division[11] — 1. theoretical politics, and 2. practical politics (see Table 2.1)

Table 2.1: Theoretical and Practical Politics

	Theoretical Politics	*Practical Politics*
a.	Theory of the state (origin, classification of forms of government, sovereignty)	The state (existing forms of government)
b.	Theory of the government (forms of institution, executive, province and limits of opposite law)	Government (constitutionally law and usage of parliamentary systems, army, navy, police, currency and budget)
c.	Theory of legislation (objects of legislation, philosophy of law or general jurisprudence, method and sanction of law, interpretation and administration, machines of lawmaking)	Laws and legislation (legislative procedure, courts of justice and their machinery, judicial precedents and authority)
d.	Theory of state and artificial person (relation to other states and bodies of men, international law)	The state personified (diplomacy, peace and war, conferences, treatise and conventions, international agreements)

[11] Pollock, 1895, *An Introduction to History of Science of Politics*, London: Macmillan, pp. 99-100.

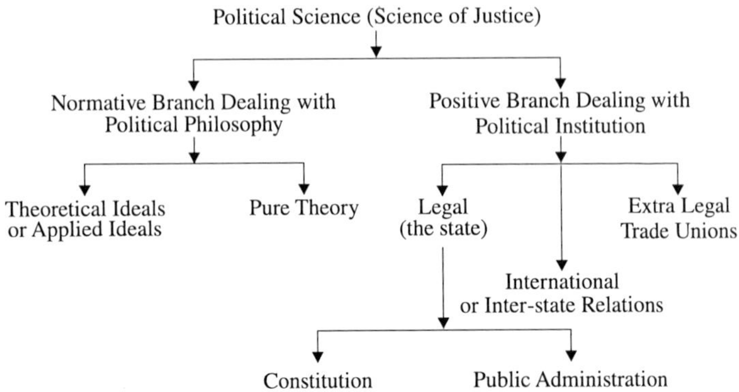

fig. 2.1: Branches of political science

So, here is no doubt, a useful division as it covers the study of the state in all its aspects. Still, majority of the writers prefer the use of the term political science instead of theoretical politics and applied politics. Political science is a comprehensive term which embraces both theoretical and applied politics. Practical politics is not the only aspect of political science.

Max Weber defines[12] political science as both a positive and normative science which studies human behaviour in its justice-seeking aspect. Krishna P. Mukherjee accepts this new definition and includes it in the scope of political science with its branches and sub-branches (*fig*. 2.1).

However, the aim of political science is not only to formulate scientific laws for political governance of man, but also to establish a way of life which, according to Aristotle, is for the sake of good life. A good life is the art of living together in a spirit of togetherness: a rational conduct of many lives, first as the citizens of a state to which man belongs and, then, as members of the common humanity. Peoples of all the states have yet to learn the art of good life in all aspects and once this art is mastered there be a happier and just life.

The mainstream of political science is divided in two parts: (1) theoretical, and (2) practical. From the above discussion, it

---

12 Kapur, 1950, *Principles of Political Science*, p. 6.

is clear that state is the core subject of political science. So here both the theoretical and practical aspects of state are discussed.

Theoretical Aspect

FOUNDATIONS OF STATE

While introducing the state we said that it originated in the bare needs of life and continues in existence for good life.

How did states get started? The first thing that anyone discovers when he begins to examine the origins of the state is the great paucity of information. Prehistoric man did not leave many records. Those he did leave are not in readily intelligible form: potsherds, implements, interments, artworks, monuments, ruins of villages and cities, and in the more advanced ancient societies, inscriptions in the form of hieroglyphics or primitive alphabets. It is not easy to interpret these remains. The science of archaeology concentrates on such interpretations, and as new archaeological evidence is uncovered, scientists have to revise their earlier judgements about life in the early history of man. Thus there is never any fine answer or permanent opinion about his life of long ago. J.W. Garner is also of the same view. To him,[13] it is well to note the limitations of archaeology. It cannot answer all these questions and the answers that it does offer are partial and tentative.

> The circumstances under which primitive men first saw the light of political consciousness and came to associate themselves together under some form of political organization are facts veiled largely, if not wholly in the mists of obscurity.[14]

One of the questions most often asked of the archaeologist is how did the state begin? What is the thing that promoted man to act politically, to come together with his fellows to form the political phenomenon called the state? The state is an abstraction and not an artefact. The archaeologist may unearth the state's grand buildings, but he gives us

---

13 Garner, 1910, *Introduction to Political Science*, p. 87.

14 Ibid., p. 27.

little help regarding its conceptual beginnings.

The question on the origin of state cannot be answered with finality and we do not exactly know when and how it came into existence, its origin is shrouded in mystery. Various guesses have been made, but they are still conjectures. The recent researches in the sciences of anthropology, ethnology and comparative philology throw some light on the subject, but all these are not sufficient to offer a logical explanation for the origin of state. Speculation is then the only alternative and we examine a number of theories that have been advanced from time to time varying with the credulity of the age. The most important of such theories are:

1. The theory of divine origin of state
2. The theory of social contract
3. The force theory
4. The patriarchal and matriarchal theories
5. The historical or evolutionary theory.

Among these theories the historical or evolutionary theory is now accepted as a correct theory of origin of state. The first four stands are rejected. But it does not mean that they have no practical utility. Each one of these theories contains some elements of truth and, thus, aids us in understanding the mysteries of the past and helps to find out how and why the state came into existence. To examine and reject a speculative theory means arriving at truth. It is only by groping in the darkness that we hope to reach the light.

Stephen Leacock has rightly said that the "rejection of what is false in the speculative theories of the past will aid in establishing more valid conclusions on the residual basis of what is true". What exists is never known. It is a monument of human effort, the result of prolonged activity. We cannot, therefore, understand any contemporary institution without some knowledge of its genetic background.

Speculative theories exhibit the spirit of the time in which they flourished and are consequently the index of the people, their thoughts, their environments and describe the forces that moduled and shaped the practice of state. Finally, speculative theories led to the development of political thought. Men of merit thought and considered, discussed and criticized the various theories presented and it paved the way for further developments in political thinking. The social contract theory replaced the theory of divine origin and the former was replaced by the historical or evolutionary theory.

The Theory of Divine Origin of the State

The theory of divine origin of state is the oldest concerning the primary origin of the state. It looks upon the state as a divine institution. According to this theory, the state, its advocates maintain, is created by God and governed by his deputy. It was his will that men should live in the world in a state of political society and sent his deputy to rule over them. The ruler is, therefore, a divinely appointed agency and he is responsible for his actions to God alone. As the ruler is the deputy of God, obedience to him is held to be a religious duty and resistance a sin.

This theory was prevailed in the society for a long time as Gettell (1949: 72) has said:

> During a large part of human history the state was viewed as of direct divine creation and its government was theocratic in nature.

In such type of state the king or ruler is regarded as the agent or representative of God on earth. And it was his religious duty to make his subject happy, and the duties of subjects are also made that they should obey their ruler and not to make him unhappy.[15]

The theory of the divine origin of the state is as old as political science itself. There is sufficient evidence to prove now that the early states were based on this conception and all political authority was connected with certain unseen powers. The earliest rulers were the combination of priest and king or the magic man and the king. Religion and politics were so inextricably mixed up in the primitive society

---

[15] Narayana, 1962, *Rājanīti-Śāstra ke Mūla Siddhānta*, p. 102.

that not a hazy line of demarcation could be drawn between the two.[16] And even today, the relation of politics and religion is found in many countries' constitution.

The Jews were the earliest advocates of this theory. According to them God is the appointer of the king, and he is the power of the king. In the words of Bluntschli, "The state was the immediate work of God, the direct revelation upon earth of the divine government." This theory was also accepted by the Greek and Romans at that time. The theory that authority has a religious origin and sanction finds unequivocal support in the scriptures of every religion. In *Mahābhārata* it has been stated that when people were tired of anarchy and lawlessness, they prayed God for respite and he appointed Manu as their ruler. And in the Bible it is said "Let every soul be subject unto the higher powers". For there is no power but to God "the powers that be are ordained of God". The God is the source of all powers and the rulers are considered his agents. The early church fathers also propounded this theory.[17] During the Middle Ages a fierce controversy developed between the state and church for supremacy on the basis of this theory. Gradually the theory of state was transformed into the theory of the divine rights of kings.

In England James I and Sir Robert Filmer were the leading exponents of the devine right of king doctrine. In his work, *The Law of Free Monarchies*, James I wrote: "Kings are justly called gods, for they exercise a manner of resemblance of divine power upon the earth."[18]

The notion of state being divinely created does not find any place in the present-day political thought. The state is essentially a human institution, and it comes into existence when a number of people occupying a definite territory organize themselves politically for achieving common ends. The laws of the state are made by men and enforced by them. The state, therefore, originated in the bare needs of the human life and continues in existence for satisfying those needs. To

---

16 Gilchrist, 1921, *Principles of Political Science*, p. 80.

17 Padhi et al., 2000, *Political Theory: Concepts, Issues and Ideologies*, p. 49.

18 Narayana, 1962, *Rājanīti-Śāstra ke Mūla Siddhānta*, p. 105.

accept it as a creation of God is to defy nature itself and to exalt it to a position above criticism and change. The divine theory is dangerous as it justifies the arbitrary exercise of royal authorities by holding that authority has religious sanction and origin, and kings are the vicars of God. When the ruler is made responsible for his actions to God, and law is held to reside ultimately "in the breast of the king", it is tantamount to preaching absolution and making the king a despot. Even if it is conceded that king is the vicegerent or deputy of God, then, how can the existence of a bad king be justified? History abounds in example of bad and vicious kings. So, this theory, according to scriptures, does not find unequivocal support.

In conclusion, this theory does not consider any other form of government except monarchy and that too, absolute monarchy. Such a form of government is antagonistic to the democratic ideal, which accepts citizen consent to be the basis of the state. Although this theory has many demerits, its importance cannot be neglected, as it occupies an important place among political ideologies.[19]

Force Theory

Leacock, gives a matter-of-fact explanation of the force theory when he says that:

> Historically it means that government is the outcome of human aggression, that the beginnings of the state are to be sought in the capture and enslavement of man by man, in the conquest and subjugation of feebler tribes, and generally speaking in the self-seeking domination acquired by superior physical force. The progressive growth from tribe to kingdom and from kingdom to empire is but a continuation of the same process.[20]

The theory, in fine, tells that the state is primarily the result of forcible subjugation through long continued warfare among primitive groups. Gettell is also of the same view about this theory. To him, "The theory

---

[19] Gilchrist, 1921, *Principles of Political Science*, p. 71.

[20] Leacock, 1912, *Elements of Political Science*, p. 32.

of force, therefore, traces the development of the state as the result of conquest."[21] Hence the idea comes out that, force is the physical power by which the state can be governed, and it is the basis of the state. The theory of force has been supported and advanced by different writers for advocating their own point of view. It was used by the church fathers in the medieval period to discredit the state, and to establish the supremacy of the church. They claimed that church was divinely created whereas the state was the outcome of the brute force.

In modern times the individualists adopted the theory to protect individual liberty against governmental encroachment. They characterized the state as a necessary evil and argued that state should let the individual remain alone and it should not interfere in his doings. The individualists based their arguments on the principle of the survival of the fittest and thereby tried to prove that it is only the strong who survive and the weak go to the wall. The socialists on the other hand held that the state is the outcome of the process of aggressive exploitation of the weaker by the stronger. They further argued that force is the origin of civil society and government represents merely the coercive organization which tends exploit the working class. Therefore, the theory of socialism is a revolt against the state, as the state is the product of force and power is its justification. So, we can see that this theory has prevailed in modern time and only light changes came into its existence till now. The words of Leacock become true for this theory. To him, "The government is the result of human struggle."[22]

Force, indeed, has played an important role in the origin and development of the state; force is the essential element of the state. Internally the state requires force to ensure obedience to its commands. Externally, it is necessary to repel aggression and to preserve the integrity of the state. Without force no state can exist and the sovereignty of the state always rests ultimately on force. Immanuel Kant said: "Even a population of devils would find it to their advantage

---

[21] Gettell, 1910, *Introduction to Political Science*, p. 79.

[22] Bluntschli, 2000, *The Theory of State*, p. 292.

to establish a coercive state by general consent."[23]

No state has emerged solely by brute force. State is the product of several factors such as kingship, religion, economic activities and political consciousness.[24] Force is an essential element of the state but not the real and ultimate basis. Common will or consent of the people is the real basis of the state. T.H. Green has said:

> It is not coercive power as such but coercive power exercised according to law, written or unwritten for maintenance of the existing rights from external or internal invasions, that makes a state.[25]

According to MacIver, "coercive power is the criterion of the state, but not its essence. No state can last long by mere use of naked force."[26] This theory is not conducive to democracy. Democracy is a government by consent, discussion and criticism. The use of force suppresses people's right to discuss and debate public issues and to control the government. Force without constitutional checks and safeguards leads to tyranny and dictatorship. Force is a means to an end, namely, public welfare.

The Social Contract Theory

The most important speculative theory relating to the origin of the state is the social contract theory. It was the most popular and influential theory relating to the origin of state and the nature of political authority during the seventeenth and eighteenth centuries.

The exponents of the theory hold that the state is the result of a deliberate and voluntary agreement (contract) entered into by primitive men who originally had no governmental organization. They divided history into two periods. The period before the state was formed, is called "the state of nature" and the period after the state was instituted by contract or volentary agreement, which is instrumental in the

---

23 Kapur, 1950, *Principles of Political Science*, pp. 67-69.

24 Padhi et al., 2000, *Political Theory*, p. 54.

25 Gilchrist, 1921, *Principles of Political Science*, p. 85.

26 MacIver, 1926, *The Modern State*, p. 222.

formation of the state, divide history into two periods. In the state of nature men were subject to no law or governmental regulation. Men were subject only to such regulations as nature was supposed to prescribe. The men were enjoying some natural rights, but the state of nature became unbearable and inconvenient for primitive men to put up it for a long time. Finally, men decided to abandon the state of nature and set up a political system as society through contract. As a result of contract, each man lost his natural liberty partly or wholly, and agreed to obey the laws prescribed by the government.

The theory of social contract found adequate support both in the East and the West. Kauṭilya, the minister of Candragupta Maurya, elaborated it in his *Arthaśāstra*. He wrote:

> People suffering from anarchy, as illustrated by the proverbial tendency of large fish swallowing a small one, first elected the king Manu to be their king, and allotted one-sixth of the grains grown and one-tenth of merchandise as sovereign dues. Fed by this payment kings took upon themselves the responsibility of maintaining the safety and security of their subjects.
>
> — Bk I, chap. XIII

The description of this theory is also found in Śānti-Parva.[27]

In Greece it was supported by the sophists first. According to them, state is an artificial institution and it is the result of a contract. This theory came against the theories of Aristotle and Plato. Aristotle and Plato have repudiated this theory simultaneously in their works — *Republics* and *Politics* — respectively by saying that state is a natural institution.

This theory assumed significance during and after the Middle Ages. Two forms of theory, viz. the governmental contract and the social contract, are found in such discussions. The first postulates a tacit agreement between the government and the people; and the second, the institution of a political society (state) by means of a contract among individuals.

---

[27] ŚP LXVII.16-17.

Social contract, as distinguished from the governmental contract, is probably first mentioned in Richard Hooker's *The Laws of Ecclesiastical Polity*.[28] The theory also received impetus from the writings of Hugo Grotius, the Dutch jurist. But it found real support at the hands of Thomas Hobbes, John Locke and Jean-Jacques Rousseau. Hobbes (1588–1679), published his book, *Leviathan*, in 1651. In this book he gave a striking exposition of the theory of social contract.

Hobbes began his thesis with the state of nature, which he characterized as the pre-social phase of human nature. The state of nature, as Hobbes described it, was a condition of unmitigated selfishness and rapacity. Men had no sense of right and wrong and they fell upon each other with savage ferocity. There was a perpetual and restless desire in them to satisfy their appetites and desires with a craving for gain and glory, which men enjoyed in the state of nature, was nothing short of might and natural liberty was nothing more than "the liberty that each man hath to use his own power for the preservation of his own nature".[29]

From the analysis of the state of nature, Hobbes concluded that man was not at all social; indeed he found "nothing but grief in the company of his fellows", all being almost equally selfish, self-seeking, cunning, egoistic, brutal, covetous and aggressive. This state of nature was a condition of perpetual war "where every man is enemy to every man". These conditions were really intolerable and could not be left to continue, indefinitely. Men naturally wish for peace and security, and to escape from the misery and the horror of their natural condition, they consented among themselves to form a civil society or a common wealth. By mutual covenant they agreed to surrender their natural rights into the hands of common superior and obey his commands.[30]

According to Hobbes social contract theory is a social contract not a governmental contract. The sovereign is not a party to the contract

---

28 Padhi et al, 2000, *Political Theory*, p. 55.

29 Hobbes, Thomas, 1651, *Leviathan*, part I, chap. XXI.

30 Lucas, 1996, *Principles of Politics*, p. 62.

as he is the creation of the contract or, as W.A. Dunning puts it, "A superior, or sovereign, exists only by virtue of the pact, not prior to it".

As a sovereign is not a party to the contract, he does not subject himself to any conditions; his authority is absolute and unlimited. All his subjects must obey him; otherwise there will be conflict, war and a return to the wretchedness of the state of nature. Hobbes denied to the people this right to revolt against the authority of the sovereign.[31] Hobbes was basically an individualist philosopher who justified absolute power of the government in the interest of peace and security which are the basic needs of human beings. Locke and Rousseau also supported this theory. Locke's theory, propounds state of nature as a pre-political and not social, as such, it does not, present to him such a dismal state of affairs as it did to Hobbes.

Locke's man in the state of nature is neither selfish, nor self-seeking, nor aggressive. He is social and sympathetic. In Locke's state of nature men are equal to free their deeds what they want, but "within the bounds of the law of nature". And his state of nature was, therefore, "a state of peace, goodwill, mutual assistance and preservation".

But men experienced three inconveniences: (1) the absence of settled and fixed laws; (2) the absence of known and impartial judge; (3) and the absence of an executive power to enforce just decisions. Men made a contract to escape from the state of nature, which was an "ill condition" and establish the civil society in which the whole community enjoyed supreme power. Each individual surrendered his natural rights of interpreting and enforcing the law of nature so that his fundamental natural rights of life, liberty and property could be secured. Supreme power was vested in the community which set up a government as a "fiduciary trust" to carry out the functions delegated by the community. Government was based on the consent of the people who could overthrow it when it acted against the trust resposed on it. His theory thus results in constitutional or limited government.[32]

---

31 Hobbes, 1651, *Leviathan*, chap. XIV.

32 Padhi et al., 2000, *Political Theory*, p. 56.

As Locke says:

> The community perceptually retains a supreme power of saving themselves from the attempts and designs of anybody . . . whenever they shall be so foolish or as wicked as the lay and carry on designs against the liberties and properties of the subjects. . . . Whenever anyone shall go about to bring them to a slavish condition, they will always have a right to get rid themselves of those who invade this fundamental, sacred and unalterable law of self-preservation.[33]

Rousseau's view in "contract social" inspired the French Revolution of 1789 and also provided the basis of theory of popular sovereignty. Man, according to Rousseau, is essentially good and sympathetic and "man is born free, however, he is everywhere in chains".[34] The state of nature was a period of idyllic happiness. Man was a "noble savage" and led a happy and simple life. With the growth of population and the idea of private property men became selfish, greedy and aggressive. With the dawn of reason, human nature becomes increasingly complex. Conflicts and tensions in the later stages of the state of nature forced men to enter into a contract whereby they surrendered all their natural rights to the community or the "general will". The people and collective body became sovereign and each member was an inseparable part of general will and decision can be made only in assembly of the whole people.

Government remains as agent of the community and exercises only executive power delegated to it by the community. Rousseau's idea inspired the movements for democratic rights in the eighteenth and nineteenth centuries; and at the same time his "doctrine of general will" has been manipulated to serve the purpose of the totalitarian states. According to him:

> The public person thus formed by the union of all particular individuals, was formerly given the name city, and is now called a republic or body politic. Its members refer to it as the state when it is passive, the sovereign, when it is active; a power when they compare

---

[33] Locke and Seal, 1924, *Of Civil Government*, XII.149, XIX.217-18, 219-22.

[34] Rousseau, 1763, *The Social Contract I,* p. 23.

> it with institutions. With regard to the associates they are collectively called the people. When they are thought of participating in the sovereign authority, they are called citizens, when they are thought of submitting to the laws of the state, they are called subjects.[35]

But this theory of social contract has been assailed from various angles. It has been characterized as bad history, bad law and bad philosophy. But the importance of this theory cannot be denied. It has the advantage of giving as perhaps the only sound assumption on which to build and maintain any system of political relationships. At the same time, this theory was practically most valuable.

The contract theory has also helped in the development of the modern concept of sovereignty. Hobbes paved the way for John Austin, the proponent of legal sovereignty; Locke was the champion of political sovereignty and Rousseau was the high priest of popular sovereignty. Rousseau also brought into prominence the ideal of direct democracy. Indirect or representative democracy lost much of its appeal after the First World War. New devices of popular participation in the work of government began to be advocated, and "the referendum is merely a modified form of Rousseau's conception of inalienable sovereignty of the people".

The modern theory of a clear separation between the state and government has really come to us from Locke. Finally the contract theory raises a common man on the pedestal of political glory. The modern cry of equal rights of voting for all citizens is, in fact, the legacy of Rousseau's ideal of equal political rights.[36]

Patriarchal and Matriarchal Theories

Then the next theories of the origin of state are the patriarchal and matriarchal theories. These theories were also valuable at that time. These theories, jointly known as "kinship theories" seek to explain the origin of state in terms of the explanation of the family which is the

---

35 Rousseau, 1763, *The Social Contract I*, p. 114.

36 Gilchrist, 1921, *Principles of Political Science*, pp. 78-79.

oldest social organization and the basic unit of a society. According to kinship theories, "the state is an expanded family". Aristotle was in support of this theory; he believed that the state came into existence as a result of the natural expansion of the family.[37] In the words of Leacock, "first a household, then a patriarchal family, then a tribe of persons of kindred decent, and finally a nation – so runs the social series erected on the basis".[38]

Sir Henry Maine, the chief advocate of the patriarchal theory, in his books *Ancient Law* (1861) and *Early History of Institutions* (1874), has defined it as "the theory of the origin of society in separate families, held together by the authority and perfection of the eldest male descendant". The chief exponents of matriarchal theory are J.F. McLennan (1827-81), L.H. Morgan (1818-81) and Edward Jenks (1861–1939). The aborigines of Australia and certain communities in India provide examples of the matriarchal system. The fundamental features of this society are: (i) transient marriage relationships, (ii) female kingship, (iii) maternal authority, and (iv) succession of only females to property and power.

But sociological and anthropological researches have proved that neither patriarchal nor matriarchal system was universal in primitive societies. It is incorrect to regard matriarchal family as the oldest form of social organization everywhere.

It is not possible to believe that a complex social organization like the state developed through the expansion of family, whether patriarchal or matriarchal. As W.W. Willoughby observes:

> It would not be true to say that the state developed out of this small social unit. The two institutions are different in essence. In the family the location of authority is natural (i.e. in the father). In the state it is one of choice. Subordination is the principle of the family: equality that of the state. Furthermost, the functions or aims of the state are essentially different from, and even contradictory to, those

37 Padhi et al., 2000, *Political Theory*, p. 61.

38 Leacock, 1912, *Elements of Political Science*, p. 381.

of family.[39]

Evolutionary Theory

The generally accepted and most satisfactory theory of the origin of state is the evolutionary or historical theory. In rejecting the earlier theories, largely based on speculation, Garner writes:

> The state is neither the handiwork of God, nor the result of superior physical force, nor the creation of resolution or conventions, nor a mere expansion of the family.[40]

It is on the other hand the product of growth, a slow and steady evolution extending over a long period of time embracing many elements in its development, prominent among which were kinship, religion, property and need for self-defence from within and without.

S. Leacock (1912) says:

> The state is a growth, an evolution, the result of gradual process, running throughout all the known history of man and remote and unknown past.

The state was not created in any single point of time. Its origin lies in the long evolutionary process through which it has passed. So it is considered as a historical creation. As Robert L. Burgess puts it:

> The proposition that the state is the product of history means that it is a gradual and continuous development of human society, out of grossly imperfect beginning, through crude and improving forms of manifestation, towards a perfect and universal organization of mankind it means, to go a little deeper into the psychology of the subject, that it is the gradual realization, in legal institutions of the universal principles of human nature and the gradual subordination of the individual side of the nature to the universal side.[41]

Slowly and imperceptibly, the state developed from simple to a complex

---

39 Willoughby, 1898, *An Examination of the Nature of the State*, p. 20.

40 Garner, 1910, *Introduction to Political Science*, chap. IV.

41 Quoted in A. Appadurai, 1954, *The Substance of Politics*, p. 38.

political organization of modern type. As Gettell (1910: 65) writes:

> Like all other social institutions, the state arose from many sources and under various conditions, and it emerged almost imperceptibly. Most of the political scientists today feel that this is the most acceptable theory of origin of state. States are of course today much bigger than they used to be, much stronger, certainly more complex, states also accept more responsibilities and thus affect the individual more markedly than did their earlier counterparts. How has all this come about?

The population of the world has increased enormously. Archaeologists find that civilized man existed in the Indus Valley in Pakistan about 7,000 years ago. At that time the population of the world probably numbered no more than a few millions. Today the world population totals more than seven-and-a-half billion people. Large and growing populations produce problems.

As the population pressure increases, people begin to spill over into territories of other states, resulting into conflicts which tend to strengthen and magnify the state. Furthermore, large populations usually require a strong government at home to address their numerous problems. There is increasing competition for land, resources and jobs. All this manifests itself in the demand by the people for the state to undertake more functions and responsibilities. Thus there has been a continuing tendency for the state to grow in authority and in the scope of its activities.

Stages in Development of the State

Greek city state → federal state → nation state (democratic state or modern state) → the future state

Hence it becomes clear that modern state (democratic state) came into existence after a great evolutionary process.

Practical Aspect: Political Institutions

THE STATE

> [A state] is a community of families and aggregations of families in well-being for the sake of a perfect and self-sufficing life. Such a

> community can only be established among those who live in the same place and intermarry. Hence there arise in cities family connexions, brotherhoods, common sacrifices, amusements which draw mass together. But these are created by friendship, for to choose to live together is friendship. The end of the state is the good life, and these are the means towards it. And the state is the union of families and villages in a perfect and self-sufficing life, by which we mean a happy and honourable life.[42]

The term "state" has a scientific meaning in political science. We do not use it with the same vagueness and ambiguity as it is used by a man in the street. It is often, but erroneously, employed as a synonym for "nation", "society", "government", etc. But all these terms have definite meaning of their own in political science and should be clearly distinguished one from the other. The term "state" is also very commonly used to express the collective action of the community, through the agency of the government, as distinguished from individual action. For example, whenever we talk about "state management", "state regulation", "state aid", etc. we actually use the word state for government.

In its scientific sense the state refers to an assemblage of human beings, occupying a definite territory, under an organized government and subject to no outside control or invasion. Without the people there can be no community to form one, and no common life without some definite piece of territory in which to make that experiment of collective living, which epitomizes the meaning of Aristotle's famous phrase, "man is a social animal".[43]

When people organize themselves for a settled life in order to secure certain elementary purposes and conditions of life, they bind themselves with some rules of common behaviour and from this emerges the state. Then Aristotle's second phrase becomes true "man is a political animal".[44] Society takes up man's need for companionship;

[42] Aristotle, *Politics* III.9.1280b32-1281b2.

[43] Aristotle, *Politics*, p. 5.

[44] Foster, 1941, *Masters of Political Thought*, vol. I, p. 126.

the state solves the problems created by the society through its agency, the government.

The state is, thus, a group of people organized for a common purpose. It is a territorial society divided into government and subjects, the former being a body of persons within the state bestowed with the duty to maintain those conditions of life which help to secure the purpose for which the state came into existence, that is, the welfare of man. The purpose or the aim of the state can best be defined in the words of the representatives of the United States of America before the United Nations' commissions for the drawing up of an international bill of rights:

> The state is created by the people, for the promotion of their welfare and the protection of their mutual rights. Everyone has the right to a fair, and equal opportunity to advance his own physical, economic, spiritual and cultural well-being, and to share the benefits of civilization. It is the duty of the state, in accordance with the maximum use of its resources, and with due regard for the liberties of the individual, to promote this purpose by legislation or by other appropriate means.[45]

Therefore, the state is a natural, a necessary and a universal institution. It is natural because it is rooted in the reality of human nature. It is necessary because, as Aristotle said:

> The state comes into existence originating in the bare needs of the life and continuing in existence for the sake of good life.[46]

Man needs the state to satisfy his diverse needs and to complete his desires what he wants. Without state he cannot rise to the full stature of his personality. In fact, in the absence of such a controlling and regulating authority, society cannot be possible and there will be disorder and chaos. In which sense the food is the most important requirement of man, in the same sense the state is to man. Both

---

45 Kapur, 1950, *Principles of Political Science,* pp. 28-29.

46 Dunning, 1970, *A History of Political Theories*: *Ancient and Medieval*, p. 55.

are indispensable for his existence and development. The state is, accordingly, a universal institution. It has existed whenever and wherever man has lived in an organized society.

Though the state is a necessary and a universal institution, and also considered as the central subject of the political science, what is a state? This is extremely a complex question of political science. As we know, each person is a member of a state. And the word "state" is used by us in many times a day, but in fact, what is a state? Very few people know it. Many political scientists have tried to define it, but because of time and situation they understood this in different forms. And also there have been many different views of what constituted the proper purpose of the state and hence its incompatible definitions. It may well seem curious, says R.M. MacIver, that so great and obvious a fact as the state should be the object of quite conflicting definitions. Some other scholars like Franz Oppenheimer and Karl Marx define the state as essentially a class structure and others regard it as the one organization that transcends class and stands for the whole community. Some interpret it as a power system, others as the welfare system, some view it entirely as a legal construction, either in the Austinian sense which made it a relationship of governors and governed or, in the language of modern jurisprudence, as a community organized for action under legal rules; some identify it with the nation, others regard nationality as incidental or unnecessary or even as a falsifying element which prevents the nature and functions of the state.[47]

Some regard it as a mutual insurance society, others as the very texture of all our life. To some it is a necessary evil, and to a very few an evil that is or will be some day unnecessary, while to others it is "the world the spirit has made for itself".

These disagreements are primarily due to the fact that every writer has defined it from his own point of view. If the author is a sociologist, like Oppenheimer or a philosopher like Hegel, or an economist, or a lawyer, his peculiar prepossessions may lend him either to distort the

47 Narayana, 1962, *Rājanīti-Śāstra ke Mūla Siddhānta*, p. 47.

reality by emphasizing some actual characteristics of the state ignoring the rest, or free himself altogether from reality and to picture the state as he thinks it ought to be.

Out of this maze of confusion we select a few definitions which fairly represent the weight of authority and by comparing them we try to understand what is common in them. T.E. Holland defines the state as "a numerous assemblage of human beings, generally occupying a certain territory, amongst whom the will of the majority, or of an ascertainable class or of persons, is by the strength of such a majority, or class, made to prevail against any of their number who opposes it". According to Marcus Tullius Cicero, "the state is a numerous society united by a common sense of right and natural participation in advantages". E.E. Hall says, "the marks of an independent state are that the community constituting it is permanently established for a political end, that it possesses a defined territory and that it is independent of external control". A state exists, according to Oppenheimer, "when a people is settled in a country under its own sovereign government". MacIver defines it as "an association which; acting through law as promulgated by a government endowed to this end with coercive power, maintains with a community territorially demarcated the universal external conditions of social order". Bluntschli says, "the state is the politically organized people of a definite territory", and according to Woodrow Wilson, it "is the people organized for law within a definite territory". Laski defines the state as "a territorial society divided into government and subjects claiming, within its allotted physical area, a supremacy over all the institutions". According to Willoughby:

> The state exists whenever there can be discovered in any community of man a supreme authority exercising a control over the social action of individuals and groups of individuals and itself subject to no such regulation.[48]

To John William Burgess:

---

[48] Willoughby, 1924, *The Fundamental Concepts of Public Law*, p. 3.

> The state is a particular portion of mankind viewed as an organized unit.[49]

Garner says:

> The state is a community of persons, more or less numerous, permanently occupying a definite portion of territory, independent or nearly so of external control and possessing an organized government to which the great body of inhabitants render habitual obedience.[50]

According to MacIver:

> The state is an association which acting through law as promulgated by a government endowed to this end with coercive power, maintains within community, territorially demarcated, the universal external condition of social order.[51]

In most of the above definitions only three elements of state are mentioned: (1) population, (2) territory, and (3) government. All these writers have same view on this, but the disagreement again becomes prominent in respect of the fourth element, i.e. sovereignty. Those who deny to the state the element of sovereignty accord a special quality to government. It is habitually obeyed, says Sedgwick; it is superior to individual wishes, says Esmien; it claims unlimited authority, says Zimmer; it is endowed with coercive power, says MacIver; it is sovereign, says Oppenheimer. When government is accorded superior quality, it is really the quality of the state. According to Herman Finer,[52] is in its monopoly of coercive power:

> This, then, is the state; and its supreme power and monopoly of coercion (which it can devolve in many ways on its own term) is sovereignty.

The sovereign is "legally supreme over any individual or group", says

[49] Burgess, 1891, *Political Science and Comparative Constitutional Law*, vol. 1, no. 8.

[50] Hacker, 1961, *Political Theory*, pp. 4-5.

[51] MacIver, 1926, *The Modern State,* Introduction.

[52] Finer, 1932, *The Theory and Practice of Modern Government*, p. 10.

Laski,[53] and the sovereign possesses "supreme coercive power". The state and government are by no means the same thing. Government is merely an essential instrument or contrivance of the state. So the writers who have not included sovereignty in their definition of state, their definition is deemed to be incomplete. But Garner has clearly mentioned all the four elements such as (1) population, (2) land (territory), (3) government, and (4) sovereignty in his definition of state. Population, territory, government and sovereignty are simultaneously defined by Garner as (1) a community of persons, (2) occupying a definite portion of territory, (3) organized government, and (4) independent or nearly so of external control and the great body of habitants render habitual obedience.[54] Hence, all the essential elements of state are available in Garner's definition. So his definition is scientific and accepted by all.[55]

From the above analysis, it becomes clear that scholars are not of the same views in defining the state. They have defined the state in different ways. According to Willoughby,[56] (1) population, (2) regime, and (3) constitution are the three essential elements of the state. Bluntschli has mentioned seven elements of state. But according to modern politicians the state has only four essential elements. Therefore, state possesses the elements of (i) population, (ii) territory, (iii) government, and (iv) sovereignty.

The first two elements — population and territory — are the physical basis or substantial basics of the state, and the last two — government and sovereignty — are the spiritual foundations of the state. We will discuss these elements separately.

Population

From above discussions we reach the conclusions that: (1) the state is a human institution; the product of man's gregarious nature and the

---

53 Laski, 1935, *The State in Theory and Practice*, p. 9.

54 Garner, 1928, *Political Science and Government*, p. 75.

55 Hacker, 1961, *Political Theory*, p. 6.

56 Willoughby, 1898, *An Examination of the Nature of State*, p. 4.

result of bare necessities of human life, and (2) population and land are the starting point of any study of man in his organized groups. It is the people which make the state, without them there can be none.

So, to the establishment of human society, population is a very important factor. But the population must be sufficient enough to make a state. The members of one single family do not make a state; there should be a series of families. No limit, however, can be placed on the number of the people constituting the state. How large a population is required for a state? Andorra, a state in the Spanish Pyrenees, has a population of about 85,000, and the Vatican City in Rome has something like 1,000 people. Are these populations sufficiently large? The question is not easy to answer. Some states, such as China and India, have huge populations, others have extremely small ones.[57]

Plato and Aristotle put definite limitations on the population of the state. Their ideal was a Greek city state like Athens and Sparta Plato and they fixed the number at 5,400 citizens. Aristotle held that neither ten or 100,000 could make a good state, both these numbers should be neither too small nor too large; it should be large enough to be self-sufficing and small enough to be well governed.[58] Rousseau, the priest of direct democracy, determined 10,000 to be an ideal number for a state.[59] And Garner has also presented his view. To him:

> The population must be sufficient in number to maintain a state organization and that it ought not be greater than, the territorial area and resources of the state are capable of supporting.[60]

Modern tendency is in the favour of states with huge population. It is believed that manpower of the state must swell, as population is the sinew of war and power. Hitler's and Mussolini's governments gave bounties to couples producing children above a given minimum. Issueless and unmarried persons were taxed.

57 Gettel, 1910, *Introduction to Political Science*, pp. 14-15.

58 Aristotle, 1984, *Politics*, Bk VII, 4 (Sowetts edn), p. 271.

59 Rousseau, 1762, *Social Contract*, Bk II, chap. 10.

60 Garner, 1928, *Political Science and Government*, p. 77.

Russia too has encouraged growth of her population. In India, the challenge is to check the ever-growing population, because of the wide disequilibrium between the population and the available means of production.

But the size of population is no criterion of the state. Increase or decrease in population makes no difference in its statehood. Though, no limit, either theoretical or practical, can be placed on the population of the state, the population must be sufficient to maintain a state organization and it should not be more than what the territorial resources of the state are capable of supporting. But behind all these quantitative and qualitative factors, there lies the problem of evaluating population. Population cannot be reckoned in mathematical terms; the kind of people a state has matters no less than their numbers.

Aristotle rightly said:

> A good citizen makes a good state and bad citizen makes a bad state. A good citizen must be intelligent, disciplined and healthy. Healthy citizens are the health of the good state. Disease diminishes intelligence, capacity for work, energy and vitality, it makes for poor production, laziness and lethargy. Similarly, good citizens will not allow religious or political differences to destroy the state's unity and good security.[61]

Territory

The second important element of the state is territory. As the population is essential for the state, in the same way it also acquires a territory in the formation of state, without it, there is no possibility to make a state. But some writers ignore territory as an element of the state. Leon Suguit says:

> The word state designates the rulers . . . or else the society itself in which the differentiation between rulers and ruled exists and in

61 Hacker, 1961, *Political Theory*, pp. 6-7, see also, Kapur, 1950, *Principles of Political Science*, p. 31.

> which, for that very reason, a public power exists.[62]

Sir John Seely, too, does not regard territory as an essential element or attribute of the state.[63] If a society is held together, he maintains, by the principle of government, it constitutes a state. Willoughby says:

> The state itself then is neither the people, the government, the magistracy, nor the constitution. Nor is it indeed the territory over which its authority extends. It is the given community of given individuals, viewed in a certain aspect namely as a political unity.[64]

But this concept or theory is refuted by modern politicians. According to them, territory is the most valuable element of state and have given their views on its importance. The names of W. Wilson, Bluntschli and Garner are famous in this context. So, the reality is that without territory the existence of a state is incomplete. It is accepted by M. Duguit:

> Modern civilized societies are in fact fixed on definite territories.[65]

William Edward Hall is also of the same view:

> There is no reason why even a wandering tribe or society should not feel itself bound as strongly as a settled community, by definite rules of conduct towards other communities.[66]

He has also accepted that:

> The circumstances of modern civilization which associate land, with sovereignty, make the possession of a fixed territory a practical necessity.[67]

According to Garner:

---

62 Gettel, 1910, *Introduction to Political Science*, pp. 31-37.

63 Ibid.

64 Hacker, 1961, *Political Theory*, p. 8.

65 M. Duguit, quoted by Garner, 1928, in *Political Sciences and Government*, p. 18.

66 Quoted in Garner, 1928, *Political Science and Government*, p. 86.

67 Hall, 1880, *International Law*, 3rd edn, p. 20.

> A people under such conditions may be a state in the making, but they do not become a state until their migration has ceased and they have established themselves permanently on a definite portion of territory.[68]

Thus, there is no state without its proper territory, large or small, and no territory that is not part of some state, large or small. And as far as we personally are concerned, it is our connection with a particular territory that normally creates our membership of a state. I am a citizen of India, because I am born there, or because my father was born there. My fellow citizens are my fellow-residents, and it is this sharing of the some territory that creates most of our common interests. Living together in a common land welds the people in a community of interests and it is a strong incentive to the feeling of fellowship. Love for territory inculcates the spirit of patriotism, which has been described in all ages and stages as a supreme virtue of man.

Moreover, the conduct of international relations would be seriously impeded without the requirement of a defined territory. All authorities on international law are now agreed that a fixed territory must be a condition of statehood. People and government are not enough. The occupation of a fixed territory is also essential, otherwise the state could not be readily identified and held to account if one attempts to conquer the other.[69]

There are at present 196 states in the world. Alongside of such giants as the United States and USSR we rank such pigmies as San Marino and Monaco as independent states. No limit, like population, can be put on the territory of the state, although opinion has differed on the political utility of a small and a big state. Plato drew a close analogy between the stature of a well-formed man and the size of a normal state. Aristotle was also favourably inclined towards the state of a moderate size.[70] Rousseau took cue from Plato's analogy and set

---

[68] Garner, 1928, *Political Science and Government*, p. 81.

[69] Gettel, 1910, *Introduction to Political Science*, p. 38.

[70] Benjamin Jowett (tr.), 1823, *The Laws of Plato*, p. 737 and *Politics*, Bk *IV, chap. 4.*

definite limits to the size of a well-governed state. He maintained that in general "a small state is proportionally stronger than a large one".[71] Montesquieu said that there is a necessary relation between the size of the state and the form of government best adapted to it.[72]

But these views were changed according to time. So, it can be said that well-formed government is not today dependent on the structure of the state (or territory) but it depends upon the population. What is the size of the state, it's not the main factor, and everywhere democracy is applied, it is not dependent on the size of the state, whether it is small or big. And in different countries states are of different sizes, because of their economic situations. Hence, it does not matter, what should be the size of the state. But, the important thing is that it should be well equipped and there should be unity for its development.

Government

The purpose for which people live together cannot be realized unless they subject themselves to certain rules of behaviour. The agency which is created for that purpose is called government. Government, in fact, is the focus of the common purpose of people occupying a definite territory and it is through this medium that common policies are determined, common affairs are regulated and common interests are promoted. Without government people will be just a babel of tongues with no means of collective action. They would divide themselves in groups, parties and even rival and antagonistic associations with rivalry, conflict and war ever ranging amongst them. It is, therefore, essential that there should be a common authority and a consequent order wherever people live. It is the prerequisite of human life and, as such, government is an essential element of the state. The state cannot and does not exist without a government, no matter what form of government may it assume.[73]

---

71 Rousseau, 1762, *Social Contract*, Bk II, chaps 6 and 8.

72 Montesquieu, 2002, *The Spirit of the Laws,* Bk VIII, chaps 19-20.

73 Kapur, 1950, *Principles of Political Science*, pp. 34-35.

Sovereignty

Sovereignty of the state is its most essential and distinguishable feature. A people inhabiting a definite portion of territory and having a government do not constitute a state. They must be internally supreme and free from external control. Sovereignty of the state has two aspects, internal sovereignty and external sovereignty. Internal sovereignty is the state's monopoly of authority inside its boundaries. This authority cannot be shared with any other state and none of its members within its territory owes obedience to any other state. If the state admits no rival within its own territory, it follows that it has no authority outside it. Each state is, therefore, independent of other states. Its will is its own, unaffected by the will of any external authority. That explains the meaning of external sovereignty.

Every state, therefore, must have its population, a definite territory, a duly established government and sovereignty. Absence of any of these elements denies to it the status of statehood. Accordingly, the term "state" generally used for the units of the Indian Republic, or any one of the fifty states, which make the United States of America, is a misnomer. None of them is sovereign. They possess the first three elements and are autonomous in their own spheres of jurisdiction. But autonomy is not sovereignty and when they lack sovereignty they cannot really be called states.

THEORIES OF STATE FUNCTION

Many ideologies originated from time to time like Marxism, Socialism, Fascism, Anarchism and Feminism, but among these the most important and valuable for present time is Liberalism. Francis Fukiama in his book *The End of History*, called it the "highest stage" of political institutions, as far as the notion of politics in Western tradition is concerned. It is necessary to know the basic idea of liberalism through which one can understand the concepts of state and government and also the Western concept of political institution.

Idea of Liberalism

Giovani Sartori observes:

> Liberalism and democracy, together with socialism and communism, are the labels which sum up the basic terms of the political context of the nineteenth and twentieth centuries.[74]

Liberalism, according to H.J. Laski, has been the outstanding doctrine of the West for centuries. The history of the past four centuries of the Western liberal democratic countries, and nearly all the socio-economic and political developments and movements of the modern Western world are closely intertwined with liberalism.

During this long period, liberalism has undergone changes with the changes in time and circumstances and there have been different shades of liberalism in various countries in different epochs, rather than one single, consistent brand of liberalism. It has been an extremely flexible and dynamic ideology, and despite numerous challenges and recurrent crises, it has survived all odds and gets going. Liberalism is not amenable to any precise definition because it does not represent any coherent body of doctrine. It is rather a historical tendency embracing diverse and even contradictory currents of thought. Explaining the difficulty of defining liberalism, Andrew Hacker writes:

> Liberalism has become so common a term in the vocabulary of politics that it is a brave man who will try to give a precise definition. It is the view of the individual, of the state, and of the relations between them.[75]

Liberalism can be defined as "an idea committed to freedom as a method and policy in government, as an organizing principle in society, and a way for the individual and community".[76] Liberalism, as Laski writes,

> is the expression less of a created than of a temperament. It implies

---

[74] Sartori, 1965, *Democratic Theory*, p. 353.

[75] Hacker, 1961, *Political Theory*, p. 237.

[76] *Encyclopaedia Britannica*, vol. III.

> a passion for liberty, and that the passion may be compelling; it requires a power to be tolerant, even sceptical, about opinions and tendencies you hold to be dangerous, which is one of the rarest human qualities.

According to Sartori, "very simply liberalism is the theory and practice of the individual liberty, juridical defence and the constitutional state".[77]

A.P. Grimes writes:

> It represents a system of ideas that aims at the realization of the pluralist society, favouring diversity in politics, economics, religion and other cultural life, it is opposed to conformity. It seeks its simplest sense to advance the freedom of the man. It is essentially anti-authoritarian. It seeks to increase individuality of man by increasing his area of choice and decision. It is essentially humanitarian in its appeal . . . finally it is flexible in the methods of its realization.[78]

Gordon Davis and Good point out:

> In the broadest sense, liberalism is rightly identified with the rise of the modern technical society availing itself of democratic political forms and of political capitalist economic institutions. This liberal society came to birth in Britain, France and America in opposition to the feudal aristocratic culture of the European past. Liberalism in the broadest sense is therefore synonymous with democracy.

Liberalism is a "psychological attitude" which embraces various facets of human activity such as religion, economics, morality and politics. It is an attitude rather than a doctrine which lays stress on man's goodness and rationality and desire for reforms to be introduced in every walk of life for a bright future. Central to the whole theme of liberalism is the doctrine of liberty. It was primarily the philosophy of the victorious middle class in Europe that came into power and prominence after the eclipse of the feudal classes. The capitalists first utilized the body of liberal ideas against the authority of the feudal barons, the government

---

77 Sartori, 1965, *Democratic Theory*, p. 364.

78 Grimes, 1956, "The Pragmatic Course of Liberalism".

by aristocrats and the power of the clergy. But with the advent of industrialization, a new opposition aroused between the capitalists and the wage earners with the result that liberalism tended to become a defence mechanism for the capitalists against the proletarian attacks.

In short, Liberalism treats market society as the model of the social organization where role of the state should be confined to the protection of the individual's life and property, enforcement of contracts and maintenance of minimum common service which would not be undertaken by the private entrepreneurs. In liberal view, the state is a necessary evil. Liberalism treats the state as the means and the individual as the end. It rules out the absolute authority of the state. Early exponents of liberalism included John Locke (1632–1704), Adam Smith (1723-90) and Jeremy Bentham (1748–1832). Locke is known as the father of liberalism. They are the founders of the classical liberalism which is called negative liberalism because it contemplates the negative role of the sphere of mutual interaction of individuals. In the twentieth century Herbert Spencer (1820–1903), sought to reaffirm negative liberalism through the application of the principles of natural science to social organization.

John Stuart Mill sought to modify utilitarianism and the principle of laissez-faire on philosophical grounds which paved the way for the theory of welfare state. Then T.H. Green (1832-82), sought to add a moral dimension to liberalism and thus advanced the theory of a full-fledged theory of welfare state. This tradition was further developed by L.T. Hobhouse, Harold J. Laski and R.H. Tawney, all of them were English philosophers. Thus the theory and practice of the welfare state flourished in the first half of the twentieth century in England. And this theory contemplates positive role of the state in securing a dignified life to individuals. It is therefore called positive liberalism.

On political perspective, liberalism promotes democracy; on economic side, it promotes capitalism. Democracy is concerned with fulfilling the needs and aspirations of ordinary people, but capitalism results in the concentration of economic power in the hands of the few who may use it against the interests of the ordinary people. This situation is sought to be rectified by the mechanism of welfare state.

Early liberal theory developed in two main directions: (a) individualism, and (b) utilitarianism. Individualism focused on an individual as a rational creature. It required that an individual's dignity, independent existence and judgement should be given full recognition while making public policy and decisions. It means, no individual shall be made to suffer in order to benefit any larger unit of the society. According to this view, only individual can have any rights; family, trade union, corporation or the state cannot have any rights which could be distinguished from the rights of their individual members. Similarly, no social unit can have any interest which could be distinguished from the interests of its individual members. Individualism supports a social and legal system which is based on voluntary transaction between individuals. This view strongly upholds market society model and holds that even taxation should be confined to the provision and maintenance of common services. John Locke and Adam Smith were the early exponents of individualism.

On the other hand, utilitarianism stands for the "greatest happiness of the greatest number" where interest of the few may be sacrificed. Happiness is defined as the balance in favour of pleasure over pain derived from various goods and services, act and policies. Founder of this school of thought, Jeremy Bentham, observed that nature has placed mankind under two sovereign masters: pleasure and pain. Human behaviour is guided by an urge to obtain pleasure and avoid pain. Moral principles and state policy should aim at promoting "greatest happiness of greatest number".

Neo-liberalism stands for contemporary version of classical liberalism. It denounces the welfare state, opposes state intervention and control of economic activities. In the second half of the twentieth-century thinkers like F.A. Hayak, M. Friedman and R. Nozick realized that the theory of welfare state was inimical to individual liberty, as it involved the forced transfer of resources from the more competent to the less competent. In order to restore individual liberty, they sought to receive the principle of laissez-faire not only in economic sphere, but also in social and political sphere. In a nutshell, neo-liberalism upholds full autonomy and freedom of the individual.

The greatest merit of liberalism lies in initiating the process of replacing traditionalism by modern rationalisṃ. In other words, it asserted that socio-economic relations of men in society, which were hitherto based on "tradition", should now be based on "reason". Liberalism has led to new insights as regards the principles of freedom, equality, justice, democracy, progress and other human values.

From this chapter it becomes clear that political science is that which concerns with the study of the state. The idea of politics is the result of the Western tradition. Practical (existing forms of government) and theoretical (origin, classification of forms of government, sovereignty) aspects of the state are also presented. This chapter also throws light on state and its elements. Main ideology known as liberalism, which comes in front of us, is relevant and a major thought for the modern society. It is quite necessary to get an overview of the political thoughts of the Western world, because the present work is based on political thought. It is necessary to get a fair idea about political thoughts, otherwise it cannot be possible to approach Śānti-Parva as a political text. It provides a great background in dealing with the political thoughts and principles in Śānti-Parva.

3

Political Ideas in Śānti-Parva

The Background

MANY Western scholars have presented their views that Indians were unknown to political ideas. According to them, modern politics is the result of the Western ideologies. But after studying the ancient Indian texts, their misunderstanding is over and they acknowledge that the early Indians were fully aware of the political system. There is a possibility that the political thoughts, which are vivid in *Arthaśāstra*, *Nītiśāstra*, *Rāmāyaṇa*, *Mahābhārata* and *Manusmṛti* had already been existing in the minds of the ancient people. In ancient India, the term *rājadharma* was used in a wider sense.[1] *Rājadharma* was a subject of discussion in the works on Dharmaśāstras from very ancient times. *Āpastamba Dharmasūtra* talks about "the general and special *dharma*s of all the *varṇas*". Except these there are also many other valuable and famous texts on *rājadharma*, such as *Yājñavalkyasmṛti* (304, 367), *Vṛhada Hārītasmṛti* (chap. 7, pp. 277-85), *Viṣṇu Dharmasūtra* (111), *Nītisāra* of Kāmandaka, *Agni Purāṇa* (chap. 218-42), *Garuḍa Purāṇa* (108-15), *Matsya Purāṇa* (215-43), *Viṣṇudharmottara Purāṇa* (11), *Mārkaṇḍeya Purāṇa* (24), *Kālikā Purāṇa* (87), *Nītiprakāśikā* (Jīvānanda edn, 1890), *Abhilāṣitārthacintāmaṇi* (first four *viṁśatiyāṅ*), *Muktikalpataru* of Bhoja, *Nītivākyāmṛta* of Somadeva, *Rājanīti-Ratnākara* of Caṇḍeśvara, *Rājanītiprakāśa* of Miśramiśra, *Nītimayūkha* of Nīlakaṇṭha and *Rājadharma-Kaustubha* of Anantadeva.[2] The discussion of *rājanīti* in these texts reveals that *rājadharma* was a core issue from ancient times.

[1] Vidyālaṁkāra, 1984, *Mahābhārata mein Śānti Parva kā Ālocanātmaka Adhyayana*, p. 80.

[2] Ibid., p. 81.

In ancient India, the term "politics" was basically conceived as *rājanīti* (the ethics of politics or political ethics). Due to different circumstances, some deviations and departures occurred from the fundamental norms of politics. Consequently, politics became a matter of convenience, expedience and selfish interest. Most of the earthly misdeeds are because of the deplorable fall in the ethics of politics from its original pedestal.

In the field of political ethics *Mahābhārata* occupies a great place because it is deeply concerned with the complex situations of political life and offers solutions to the various problems in politics. In *Mahābhārata* there is a specific and valuable description on *rājadharma* because here we find the delineation of a great war with the description of genealogy of the kings of the main narrative. In *Mahābhārata, rājadharma* is regarded as the most important science and it also consists of all other branches of knowlegde (*vidyās*)[3] in itself. *Rājadharma* has been called *kṣātra-dharma* in *Mahābhārata* because kṣatriyas were the ruling class. *Kṣātra-vidyā* is another term used in the sense of politics; the earliest references to it can be traced in *Chāndogyopaniṣad* VII.1.2 which thrice refers to this term.

Rājadharma. is regarded as the root of or the quintessence of all *dharmas*. Śānti-Parva of *Mahābhārata* states: "know that all the *dharmas* are merged in *rājadharma*; that *rājadharmas* are at the head of all the *dharmas*" and the welfare, good rains, sickness, calamities and death among people owe their origin to the king.[4]

---

3 ŚP LIII.29.

4 *evaṁ dharmān rājadharmeṣu sarvām sarvāvasthān sampralīnān nibodha*||
sarve dharmā rājadharmapradhānāḥ ||
sarvā vidyā rājadharmeṣu yuktāḥ sarve lokā rājadharme praviṣṭāḥ |
— ŚP 2LXIII.25, 26, 29

rājamūlā mahābhāho yogakṣemasuvr̥ṣṭayaḥ |
prajāsu vyādhayaścaiva maraṇaṁ ca bhayāni ca ||
kr̥taṁ tretā dvāparaṁ ca kaliśca bharatarṣabha |
rājamūlā iti matirmama nāstyatra saṁśayaḥ|| — Ibid. CXLI.9-10
sarvasya jīvalokasya rājadharmaḥ parāyaṇam| — Ibid. LVI.3

In ancient India, political science was known by several terms like *daṇḍanīti*, *nītiśāstra*, *arthaśāstra*, *rājanīti*, *rājadharma* and *rājyaśāstra*. These terms were used to denote what we call politics today. We will discuss about them, for what they were used and what were their importance and meaning.

Daṇḍanīti

The term *daṇḍanīti* is self-explanatory and was the most commonly used term. It occurs frequently in *Mahābhārata*,[5] *Arthaśāstra* of Kauṭilya,[6] *Manusmṛti*,[7] Purāṇas,[8] and the later works like *Kāmandaka Nītisāra*[9] and *Śukra Nītisāra*.[10]

Mahābhārata defines *daṇḍanīti* in these words: "because men are led (to the acquisition of the object of their existence) by chastisement, or again chastisement leads or governs everything", therefore, this science is known in all the three worlds as *daṇḍanīti*.[11] *Mahābhārata* describes *daṇḍanīti* in the fifteenth chapter of Śānti-Parva. It is used many times in this chapter. The whole Rājadharmānuśāsana chapter is a great source of ancient Indian politics.

Some other writers like Kauṭilya, however, do not understand *daṇḍa* in a narrow sense. He points out that punishment is not be viewed only in its prohibitive aspect. It establishes law and order in society and thus brings about a natural tendency in the average individuals to obey the law of the land, which renders the frequent use of force unnecessary.

---

5 ŚP XXIV, see also *Mbh*. CCVII.24; Udyoga, CXXXII.14-15 (Southern Recension, G.P. edn).

6 Bk I, chap. 2, 1-6; Bk I, chap. 4.

7 VII.43.

8 *Agni Purāṇa* CCXXV.21, CCXXXVIII.8-9, CCXXXIX.12-16; *Matsya Purāṇa* CCXV.53.

9 *NK* II.1-5, 7, 9, 15, 44.

10 I.151 and 156.

11 *daṇḍena nīyate cedaṁ daṇḍaṁ nayati vā punaḥ* |
daṇḍanītiriti khyātā triḻlokānabhivartate || — ŚP LIX.78

It ultimately secures the proper progress in religion, philosophy and economic well-being. It can be said in another way that *daṇḍa* is a means for the progress of *ānvīkṣikī* (philosophy), *trayī* (three Vedas) and *vārttā* (economics). The way to realize these is *daṇḍanīti*.[12]

According to Kāmandaka "restraint is known as *daṇḍa*, *daṇḍa* is the king, since it resides in him, the direction of *daṇḍa* is *daṇḍanīti*. *Nīti* is so called because it directs.[13] Generally the term *daṇḍanīti* means the policy of punishment. But this is a narrow meaning of the word. Its contents and scope show that it deals with all the aspects of state and government, not with punishment alone. The term *daṇḍanīti* has been variously translated and interpreted by modern scholars. According to Beni Prasad (1927), it is "the science of government".[14] To, Dikshitar (1951), "*daṇḍanīti* is the science of politics".[15] To C.V. Vaidya (1907), *daṇḍanīti* stands for "the rules of government".[16] P.C. Roy (1890) translates the word as the science of chastisement.[17]

Nītiśāstra

The word *nīti* has its origin from the root *nī* to lead; therefore it means guidance or direction. *Nītiśāstra* literally means the science of *nīti*. *Nīti* has also been used in *Mahābhārata*,[18] as well as in other ancient works. In *Mahābhārata*, *nītiśāstra* stands for both politics and as well as ethics. In the time period of Kāmandaka *nīti* came into existence in the form of politics. That is why Kāmandaka and Śukra have entitled

---

12 *ānvīkṣikitrayīvārtānaṁ yogakṣemasādhanodaṇḍaḥ, tasya nītiḥ daṇḍanītiḥ, alabdhlābhārthā labdhparirakṣiṇī, rakṣitavardhini vr̥dhasya tīrtheṣu pratipādinī* || — *Arthaśāstra*, Bk I, chap. 4, see also *Mbh* XII.59.78-79.

13 *damo daṇḍa iti khyātaḥ tātsthyāta daṇḍo mahīpatiḥ* |
tasya nītiḥ daṇḍanītiḥ nayanānnītirucyate || — *NK* II.15

14 Prasad, 1927a, *Theory of Government in Ancient India*, p. 21.

15 Dikshitar, 1951, *Purāṇa Index*, vol. II, p. 61.

16 Vaidya, 1907, *Epic India*, p. 197.

17 *Mbh*, tr. Ray, vol. VII, p. 283.

18 Ādi Parva CXL.26.

their treatise on polity as *nitiśāstra*. Bhartṛhari used this term as "science of wisdom and right course" in his book *Nītiśataka*. Śukra points out how *nītiśāstra* is a *sine qua non* (an essential element) for the stability and progress of a society in all directions and how it enables the realization of the fourfold goals connected with *dharma*, *artha, kāma* and *mokṣa*.[19] Monier-Williams and Sorensen have also interpreted the word *nītiśāstra*, respectively as the "science of, or a work on, political ethics and morals"[20] and "treatise on political ethics".[21]

Arthaśāstra

It is another term for the science of politics, which calls for a detailed discussion. And this term is also used in *Mahābhārata* to denote politics.[22] Nīlakaṇṭha explains it as the science of deceit (*vañcanā śāstra*).[23] *Arthaśāstra* according to Kauṭilya, is "the subsistence of mankind is termed *artha*, wealth; the earth which contains mankind is termed *artha*, wealth; that science which treats the means of acquiring and maintaining the earth is *arthaśāstra* and it is a science of polity".[24] The aim of *arthaśāstra* is to acquire the realization of *trivarga* which we call the threefold end of human life, viz. *dharma, artha* and *kāma*. *Arthaśāstra* helps one in this world and also in the *loka*, hereafter.[25] *Amarakośa* also equates *daṇḍanīti* with *arthaśāstra*. *Śukra Nītisāra* defines that *Arthaśāstra* discusses instructions about the government

---

19 *saropajīvakaṁ lokasthitikṛnnītiśāstrakam* ।
dharmārthakāmamokṣaṇāṁ hi smṛtaṁ mokṣapradaṁ yataḥ ॥ — *NŚ* I.5

20 Altekar, 1977, *State and Government in Ancient India*, p. 3.

21 Sorensen, 1925, *An Index to the Names in Mahābhārata*, p. 520.

22 Sabhā XLIX, p. 853.

23 *strībuddhimanusṛtya vṛhaspatyādibhirvañcanāśāstarṁ pravartitavyam-ityukti* ।
etāḥ pūjitā dhikkṛtā vā tulyavadvikāraṁ janayantītyarthaḥ ॥

24 *manuṣyāṇāṁ vṛttirarthaḥ* । *manuṣyavatī bhūmirityarthaḥ*। *tasyāḥ pṛthivyāḥ lābhapālanopāyaḥ śāstramarthaśāstramiti* ॥ — Bk XV, chap. I, 1-3, p. 667

25 Bk XV.7-9.

along with the acquisition of wealth.

dharmaśāstravirodhena hyarthaśāstraṁ vicārayet ।[26]

In *Viṣṇu Purāṇa, arthaśāstra* has been placed in the list of eighteen *vidyās* (sciences).[27]

Rājyaśāstra

It means the Śāstra of the kings which is similar to *daṇḍanīti*. *Rājyaśāstra* was an ancient Indian term for politics. In Śānti-Parva this term is also mentioned, it becomes clear when Bhīṣma introduces to ancient Indian political thinkers and calls them as *rājyaśāstrapraṇetā*[28] (composers of *rājyaśāstra*).

Rājanīti

This term has been explained in different ways: first one being the policy (*nīti*) of the king (*rājā*) and second one as the policy which pleases the people because the word *rājā* is derived from the root *rañj*, which means to please. Word *rājanīti* has been used in *Mahābhārata*, in the sense of politics. In Śānti-Parva this verse

bṛhaspatipurogāṁstu devarṣīnasakṛt prabhuḥ ।
toṣayitvopacāreṇa rājanītimadhītavān ॥ — ŚP XXXVII.9

shows that Bhīṣma has thorough knowledge of *rājanīti*. B.K.Sarkar describes it as "statecraft".[29]

Rājadharma

This term is used in *Mahābhārata* with different meanings. First one is for the royal duties[30] and the second one for politics. The latter sense of *rājadharma* is confirmed by seeing the fact that one whole or complete section of Śānti-Parva, dealing with rules, relating specially to the art

[26] IV.785, see also ibid. IV.296-97.

[27] *Viṣṇu Purāṇa* III.6.28-29.

[28] ŚP LVIII.2-3.

[29] Ibid., XXXVII.9.

[30] *aśrauṣīstvaṁ rājadharmān yathā vai manubravīt* । — Vana XXXV.21

of government, is known as "Rājadharmānuśāsana-Prava".[31] In Śānti-Parva, *rājadharma* has been regarded as the most important science and it also consists of all other branches of knowlegde (*vidyā*s)[32] in itself.

In Śānti-Parva there is another term for *daṇḍanīti*. In its origin, it refers to Brahmakanyā. It has been originated from Brahmā. It is known as Jagaddhātrī because it sustains the world. It is also identified with Lakṣmī, which is the source of prosperity to the people. It also stands for *vr̥tti* because it provides the means of livelihood to the people.

In the age of Vedas and the Brāhmaṇas, the thinkers had also speculated in connection with the exaltation of kingship, inter-tribal warfare, elective principles of the king as well as administration at the village and city levels. In this context various Maṇḍalas of *R̥gveda* such as first, third, fourth, sixth, eighth, ninth and tenth are informative. Similarly, the hymns of *Atharvaveda* refer to the coronation of the king, principles of the election, divinity of kingship, timetable of the kingly duties, taxation, ethics of war, etc. Importance of *bala* also finds mention in the Vedic sources. The description of these is given herewith.

In Vedic era development of politics became possible when five organizations, namely, *gotra*, *grāma, viśa, jana* and *rāṣṭra* combined together. These were considered as the political units; without these there was no possibility of any societal institution. In these institutions there was no space for discrimination like untouchability, and concepts like forward or backward. These were in the complete form and were indivisible. Unity was the most important and fundamental basis of these units. *Rāṣṭra* and *rājya* played an important role in the formation and development of the society. According to Bandyopadhyaya, in the initial stage of Indian community, *grāma* was the smallest and *jana* (people) was the highest political unit.[33] To H.N. Sinha *rāṣṭra* was a developed form of *grāma* (village). In Indian army, judiciary and

31 Jauhari, 1968, *Politics and Ethics in Ancient India*, p. 37.

32 ŚP LIII.29.

33 Bandyopadhyaya, 1927a, *The Development of Hindu Polity*, p. 60.

taxation, *grāma* had a major role in the Vedic period. On this basis, it can be said that the characteristics of *grāma* were political and by the combination of many villages *rāṣṭra* came into existence.[34] So according to the area and mode of administration it can be said that *grāma* was the smallest and *rāṣṭra* was the biggest unit. *Rājya, deśa, jāti* and *saṁskāra* were included in *rāṣṭra*. All were considered to be its part.

In ancient India the form of *rāṣṭra* was monarchical. Monarchy was the most comprehensive and people-oriented system of governance than modern democracy. We found the references of *gaṇa*s (republics) in *Ṛgveda*.[35] To R.S. Sharma, Vedic *gaṇa* was probably in nature a primitive tribal democracy centring in itself the military, distributive, religious and social activities of the early ideologies of war and peace.[36] According to Jayaswal, the republic came after the early Vedic age and after monarchy. Rejecting the above views about the Vedic republics R.S. Sharma presents his view that when the office of *gaṇapati* became transformed into *rājan*, the tribal republics passed into the phase of monarchical states. This fact is also supported by anthropological evidence. Some scholars are in support of R.S. Sharma but some by rejecting his views on *gaṇa*s, forcefully recommend it as the democratic. In Vedic *gaṇa*s we find all the characteristics like labour division, societal classification and equality. The early Vedic period doesn't present the clear picture of *gaṇa*s but in the later stage, there is more clarity.

In *Ṛgveda*, many words like *ekarājya, adhirājya, samrāṭa* and *svarāja* are mentioned, by which the development and respective classification could be understood properly. We can see the development of *rāṣṭra* and philosophies regarding this nation from very early Vedic period. So from the above facts, the logic that Indian ideologies have

---

34 Sinha, 1938, *Sovereignty in Ancient Indian Polity*, pp. 22-24.

35 *Ṛgveda* I.64.12, V.52.13-14.

36 Sharma, 1959, *Aspects of Political Ideas and Institutions in Ancient India*, pp. 120-21.

been taken from the outside world becomes redundant.

The chief of Vedic *rāṣṭra* was the king and he was called *antarbhū*, which means he was one from all peoples of *viśā*. He was considered as the most civilized person within the society. It means that the king was the member of Indian civil society. Stability of the king depended on *rāṣṭra*. We get the concepts of unity, stability and integrity of *rāṣṭra* from the very early period. There was an election process in the selection of a king and it was performed by *rājakṛta* and *grāmīṇa*. Thus, the king was an elected personality. According to Altekar the power of the king was hereditary, but the view presented by him doesn't belong to the period of Saṁhitās, but to the period of Brāhmaṇas. Ghoshal and Bandyopadhyaya are of the same view. Hence, it becomes clear that in ancient India there was the process of an election method. We find many examples of it in Vedas.

The king was elected by the people, assembled in the *samiti*. The people assembled to elect him to rulership unanimously. The *samiti* appointed him. He was asked to hold the state. It is hoped that he would not fall from his office. He was expected to crush enemies. As stated in *Atharvaveda* VI.87-88:

> *ā tvāhārṣamantarabhūrdhruvastiṣṭhāvicācacalat* ।
> *viśastvā sarvā vāñchantu mā tvadrāṣṭramadhi bhaṛśat* ॥
>
> *ihaivaidhi māpa cyoṣṭhāḥ parvata ivāvīcācalat* ।
> *indra iveha dhruvastiṣṭheha rāṣṭramu dhāraya* ॥
>
> *indra etamadīdharad dhruvaṁ dhruveṇa haviṣā* ।
> *tasmai somo adhi bravadayaṁ ca brahamaṇaspatiḥ* ॥

> Gladly you come among us, remain firmly without faltering, all the people want you; may you not fall the state. Here be you firm like mountain and may you not come down. Be you firm here like Indra, remain you here and hold the state. Indra has held it (the state) firm on account of firm *havi* offering; for it *soma* as well as Brahmaṇaspati has said the same.

Here we also find the process of re-election of *rājā* who had been apparently driven out.

tvāṁ viśo vr̥ṇatāṁ rājyāya tvāmimāḥ prādiśāḥ pañca devīḥ ।
varṣman rāṣṭrasya kakudi śrayasva tato na ugro vi bhajā vasūni ॥ — *Atharvaveda* III.4.2

The people elect you to rulership; the wide glorious quarters elect you. Be seated on this high point in the body of the state and from there vigorously distribute the natural wealth.

Here in this verse *kakud* literally means "the hump" of the bull. The allusion is to the throne which is regarded as the highest place in the body politic.

According to the last verse of hymn in *R̥gveda* corresponding to the song of election,[37] he becomes the sole taker of the taxes from the people; he becomes the king of the people. The "sole taker" signifies that the regular tax, as a royal due, had already developed. No one else but the king alone was entitled to it. The king is asked to ascend a raised seat which is significantly described as the highest point of the body of state. It shows that the idea of the state as an organism was realized as early as Vedic kingship. In this way we find many references regarding the election process of a king.

In Vedic period, we find clear indications of some state elements like *rāṣṭra*, *viśā* and sovereignty. Land and government are included in *rāṣṭra*; they are considered as very important constituents. *Kṣatra* and *kṣatraśrī,* the R̥gvedic terms are seemed to be the synonyms of the political sovereign. *R̥ta* was considered as the highest in the field of law and administration. To protect, *r̥ta* was the fundamental duty of Vedic politics. Politics was then *kṣatra* and *kṣatrī*. The development of state sovereignty depended on the king. He established *r̥ta* and removed the situation of untruthfulness and chaos.

There was no concept of autocracy in Vedic politics. Legal institutions like *sabhā samiti* and *vidatha* were free from autocratic

---

[37] *dhruvaṁ dhruveṇa haviṣābhi somaṁ mr̥śāmasi* ।
atho ta indraḥ kevalīrviśo balihr̥taskarat ॥ — *R̥gveda* X.173.6

concepts. Though there is no proof of texture of these institutions, Vedic *sabhā* was sovereign in its nature. As to the composition of the *samiti*, Ludwig holds that it included all the people, primarily the *viśaḥ* (subjects), but also the brāhmaṇas and *maghvans* (rich persons) if they desired, though the *sabhā* was a special assembly.

Sabhā was described as the sister of *samiti*, one of the two daughters of Prajāpati.[38] *Sabhā* was called *nariṣṭa* which Sāyaṇa explains as a resolution of "many" that cannot be broken or violated. As stated:

> *nariṣṭā; ahiṁsitā parairananhibhāvya . . . bhāvaiḥ saṁbhūya yadyekaṁ vākyaṁ vadeyusataddha na parairtilaṅghyate ataḥ anatilañghyavākya tvāt nariṣṭeti nāma* I —*Atharvaveda* VII.12.2

Hence from inviolability the name is derived. Free discussion was held in the *sabhā* and the resolution of the *sabhā* was considered binding in all and inviolable. Evidently *sabhā* was as important as *samiti*. *Sabhā* means, "a body of men sitting together".[39] *Sabhā* acted as the national judicature. In Puruṣamedha of *Śukla Yajurveda* 30.6, the term *sabhā* is used which means "one going to the *sabhā*" and it is dedicated as a victim to justice — *dharmāya sabhācaraṁ*.

Again, *R̥gveda*, describes the friend of one who comes back successfully from the *sabhā*, "joyfully and delighted" and the man himself is "free from blame". As stated:

> *sarve nandanti yaśasāgatena sabhāsāhena sakhyā sakhāyaḥ* I
> *kilbiṣaspr̥tpituṣaṇirhyeṣāmaraṁ hito bhavati vājināya* II
> —*R̥gveda* X.71.10

Thus, we find that the main function of the *sabhā* was judiciary, while the most important business of *samiti* was to elect the king (*rājan*) (*AV* V.19.15). It could also re-elect a king who had been banished. Thus, it was a sovereign body from the constitutional point of view.

---

[38] *Atharvaveda* VII.12.1:
sabhā ca mā samitiścāvatāṃ prajāpaterduhitaravsaṁvidāne I
yenā saṁgacchā upa mā sa śikṣācchāru vadāni pitaraḥ saṁgateṣu II

[39] *saha dharmeṇa sadbhirvā bhātīti sabhā.* — *Pāraskara Gr̥hyasūtra* III.1

In *Ṛgveda* there is also the indication of *samiti*, common policy of state (*samāno mantraḥ samitiḥ samānī*), a common aim and common mind (*samānaṁ vārtā sam cittameṣāma*). The reference is that it was the king's duty to attend the *samiti* and if didn't attend, he would be considered "untrue". The practice of the king is to present himself before the *samiti*, continued probably as long as *samiti* existed. *Chāndogyopaniṣad* V.3, relating the visits of Śvetaketu Āruṇeya Gautama to the *samiti* of Pāñcālas, mentions the king (*pravahaṇa jaivāla*) as present in the *samiti*.[40] There are some other major characteristics of the Vedic politics. Society and people were the two important sources of political set-up. Population is the most important constituent. The fundamental principle of the Vedic polity was social welfare. For the attainment of these aims political institutions were established. The duty of the king was to serve his people and not to be served by them. The main aim of the king should be the development of state (*rāṣṭra*) from which he belongs, and to remove the chaos and disorder from the society. On the basis of the military and defence, the power of the state was assumed and by these presumptions the power of the king was also guessed.

Ṛta is the fundamental principle of the Vedic society. It was the duty of the king to protect *ṛta*; when he performed this duty, he was considered as *ṛtasyagopā*. As the upholder and protector of *rāṣṭra* he was *rāṣṭramūrdhāya*. This definition includes all the values of democracy. Being the *gopajanasya* he established peace and order in the society. When there was a situation of debate and struggle, it was the king who made the judgement. It was the duty of the king to set spies out to identify the corrupt, thieves, terrorists, unethical people, the factious and chaotic people, and to eliminate them from the society.

King performed all his duties for the development of state. Ancient *rāṣṭra* was not like the modern state. Some of the scholars have presented some spurious explanation of the state saying that ancient

---

40 Cf. *BṛUp* VI.2.

rāṣṭra in some ways was similar to that of a modern state.[41] From this viewpoint one comes to know that some scholars have tried to find out Western concepts of state in ancient Indian politics. Western concepts of state are totally different from the Indian political values. In Vedic period state was conceived as a *rāṣṭra* for proper administration. The duties and functions of the high command (king) were described.

In the early Vedic era, one finds political and economic ideas in a more organized form, but there is still no systematic exposition of political doctrines, and the subject is not treated as an independent branch of learning. Dharmasūtras lay down the norms of political organization, mainly a monarchy. The Sūtras emphasize the reciprocal duties of the king as well as the people and prescribe the principal functions of the king as a protector of the subjects and promoter of their allround welfare; and this function entitles him to receive taxes more or less in the form of pay. Examples of hereditary nature of succession on kingship and references to the special status of brāhmaṇas in upholding the moral order of society and in exercising effective curbs on the king's conduct are among the highlights of Sūtra literature. Dharmaśāstras as a genre of literature represent the efforts of successive generation to adjust human behaviour to a just and valid form. Dharmaśātras make it significant that "religion" in India is not a dogma, but a working hypothesis of human conduct adopted to different stages of spiritual development and different conditions of life. While the early Dharmasūtras attempted to set out the norms of political organization as an essential part of social complex, and they did so only inadequately, it is in the Dharmaśāstras that one finds the desired elaboration of these early political ideas. A lot of rules and regulations were defined by the Dharmaśāstra writers. *Rājadharma* formed a legitimate part of it, since the king's rule and administration drove the smooth functioning of the social organization.

The oldest and most famous text of Dharmaśāstra is *Mānava Dharmaśāstra* which is known as *Manusmr̥ti*. It is a book of 12

---

[41] Vidyalankar, 1978, "Rāṣṭra ke Lakṣaṇa tathā Vicāra".

chapters. According to P.V. Kane, *Manusmṛti* must have been composed in the first century BCE. Ghoshal and other scholars place it between 200 BCE and 200 CE. Chapters 7 and 8 and a part of chapter 9 of *Manusmṛti* deal with *rājadharma*. These chapters describe the qualities and duties of the king or rulers, and the principles of statecraft in peace and war. Chapter 7 deals with the entire range of state activity such as the appointment of ministers and their responsibilities, diplomacy and interstate relations, the deployment of massengers and spies.

Manu looks upon *daṇḍa* as the real king, leader and administrator; it is *daṇḍa* which governs the people, protects all and is the custodian of *dharma*.[42] Manu in his Smṛti inunciates the role of *daṇḍa* in the maintenance of social cohesion and political order. If the king does not exercise coercive power, the strong devour the weak in the same manner as the fishes are fried. In *Yājñavalkyasmṛti* it has been stated that having obtained the seven elements of state the king should use his authority in punishing the wicked because *dharma* was created in the form of *daṇḍa* by Brahmā in ancient India.[43] For the realization of universal prosperity, Śukra recommends both *nīti* and *daṇḍa*. The king, therefore, should weild the sceptre of *daṇḍa* and be an adherent of paths leading to the maximization of intelligence, power, vigour and *nīti*.[44]

Thus the elements of *daṇḍa* seem to have assumed considerable importance in the age of Kauṭilya, when centrifugal forces had been set in motion on account of foreign invasion and internal uprising.

Rāmāyaṇa and *Mahābhārata* are replete with political and economic theories of good governance. The origin of these epics, as that of all forms of Indian literature, has been traced to the Vedas. These epics deal with the deeds of kings and heroes, the description of wars and political philosophy. The epics are the good answer to those tall thinkers and pseudo-intellectuals who make some sweeping statements that Indian political theory has so far not been constructed even in a

---

42 *Manu* VII.17-18.

43 ŚP I.353-4.

44 *Śukra* I.45, VII.11.

rudimentary form. In fact, the two great epics are of perennial interest to understand the ancient Indian social and political set-ups.

Rāmāyaṇa, which is earlier than *Mahābhārata,* contains references of *rājadharma*, the whole 100 cantons of Ayodhyā-Kāṇḍa are full of political thoughts. When Rāma was on the exile for fourteen years and was staying in Citrakūṭa mountain, then King Bharata came to him with his ministers. At that time Rāma gave some preachings on some *daṇḍanīti,* including some questions to Bharata. He asked Bharata:

> *kaccidātmasamāḥ śūrāḥ śrutavanto jitendriyāḥ* ।
> *kūlīnāścergitajñāśca kṛtāste tāta mantrinaḥ* ॥
>
> *kaccinnidrāvaśaṁ naiṣi kaccit kāle 'vabudhyase* ।
> *kacciccāpararātreṣu cintayasyarthanaipuṇaṁ* ॥[45]

In this way, it also gives the description of good governance, diplomacy of war and peace. It contains the prescriptions regarding the manner in which the king should consult his ministers, learned men and the principal officers of army in formulating state policy on different matters.

On the other hand, *Mahābhārata* is a class by itself. It is an electric work, in a sense, it brings together the various standpoints expressed in the works on polity. It contains well-developed political schools of thought and formulations. It is an authoritative book of law, morality, and social and political principles. Laying down the rules for the attainment of *dharma, artha, kāma,* called *trivarga,* and showing the way to liberation, the highest religious philosophy of India. As an encyclopaedia of ancient India it deals with the diverse subjects in various aspects but importantly, it also discusses the issue of politics. It contributes significantaly to the reinforcement of Indian political tradition of thought and condenses the political wisdom of the ages.

The existing Western methodology may prove inadequate to decipher the character of this treatise dealing with the classical Indian political tradition and its various implications. As an indispensable

---

45 Ayodhyā-Kāṇḍa, C.15,17, see also the whole chapter for more information regarding *daṇḍanīti*.

source of ancient Indian political theory the prime significance of *Mahābhārata* over the modern political theory comes from the sole fact that the epic itself advances the view that the state emerged within the society and the ties of kingship, religion and economic needs were primarly representative of the formations of the rudiments of the state. In *Mahābhārata* the major political ideas were described in Śānti-Parva's Rājadhramānuśāsana chapter, in which the kingly duties (*rājadharma*), origin of states and *saptāṅgas*, state relations, council of ministers, judiciary, etc. are discussed in a proper manner. The king is considered as the holder of *daṇḍa* in order to protect his subjects and is of the divine origin in its form.[46]

To conclude, in the early stages of the development of the political science, it was known as *rājadharma*; *daṇḍanīti* became a more acceptable term a little later and *arthaśāstra* was suggested as an alternative to it. In course of time, however, the word *rājanītīśāstra*, abridged into *nītiśāstra*, became most popular and supplanted other terms. So gradually changes took place in the development of political science in the Indian tradition. Many other texts were also written time to time on the same subject, but they failed to acquire the status of *Mahābhārata*, *Arthaśāstra* and *Nītiśāstra*. These books became famous in India as major texts of political science. This study is confined to Śānti-Parva only hence it is not necessary to discuss the political concepts of all the ages in vague but in brief. Let us approach the political concepts of Śānti-Parva systematically.

Political Ideas in Śānti-Parva

Śānti-Parva is the repositary of traditional knowledge and deals extensively with the political, social, moral, religious, philosophical, and cultural aspects of ancient Indian society. Śānti-Parva is divided into three sections: (1) Rājadharmānuśāsana, (2) Paddharma, and (3) Mokṣadharma. Out of these three sections Rājadharma section has special importance, inasmuch as it perhaps embodies the earliest systematic thought on the science of polity (*rājanīti*) in Indian

46 ŚP XII.68.40.

literature. This *parva* deals with some fundamental aspects of polity such as the origin of the science of polity (the origin of state), the importance of *daṇḍa* (punishment), and the importance and duties of the king. It also deals with the duties of *varṇa*s and *āśrama*s, the seven *prakṛti*s (constituents) of state and their significance, foreign policy, taxation, the importance of *vārttā* (agriculture) and commercial activities, the various tactics of war, battle formations, etc. A very refreshing discussion is also found about republics and their functions.

According to Śānti-Parva, *dharma* is the fundamental principle of politics, it is considered as the root of all the political ideas. All the acts and functions of the state and its components are under the guardianship of *dharma*. In Śānti-Parva various types of *dharma*s are discussed: *rājadharma, varṇa-dharma, āśrama-dharma,* etc. But here the main focus is on *rājadharma*. Śānti-Parva many times is considered as the "Rājadharmānuśāsana-Parva", because it has given all the major instructions and information on *rājadharma*, which is otherwise not found anywhere. *Rājadharma* is the central point of all the *dharma*s, and it is not erroneous to say that it is the refuge to all the *dharma*s:

> *sarve dharmā rājadharmapradhānāḥ*
> *sarve varṇāḥ pālyamānā bhavanti* ।
> *sarvastyāgo rājadharmeṣu rājaṁstyāgaṁ*
> *dharmaṁ cāhuragrayaṁ purāṇaṁ* ॥
> — ŚP LXIII.27, see also 28-30

In the Rājadharmānuśāsana chapter Bhīṣma gives instructions to Yudhiṣṭhira, that *rājadharma* is the greatest one, which includes all the *trivarga*s in itself:

> *trivargo hi samāsakto rājadharmeṣu kaurava* ।
> *mokṣadharmaśca vispaṣṭaḥ sakalo 'atra samāhitaḥ* ॥
> — ŚP LVI.4

So he should act according to this and says that it is the duty of the king to seek and promote the welfare of his citizens. The king must be compassionate to the people of all sections of the society and he should concentrate on the welfare of his citizens. His main functions were protection, prosperity, maintenance of righteousness and doing justice according to *dharma*. He was not expected to act according to his personal likes or dislikes but only according to the wishes and will of the people. Śānti-Parva states that *dharma* upholds all the creatures. The king has to perform his duties according to *dharma* otherwise he would invite hell and this notion supposedly served as a great deterrent. The king has to come to existence for the maintenance of peace and *dharma* on the earth.

While requesting Bhīṣma to suggest him the way of good governance, Yudhiṣṭhira himself says that *rājadharma* is all comprehensive. It is inclusive of *dharma*, *artha* and *kāma* (*trivarga*s). *Rājadharma* only is able to control the world and keep the people under the restraint of *maryādā*.[47] It prevents the people from committing sins and wrongs.[48] Bhīṣma says that one should first acquire the king then only wife and wealth because unless there is no king to prevent him, there will be no security either for his wife or his wealth.[49] Bhīṣma enumerates Bṛhaspati, Viśālākṣa, Śukra, Indra, Manu, Bharadvāja and Gauraśira as main propounders of *rājadharma* before him.[50] Bṛhaspati says that whatever *dharma* is there on the earth that is all because of the king. It is his presence that prevents people from killing and molesting each other. It is his duty to make necessary arrangements so that people may not deviate from the path of *dharma*.

The king's main function was to establish social discipline. The king's *dharma* consisted in maintaining the rule of *dharma* in the society at large. In concrete terms, this meant that he was to facilitate the study of Vedas and philosophy, encourage the development of industry and commerce, maintain proper relations between different castes, ensure the observation of parental, filial, matrimonial and other duties, and enforce *dharma* pertaining to different stages of individual life and

---

47 ŚP LXV.3-4.

48 Ibid. LV.7.

49 Ibid. LVII.11.

50 Ibid. LVIII.1-4.

so on. The king derived his authority from the fact that he needed it to maintain *dharma*. Hence, the main purpose of the kingly duties is to maintain peace and order in the society. Then the question arises: which type of peace is concerned here, only physical peace? No, it is not the criterion. To establish social, economic and political peace in the society is the aim; peace related with all the citizens and institutions of society. Through justice (justice is a concept of moral rightness based on ethics, rationality, law, natural law, fairness, or equity, along with the punishment for the breach of ethics)[51] and law, peace remains in the society. In the absence of these moral values, degeneration gets started and no possibility of peace is regarded. The king all alone is not able to maintain peace in the society; because he is not enough to control over the citizens of the large society; he needs such an institution which can help him in all situations and in completing all the purposes related to *rājadharma*. To fulfil these purposes and for maintaining peace and order in the society the importance of politics is felt and after that *daṇḍanīti* came into existence.

ORIGIN OF POLITICS

Śānti-Parva gives invaluable information about the origin of politics. In this *parva* the term *daṇḍanīti* is used in the place of politics. Brahmadeva is regarded as one of the composers of *daṇḍanīti*. *Mahābhārata* gives first a divine and second a human origin to *daṇḍanīti* (state). But before discussing *daṇḍanīti*, it is desirable to know the process of its evolution. But before discussing its evolution it is necessary to know actually what is *daṇḍanīti*? What is its relevance to present time? Has it got any historicity? What is its subject matter and scope? Is it an art or science? In the light of these questions, a fresh approach is needed for its interpretation.

The word *daṇḍanīti* is made up of the two parts: *daṇḍa* and *nīti*, the former is used in many senses, but generally, it stands for punishment and denotes a staff that was meant to ward off demons who used to disturb the sacrificial performances or for driving away the cattles. The

51 Konow, 2003, "Which Is the Fairest One of All?", p. 1188.

latter part *nīti* stands for the science of guidance. It leads and guides the people towards the righteous path and makes the ruler punish the evil-doers. Hence *daṇḍanīti* has been termed as both a science and an art. *Daṇḍanīti* controls four *varṇa*s, prevents them from following wrong path and engages them in their respective duties. Though, it is identified with *rājadharma*, it is not only the science of punishment and government. It is the means with which the unacquired is acquired and protected well.[52] After discussing the meaning of *daṇḍanīti*, let us come to theory of its evolution.

It has been stated in Śānti-Parva that because of lawlessness, there was a state of complete anarchy. But prior to that, the people were living a life of peace and happiness. And this was regarded as the golden age of the epic, at that time, people used to protect one another according to *dharma*, though there was neither state nor any ruler. Even there was neither any jurist nor science of chastisement, nevertheless, there was as perfect happiness and peace.

niyatastvaṁ naravyāghra śṛṇu sarvamaśeṣataḥ ।
yathā rājyaṁ samutpannamādau kṛtayuge 'abhavata ॥

na vai rājyaṁ na rāja "sīnna ca daṇḍo na dāṇḍikaḥ ।
dharmeṇaiva prajāḥ sarvā rakṣanti sma parasparam ॥
— ŚP LIX.13-14

But after some time the condition changed and moral degeneration started. People fell from rectitude; greed, selfishness and cupidity began to sway and the earthly paradise which they had been enjoying[53] was soon converted into veritable hell. The law of morality came to an end and people had no sense of righteousness. What should be done and what should not.[54] They discarded

52 ŚP LXX.29.

53 Altekar, 1977, *State and Government in Ancient India*, p. 27.

54 *te mohavaśamāpannā manujā manujarṣabhaḥ* ।
pratipattivimohācca dharmasteṣāmanīnaśat ॥

naṣṭāyāṁ pratipattau ca mohavaśyā narāstadā ।
lobhasya vaśamāpannāḥ sarve bharatasattama ॥ — ŚP LIX.16-17

religious practices and began to loot other's property. They also started molesting others' women.[55] Then the existence of gods was threatened and they (people) approached Brahmā (creator) for ensuring law and order in society, and to prevent people from doing bad things. God got alarmed and decided to remedy the situation. Brahmadeva, the chief God, thought over the whole matter and finally came to the conclusion that human society could survive only if a code of law was framed and enforced through the instrumentality of a king.[56] It was He who at the request of gods not only established the law and order but also combined the science of punishment (*daṇḍanīti*). Hence, politics came into existence:

tato 'adhyāyasahasrāṇāṁ śataṁ cakre svabuddhijaṁ ।
yatra dharmastathaivārthaḥ kāmaścaivābhivarṇitaḥ ॥
— ŚP LIX.29

Daṇḍanīti was later on abridged by Śiva, Viśālākṣa, Bāhudantriputra, Bṛhaspati and Uśanasa respectively in ten, five, three and one thousand sections.[57] In Śānti-Parva, it has been stated that Brahmā, keeping the painful situation of the world in view (mind), requested Śiva to show his sympathy on the world.

tataḥ pitāmaho viṣṇuṁ bhagavantaṁ sanātanam ।
sampūjya varadaṁ devaṁ mahādevamathābravīt ॥

atra tvamanukampāṁ vai karturmahasi śaṅkara ।
saìkaro na bhavedatra yathā tad vai vidhīyatām ॥
— CXXII.22-23

After thinking a lot, on this painful situation Lord Śiva transformed himself into *daṇḍa*.[58] Then Goddess Sarasvatī has also created *daṇḍanīti* (science of punishment) which very soon became celebrated all over the world, with the view to regulate human life and to protect

55 ŚP LIX.67.

56 Altekar, 1977, *State and Government in Ancient India*, p. 27.

57 ŚP LIX.29, 86-91.

58 ŚP CXXII.24-25.

dharma.[59] According to these accounts of divine origin, the information comes out that *daṇḍa* and *daṇḍanīti* have been defined respectively by Śiva and Sarasvatī. This is considered as the divine origin of *daṇḍanīti*. In Śānti-Parva, it is also stated that a group of seven persons (Marīci, Atri, Aṅgirā, Pulastya, Pulaha, Kṛta and Vasiṣṭha) known as the Citraśikhaṇḍinaḥ composed a science (of *daṇḍanīti*). They composed their respective works in order to regulate *loka-dharma* for the sake of prosperity and happiness of the people.[60] This type of *daṇḍanīti* is regarded as of human origin, because it was created by the sages (human beings).

Though the above seven writers are not recognized as the original authors on polity (*rājaśāstrapraṇetāraḥ*), their works are said to be a source of inspiration to Manu, Bṛhaspati and Śukra.[61] It appears that these were probably the first persons dealt with the branch of *daṇḍanīti* from the general body of learning and are regarded as the pioneers in the field of classical Indian tradition. The purpose of their work is not only related with *daṇḍanīti* but it also deals with the other aspects of human life. It is also stated that they were inspired by the divine agency (Nārāyaṇa), and thus they are authentic like the Vedas.

Whatever be the origin of *daṇḍanīti* (divine or human), it is not important here. The important and valuable thing is that it originated for the establishment of peace and order. To make the world peaceful and prosperous this was created. According to scholars the main purpose of composition of it was to make the people obedient and moral. Knowledge of *daṇḍanīti* was an essential qualification for both the king and his ministers.

Many scholars have also presented their views on *daṇḍanīti*.

---

59 *tataḥ sa bhagavān dhyātvā ciraṁ śūlavarāyudhaḥ* ।
ātmānamātmanā daṇḍaṁ sasṛje devasattamaḥ ॥
tasmācca dharmacaraṇānnītirdevī sarasvatī ।
sasṛje daṇḍanītiṁ sā triṣu lokeṣu viśrutā ॥ — Ibid. CXXI.24-25

60 Ibid. CCCXXII.26-28.

61 Ibid. CCCXXII.41-44.

Bal Gangadhar Tilak does not agree with the idea of divine origin of *daṇḍanīti*. To him, Brahmā is only a mythological being.[62] In this context the differing views of Winternitz, Kane, Law, Aiyangar and Keith are significant and instructive. According to both Kane and Winternitz, *daṇḍanīti* is not only prior to Kauṭilya but it evolved from the Dharmaśāstras. M.N. Law and Rangaswami Aiyangar did not agree with the above views. According to them, *daṇḍanīti* evolved on independent lines and it was born out the Dharmaśāstras.

A.B. Keith is of the opinion that question of evolution from Dharmaśāstras does not arise because *daṇḍanīti* was opposed to Dharmaśāstras. But he agrees with the fact that *rājaśāstrapraṇetāra*s were considered as historical persons. Their names are not only mentioned in *Mahābhārata*, but they are also noticeable in *Arthaśāstra* of Kauṭilya. It appears that Kauṭilya might have read their books before writing his book on statecraft.[63]

SUBJECT MATTER OF DAṆDANĪTI

The subject matter of *daṇḍanīti* is very comprehensive, as described by many thinkers. According to them, it concerns all the aspects of statecraft. Śānti-Parva gives a clear account of Indian political thought. The contents of *Nītisāra*, composed by Brahmā, show all the aspects of *daṇḍanīti*. It also discusses about the characteristics of the princes, their needs and also their bad habits (*vyasana*s). To remove the anarchy (disorder) the epic itself informs that ten types of *vyasana*s originated from excess pleasure (*kāma*) and wrath (*krodha*) should be discarded. And also been suggested that the king should himself discard them (*vyasana*s), before expecting the people to be free from these *vyasana*s.

Daṇḍanīti includes within its fold all matters concerning the state such as formation of government consisting of ministers, population-cum-territory, forts, army and treasury, known as *pañcavigraha*.[64]

---

62 Tilak, 1965, *Śrīmadbhagavadgītā Rahasya*, p. 24.

63 Saletore, 1958, *India's Diplomatic Relation with the West*, pp. 16-23.

64 ŚP LXX.25-28.

It is *daṇḍanīti* which highlights the importance of a king in *Mahābhaārata*. *Daṇḍanīti* is the one by which the king is able to transform the iron-age (Kali) into the golden age, as discussed in Śānti-Parva. The king appears like a magician due to applications of *daṇḍanīti*. And he should must follow the injections of *daṇḍanīti*. So *daṇḍanīti* is an art in the sense that it teaches the king how to rule over his kingdom. In its subject matter *daṇḍanīti* seems to be more comprehensive and applicable than modern political science. It is helpful to solve the modern socio-economic and political problems. In other words, the content of *daṇḍanīti* reveals that it is not only problem-oriented but also solution-oriented. *Daṇḍanīti* is mainly concerned with the statecraft, yet its association with fourfold objectives of human life (*dharma, artha, kāma* and *mokṣa*)[65] enriches its subject matter. According to it "man is the measure of all things".

It studies man in relation to *dharma, artha* and *kāma*, which have values in man's life. According to many thinkers who have done their study on the epic, a man whether he is a prince, minister, or an officer, is under the superior command of *dharma, artha* and *kāma*. It is not out of place to mention that *daṇḍanīti* is also discussed with psychological and sociological approaches, for example, modern politics has nothing to do with the individual traits such as *sattva*, *rajas* and *tamas*, the *daṇḍa* and *trivarga,* namely, *sthāna vr̥ddhi*, *kāya* and *ṣaḍvarga*. But these are also included in the subject matter of *daṇḍanīti*. All the aspects of *daṇḍanīti*, connected with internal and external affairs, administrative machinery, ministers, espionage, fiscal administration, means of enriching the treasury, legal affairs, establishment of peace, etc. come under the ambit of *daṇḍanīti.*

Under the subject matter of *daṇḍanīti* the four strategem (strategies) and sixfold policies are also mentioned. It also discusses about the importance of *sāma* (conciliation), *dāna* (appeasing by suitable gifts), *daṇḍa* (use of force) and *bheda* (necessity of creating dissensions), and the knowledge of these is very important for the success of temporal

---

65 ŚP LIX.29-74.

or worldly power. It also concerns with the principles of international relation. It is (relevant) appropriate or suitable for determining the foreign policy of our country, even in the present-day scenario.

It is worth to note that whatever models suggested by the recent researchers on foreign policies in developing countries, find interwoven in the dialogues between the sages and kings in the individual *parva*s of the epic. Bhīṣma has quoted the extracts and stories as oral evidences in the context of *sāma, dāna, daṇḍa* and *bheda* which widens the scope and subject matter of *daṇḍanīti*. It also includes the purpose of keeping an army. We also find mention of the laws of war and peace, the fourfold army and its strength, method of fighting, principles of capturing booty, treatment to the prisoners of war as well as medical facilities to the soldiers. It also refers to the idea of law and court: different types of laws and courts, how to appoint judges, related rules, proper punishment of the guilty, freedom and right to defend, all these aspects are included in *daṇḍanīti*.

Finance and fiscal policies are discussed as the root of the state or *daṇḍanīti*. Hence, it deals with the principles of taxation, budget, establishment and development of industries. Emergency taxes, state's policy towards merchants and farmers, salaries and facilities to civil servants are the major topics of *daṇḍanīti*. Whether it is *Arthaśāstra* of Kauṭilya or *daṇḍanīti* of Bhīṣma, it is not only a science of wealth, but it studies both man and state.

So far as the scope of *daṇḍanīti* is concerned on the scientific aspect, it deals with the past, present and future. In this respect, *daṇḍanīti* stands for science but not in an absolute sense. All these things indicate that according to *Mahābhārata* the subject matter of *daṇḍanīti* is wide and includes all aspects of the statecraft. Regarding its scope, it furnishes remarkable information. It also remarks that the footprints of all the living being come within the fold of wide footprints of the elephant, likewise all the *dharma*s are included (*sampralīna*) in the wide range of *rājadharma* or *daṇḍanīti*, as quoted in Śānti-Parva:

yathā rājan hastipade padāni
saṁlīyante savasattvodbhavāni |

evaṁ dharmān rājadharmeṣu sarvān
sarvāvasthān sampralīnān nibodha ||
— ŚP LXIII.25

By *daṇḍanīti*, the king protects his people and adopts the four *upāya*s in normalizing his relation with other states. So, it is *daṇḍanīti* which enlightens the king to take suitable measures. Therefore, it is justified to say that *daṇḍanīti* looks to the future of the state as it should be, with the aim of improving political organization and activities in the light of changing conditions and ethical standards. It is thus a study of relation between man and state in the past, present and future. *Daṇḍanīti* describes the structure and analyses the functions of state in terms of human anatomy and physiology. It also studies the motives of human behaviour. It explains the issues on which the interstate relations in ancient India were based. Though the science of chastisement is concerned with the narrative aspect of history, it studies the same from the psychological, ethical and philosophical angles. It studies the problem of "what" (*kim*), "where" (*kutra*), "who" and "why"?

tadahaṁ jñātumicchāmi daṇḍaḥ utpdyate kathaṁ |
kiṁ cāsya pūrve jāgarti kiṁ vā pramucyate || — ŚP LXIV.12

The problems regarding the origin of state, justification for monarchy, composition of council of ministers, principles of adjunction, code of conduct of officials, and also the relation between *dharma* and *daṇḍa* find solution in the above terms, though explanations are not satisfactory and systematic. *Daṇḍanīti* deals with the four *varṇa*s and four orders (*āśrama*s). It also highlights the issues related with the interdependence of temporal and spiritual powers in the context of epic tradition.

IMPORTANCE OF DAṆDANĪTI

Śānti-Parva greatly stresses the necessity and importance of *daṇḍanīti*, it being "a favourite theme of the epic".[66] While answering the enquiries

[66] Anjaria, 1935, *Nature and Grounds of Political Obligation in Hindu State*, p. 59.

of Yudhiṣṭhira, Bhīṣma says that *rājadharma* is the refugee of the whole world. *Trivarga* (threefold end of human life, viz. *dharma, artha* and *kāma*) is also dependent on it.

trivargo hi samāsakto rājadharmeṣu kaurava ।
mokṣadharmaśca vispaṣṭaḥ sakalo 'tra samāhitaḥ ॥
— ŚP LVI.4

Not only this, the practices and conditions required for salvation also depend on it. It is *daṇḍanīti* which keeps the whole world under control. Thus it is just like reigns, which is necessary for controlling the horses, and like the hook, in the case of elephants. This science destroys all the evil consequences of the world like the sun which removes darkness. Its absence leads to confusion, disorder and unrighteousness.

tatra cet sampramuhyeta dharme rājarṣisevite ।
lokasya saṁsthā na bhavet sarvaṁ ca vyākulībhavet ॥

udayan hi yathā sūryo nāśayatyaśubhaṁ tamaḥ ।
rājadharmāstathālokyāṁ nikṣipantyaśubhāṁ gatim ॥
— ŚP LVI.6-7

Daṇḍanīti is an essential element for the maintenance of human society, and being associated with the *trayī* and *vārttā*, it causes prosperity to the people and regulates law and order. It being properly handled by the king, prevents people from following *adharma* and protects *varṇa-dharma* and *āśrama-dharma*.[67] People were instructed by this to follow their duties reminding them that non-following of their duties would result in disorder in the society.

sāmānyārthe vyavahāre pravṛtte
priyāpriye varjayanneva yatnāt ।
cāturvarṇyasthāpanāt pālanācca
taistairyogairniyamairaursaiśca ॥

sarvodyogairāśramaṁ dharmamāhuḥ
kṣātraṁ śreṣṭhaṁ sarvadharmopapannam ।

[67] ŚP LIX.14-27.

svaṁ svaṁ dharmaṁ yena caranti
varṇāstāṁstān dharmānamyathārthān vadanti ||
— ŚP LXV.5-6

It also protects the Vedas which are the sources of *dharma*.[68] The epic itself claims that Vedic tradition and studies come to an end when *daṇḍanīti* disappears, and due to it, *dharma* comes to an end causing disorder in the society.[69] Protection of *dharma* also depends upon *daṇḍanīti*.

It stands for the elements of morality. When the people deviate from the right path,[70] then the king is the one, who with its help bring them into the right path. By the help of king it can transform the Kali Age into Satya Yuga and vice versa.[71] On account of all these reasons, *daṇḍanīti* is of more importance, as it is *lokarakṣaṇakārikā*[72] or protects the people. The code of Brahmā was composed for the welfare of people and for the realization of *trivarga*. The *kṣātra-dharma* ensures best protection to the people. The utmost happiness and welfare to all being are caused by *daṇḍanīti*, otherwise complete annihilation is sure.[73]

It is interesting to note that other political thinkers also express similar views regarding the importance of *daṇḍanīti*. According to Kauṭilya, success of human society depends on it. So the king wishing to guide people to the right path should enforce the rules of *daṇḍanīti*.[74]

---

68 ŚP CCLXXXVI.40.

69 *majjet trayī daṇḍanītau hatāyāṁ*
sarve dharmāḥ prakṣayeyurvibuddhāḥ |
sarve dharmāścāśramāṇāṁ hatāḥ syuḥ
kṣātre tyakte rājadharme purāṇe || — Ibid. LXIII.28

70 Ibid. LIX.77.

71 Ibid. LXX.1-37.

72 Ibid. LIX.77.

73 Ibid. LXIV.1-5 & LXV.1.

74 *KA* 1.3-4.

Manu also expressed the same view.[75] According to *Matsya Purāṇa*, *daṇḍanīti* is necessary for the establishment of orderly progress.[76] *Vāyu Purāṇa* says that it aims at the performance of one's ordained duties.[77]

Therefore, it is for the establishment of peace and order in the society that *daṇḍanīti* was created. Because human progress and prosperity were possible only in the atmosphere of peace and rule of the law, and hence the anxiety to establish the rule of law at any cost. It was possible only by the state. Then the question comes out: what is state and what are its structure and functions?

STATE

There must be a legal machinery to ensure the proper implementation of *daṇḍa* and to deal with its misuse. This machinery is obviously the *rājya* (state), which exercises the rule of *daṇḍa* through the power of the king. In Śānti-Parva terms such as *deśa, rāṣṭra, janapada* and *rājya* have been used to denote a state. It is made up of the seven elements, called *aṅgas* or *prakṛtis*. These are *svāmī*, *amātya*, *janapada*, *durga*, *kośa*, *daṇḍa* or *bala* and *suhṛd* or *mitra*.[78] Kauṭilya also presents a similar list of *saptāṅgas*.[79] *Manusmṛti* IX.294, *Yājñavalkyasmṛti* I.353, *Viṣṇu Dharmasūtra* III.33, *Kāmandakīya Nītisāra* I.16 and *Śukra Nītisāra* I.61 have presented the same number of *aṅgas* of the state. In *Mahābhārata* it is stated that they exist, depending upon one another like three sticks standing with one another's support. The merits of one are expected to set off the merits of others. All are of the

---

75 *Manu* VII.15-25.

76 *Matsya Purāṇa* CXXIII.24; CXLII.74; CXLV.36; CCXV.54; see also Dikshitar, 1951, *Purāṇa Index*, vol. 2, p. 66.

77 *Vāyu Purāṇa* 49.117-18; 57.82; 59.26; 61.14.

78 *ātmāmātyāśca kośāśca daṇḍo mitrāṇī caiva hi* ||
tathā janapadāścaiva puraṁ ca kurunandana |
etat saptātmakaṁ ārājyaṁ paripālyaṁ prayatnataḥ || — ŚP LXIX.64-65

79 *svāmyamātyajanapadadurgakośadaṇḍamitrāṇi prakṛtayaḥ* |
— *Arthaśāstra* VI.1

same importance.[80] After discussing all the importance of state and its constituents, a few questions come to mind that how did the state come into existence? What was the necessity of that? And what is the process of its evolution? Śānti-Parva has answers for all these questions.

THEORY OF THE ORIGIN OF STATE

Philosophers in all ages and of all countries have loved to speculate on the origin of the state. As a matter of fact, the authors of *Mahābhārata* have also devoted their attention to this matter, and have advanced many theories, perusal of which indicates that they approached the issue from a religious point of view, and more or less ascribed it to the divine agencies. While analysing the different theories one should be careful in separating the grains from the chaff. It also is to be noted that several theories are interwoven in the same statements regarding a particular theory of the origin of state.

The topic of the origin of state has been discussed in the epic in a questionnaire form. In other words the curiosity and enquiry of Yudhiṣṭhira find mention in terms such as "whence", "why" and "what" pertaining to the origin of state in the epic tradition. As said in Śānti-Parva:

> *ya eṣa rājan rājeti śabdaścarati bhārata* ।
> *kathameṣa samutpannastanme brūhi paraṁtapaḥ* ॥
> — LIX.5

It will not be out of place to say that the origin of state has been discussed in the Western political thought in the same perspective.[81] Śānti-Parva gives a great account of discussion on the origin of state.

---

80 ŚP CCCXX.156-58.

81 Cf. Bhīṣma 12.36, cf. section XI, p. 26. " Whence arose the word, *rājan* (king), that is used, O Bharata, on earth? . . . for what reason does one man, viz. the king governs the rest of the world . . . ? Becomes delighted . . . ?" — Ibid. ŚP LIX.5

Cf. St. Thomas Aquinas: "whether the world is governed by someone? What is the end of the government? Whether all things are immediately governed by God?"

This being important to *daṇḍa*, naturally follows that there must be a legal machinery to ensure the proper use of *daṇḍa* and to avoid its misuse. This machinery is obviously the *rājya*, which exercises the rule of *daṇḍa* through the power of the ruler, i.e. the king. In this way the importance of state has come into existence.

In Śānti-Parva Bhīṣma gives two different accounts regarding the origin of state. According to the first account the beginning of humanity enjoyed a golden age, when there was neither the king, nor the kingdom, neither *daṇḍa* nor the one who enforced *daṇḍa*. It was an ideal state of things, wherein people protected each other by means of *dharma*.[82] But after some time the situation changed and golden age did not last long and very soon they were overcome by fatigue, lust and greed. Their behaviour resulted in all sorts of improper things, leading to disappearance of Brahmā (Vedic lore) and *dharma*. After some time the situation became more and more miserable under the influence of ignorance (*moha*), illusion (*māyā*), greed (*lobha*), passion (*kāma*) and attachment (*rāga*). Seeing this imbalance in the society all the gods approached Brahmā for a solution. Brahmā assured them by creating a Śāstra of one lakh chapters, describing all four *puruṣārtha*s therein. It included everything connected with the affairs of state and government.

Thereafter they requested Viṣṇu to appoint the strongest one among them who could rule over the mortals. Lord Viṣṇu created Virājas, but he was interested in the attainment of salvation (*mokṣa*) and finally he refused the rule. Even his sons, Kīrtiman and grandson Kardama also refused to rule. Kardama's son Anaṅga accepted the proposal and ruled for sometimes. After him, his son Atibala assumed the reigns of government. He was a slave of his sense-organs hence, seems to have become unpopular. After him Veṇā's reign started, who on account of his cruel behaviour and unsympathetic attitude towards the sages and brāhmaṇas, was finally killed by them. They churned his right arm. Consequently Pṛthu came out; he established the rule of *dharma* over the earth and made the people happy. Lord Viṣṇu himself

---

[82] *na vai rājyaṁ na rājā "sīnna ca daṇḍo na daṇḍikaḥ* |
dharmeṇaiva prajāḥ sarvā rakṣanti sma parasparam || — ŚP LIX.14

had entered Pṛthu's body and hence the whole world bowed to the god amongst men. This clearly indicates the divine origin of kingship. In this way the state came into the existence.

ENDS AND FUNCTIONS OF STATE

An analysis of different theories of origin of states reveals that state was originated for the protection of life and property of people. But does it mean that it stands only for the police work? If it is not, then what are the ends that it should strive at? Then what are the functions to be discharged by it? In Śānti-Parva, the establishment of *dharma* was the most important function of the state. It justifies the existence of sovereignty on the ground that it maintains *dharma*. It goes to the extent of saying that it is for the sake of *dharma* that sovereignty exists.[83] The foremost aim of the state is to protect people from evil-doers. The prosperity of the people depends on their duties which they have to perform and it should be according to injunctions of *dharma*, so it is the duty of the state to persuade all its subjects to perform their duties. All these things cannot be achieved without economic prosperity, so the king should do more for the economic well-being of his people.

One's life is incomplete without attempts made for the attainment of *mokṣa* from sorrows, so it is the foremost duty of the state to help people in this respect. It promotes the cause of *dharma*, persuades people to perform their duties and to follow the rules of morality. These are the factors that lead one to liberation.

Thus, the welfare of the people is the main objective of the state. It stands for the fulfilment of fourfold objectives of human life. It is the duty of the king to protect and nourish his subjects like his children. The next challenge was the proper functioning of the state machinery. To address this challenge there felt the need for instituting seven constituents as parts of the state machinery.

CONSTITUENTS OF THE STATE

In Śānti-Parva, an instruction is given to Yudhiṣṭhira that he should

---

83 *dharmāya bhavati rājā na kāmakaraṇāya tu* । — ŚP XC.20

appoint able and intelligent ministers to run the state in a proper way. The proper functioning of the state is only possible by a machinery, i.e. political institution. A king alone cannot perform all the duties and functions in a proper manner, it is only possible when there is a machinery to help him. This was the reason why the institutions (seven constituents) came into existence. In Śānti-Parva these institutions are referred as the seven constituents of the state. It is mentioned that there should be unity between the king and institutions which are made by him, for the maintenance of peace according to *dharma*. These seven constituents are considered as political institutions. They provide help in accomplishing the duties of the king which are generally related to the welfare of the society.

The *saptāṅga* theory stands for seven elements (*aṅga*s) of the state (*rājya*), and this not only deals with constituent elements of state, but also with different stages of its formation, composition, nature, functions, interrelations, growth and decline, etc. *Saptāṅga* plays an important role because in the absence of these there is no value of state, and it could not be possible to work properly without the help of them. The *saptāṅga* theory is also propounded by many other texts such as Purāṇas, Dharmaśāstras, *Nītiśāstra* and *Arthaśāstra*, with meticulous detailing.

Before discussing further, it is desirable to know the meaning of *rājya*. The epic uses the word *rājya* from *rañj* (to please). The real meaning of the word, however, seems to be "one who shines".[84] In recent times, *rājya* has been taken in the sense of "state" and "sovereign ruler".[85] In Śānti-Parva, the terms *rājā* or *rājya* and *ātman* have been interchangeably used for state.[86]

After discussing the origin of state, Bhīṣma also discusses the

---

[84] Kane, 1965, *History of Dharmaśāstra*, vol. III, p. 17, see also V.P. Varma (1959), "The root *rāj* (*Nirukta* II) means to be luminous and in the *Mahābhārata*, the root *raj* stands for *rājā* (to please)". — *Studies in Hindu Political Thought and its Metaphysical Foundations,* p. 148 n.

[85] Mishra, 1984, *Approach to the Study of the Arthaśāstra of Kauṭilya*, p. 63.

[86] ŚP LXIX.62-63.

various constituents or components of the state technically known as seven *aṅga*s or *prakṛti*s of the state.[87] The former word stands for an organ of the body. The latter denotes nature. Both of these terms are used in the epic in the sense of constituents of a state. What are the seven elements of state in the epic tradition? Śānti-Parva alludes to the seven constituents of *rājya*. But in Śānti-Parva we do not find the explanation of these seven elements in a systematic order like in the writings of Kauṭilya and Manu. Śānti-Parva gives traditional order of the seven constituents of state: i.e. king (*ātman*), minister (*amātya*), treasury (*kośa*), chastisement (*daṇḍa*), ally (*mitra*), territory-cum-population (*janapada*) and capital (*pura*).[88]

These institutions were also discussed by many ancient Indian thinkers. Their conception of state was solely based on the principles of organic unity. They regarded the state as an organic whole like a human body and looked upon its constituents as its limbs. Śukra while comparing the seven elements of the state with the organs of the body, called the king as head, ministers as eyes, friends as ears, the *kośa* as mouth, the army as mind, the *durga*s as hands and *rāṣṭra* as legs.[89]

All the limbs of its body politic have been considered equally important and complementary to each other. An emphasis has been laid upon their coordination and integration as a necessary factor for the existence, growth and proper functioning of the state. None of them could function independently. All the organs of the state moved like the wheels of the chariot. Their equal importance, mutual interdependence and indispensability are focused in the *rājadharma* section of Śānti-

87 ŚP CXXI.46. Cf. Kane, 1965, *History of Dharmaśāstra*, vol. III, p. 17.

88 *rājñā saptaiva rakṣyāṇi tāni caiva nibodha me* ।
ātmāmātyāśca kośāśca daṇḍo mitrāṇi caiva hi ॥ — ŚP LXIX.64
Cf. *MatsyaP*, CCXX.19; *KA* VI.1; *Manu* IX.294.

89 *saptāṅgamucyate rājyaṁ tatra mūrdhā nṛpaḥ smṛtaḥ* ।
durgāmātya suhṛtkṣotraṁ mukha kośo balaṁ manaḥ ॥ — NS I.61-62

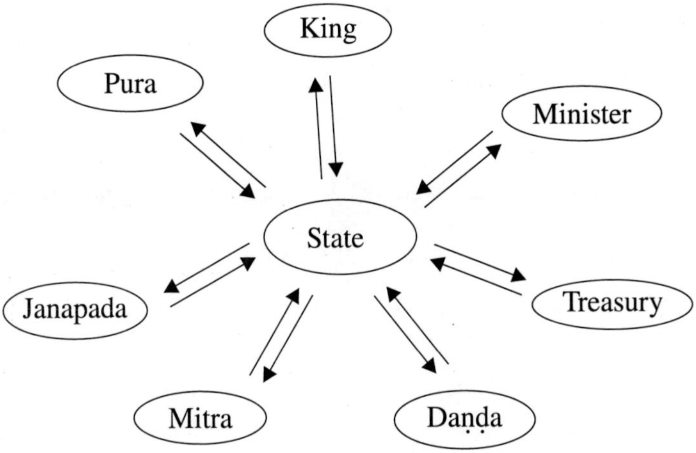

fig. 3.1: Seven constituents of the state

Parva,[90] but also in other texts like Purāṇas,[91] *Arthaśāstra*,[92] *Manusmṛti*[93] and *Kāmandakīya Nītisāra.*[94] All the seven elements constituted the wealth of the state.[95] These seven constituents played an equal role in the formation and functioning of the state (*fig.* 3.1).

SVĀMĪ (KING)

All the authorities admit that the king (*svāmī, ātman*) is an important element of the state. In *Arthaśāstra* and *Manusmṛti*, the king occupies an important place among the *saptāṅga*s of the state. It is first and foremost of constituents of the state. In Śānti-Parva, Bhīṣma details his importance, qualities, duties and responsibilities at great length. According to him king is an inevitable agency for the welfare of the

90 ŚP LVI.128.

91 *AgniP* 239.1.

92 *KA* VI.1.

93 *Manu* IX.296-97.

94 *NK* IV.1.

95 *KA* VI.1.

people. It is clearly stated that without a king, even one's better half and property are not safe. While discussing the importance of king, Bhīṣma tells about the kingless state, i.e. anarchical state. Bhīṣma condemns anarchy by saying that in a kingless state *dharma* is totally absent.[96] Sinners and robbers get an opportunity to deprive others of their belongings. Human welfare becomes impossible. Those who are not slaves are forcibly made slaves *matsya-nyāya* (law of fish), in the other words, "might is right" is practised. King is the only one who can get rid of such a situation:

rājā cenna bhavelloke pr̥thivyāṁ daṇḍadhārakaḥ ।
jale matsyānivābhakṣyan durbalaṁ balavattarāḥ ॥
— ŚP LXVII.16

It is also stated that without a king the people are as a herd of cattle without a herdsman.[97] In Śānti-Parva, it has also been stated that in an anarchical state, fire (Agni) does not convey the libation to the gods.[98]

A kingless state is deplorable[99] because the kingless subject (*prajānātha*) meets its end, all the acts prove futile, rain do not pour and gods are not worshipped.[100] Nobody follows the *dharma* in an anarchical state, because it is the king on whom *dharma* depends.[101] Thus in the absence of a king, peace, order, justice, religion, morality and life become impossible and their contraries prevail prominently. Bhīṣma suggests that one should not live in such a state. Manu has also expressed his view about such a state. According to him the

---

96 *arājakeṣu rāṣṭreṣu dharmo na vyatiṣṭhate* । — ŚP LXVII.3

97 ŚP LXVII.11. Cf. "Guided by those instances, O hero, men should bend before those that are powerful person really bends his head to Indra." — Ibid. LXII, p. 145

98 *nārājakeṣu rāṣṭreṣu vastavyamiti rocaye* ।
nārājakeṣu rāṣṭreṣu havyamagnirvahatyuta ॥ — Ibid. LXVII.5

99 *śocyaṁ rāṣṭramarājakaṁ* ॥ — Ibid. LXVIII

100 *arājakeṣu rāṣṭreṣu prajānāthā vinaśyati* ।
naśyanti ca kriyāḥ sarvā nāsti vr̥ṣṭirna devatā ॥ — Ādi CIV.44

101 ŚP LXXIII.20-22.

condition of a kingless state is dreadful. Therein people run about out of terror.[102] *Viṣṇu Purāṇa* I.13.31-32 favours the same view. In the opinion of Śukra, life becomes miserable in the absence of a king, like a boat drowned in a sea in the absence of a pilot. People do not perform their prescribed duties (*svadharma*).[103]

So by emphasizing the necessity and importance of a king, Bhīṣma regards the appointment of a king as the foremost duty of the people, because king is the one who could remove chaos and establish *dharma*.[104] Those who desire prosperity should first elect and crown a king for the protection of all. As stated:

> *tato mahīṁ pariyayau parjanya iva vr̥ṣṭimān* ।
> *śāmayan sarvataḥ pāpān svakarmasu ca yojayan* ॥
> — ŚP LXVII.32

From these accounts it becomes clear that the necessity of king was felt in order to maintain *dharma* and to get rid of disorder. Śānti-Parva focuses right on the necessity of the king because he is the maker of age. It is the king who causes Kr̥ta, Tretā or Dvāpara and Kali. The king should be righteous because only in the kingdom of the righteous king, people sleep and wake up in happiness. The institution of the kingship stands for the protection of helpless people who are oppressed by the powerful ones.

Bhīṣma justifies the kingship because peace and prosperity of subjects, sufficiency, and reasonableness of rain, disease, death and other fears are dependent upon the king, hence he is considered as *rājamūla* (root of the kingdom).[105] The king is a writ in large. State is a trust and he is the trustee. Śānti-Parva asserts that the people follow the great ones and the subjects follow the king. Hence king should observe his duties without wrath and malice. He should not abandon kindness. He should acquire wealth without persecution and cruelty. He should pursue

102 *Manu* VII.3.

103 ŚP LXV.6.

104 ŚP LXVII.2.

105 Ibid. LIX.138.

pleasure without attachment.[106] A code of conduct is prescribed for the king. King is the head of the state. He has to deal with judicial, taxation, religious and cultural issues. He has to protect and regulate the *varṇa* and *āśrama* systems. He is more important than others.

It has been stated that the king is the one who can establish the social order and is responsible for the economic and social progress of the people. It is his duty to command his *amātya*s and *tīrtha*s to streamline the administration. He is under the command of *dharma* and *daṇḍa*. He has to take care of all the constituents of state.[107] In all ages the king, by and large, proved to be the backbone of the state.

AMĀTYA (MINISTER)

Amātya is the second constituent of the state.[108] It has been already asserted that the king cannot do the multifarious duties without the help of his ministers and officials. In Śānti-Parva different terms have been used for ministers such as *saciva*[109] and *mantrin*.[110] Sometimes the word *sahayavān* also stands for a minister. But the use of *sahayavān* is not numerous as *mantrin*, *saciva* and *amātya*. *Amātya* is not a different person as it exists in *Arthaśāstra*. Thus it becomes clear without any doubt that *amātya* is used in the sense of minister. The word *sabhāsada*[111] is also used in the epic. We also find a reference to minister of war, the courtiers and *parichada* in Śānti-Parva. These terms are used in a dialogue between Yudhiṣṭhira and Bhīṣma. According to Kauṭilya, a minister is the eye of the kingdom.[112] Manu has also given his opinion that king has to sit in the assembly and deliberate with

---

106 ŚP LXXI.3.

107 Ibid. LIX.64.

108 Ibid. XCII.28.

109 Ibid. XVIII.4.

110 Ibid. LXXXIII.9.

111 *sabhāsadaḥ sahāyāśca suhṛdaśca viśampate* I
paricchahāstathāmātyāḥ kīdṛśāḥ syuḥ pitāmaḥ II — Ibid. LXXXIII.1

112 *KA* I.14.5.

his ministers. According to Śānti-Parva, a *saciva* is king's helper and *amātya* is regarded as his private secretary.

It is obviously laid down that the minister must possess eight virtues to serve the king and to hear matters of state's welfare. He should hear minutely, understand clearly and he must have sharp memory. He must think over the state matter perfectly and deliberately. He is responsible to accept things after logical thinking and consideration.[113] In Śānti-Parva Bhīṣma states that the ministers should possess modesty, self-restraint, truth, sincerity and courage. It has been stated further that ministers should be of high birth.[114] They must be the citizens of the state. They should have great learning and dignity of behaviour. So, it is stated that king should have to be very careful in selecting his ministers and officials. Stress has been laid down that ministers should be very firm and have resolve and very efficient in knowing the movement of the forces.

An *amātya* is an important constituent for the formation of state. It is *amātya* who formulates the state's policies and advises the king to act accordingly, though the king is not always supposed to do so. The king has authority to appoint his ministers. The duty of the minister is to contemplate on the king's decision and suggest him what is right and what is wrong and to prevent him from misusing his power. The importance of *amātya* is such that in the absence of the king, he has to carry out the administrative affairs. The ministers are required to look after the state's affairs. Such a state under the charge of a minister for a long period is known as *amātyasaṁstha*. He virtually rules as a king. In case of any doubtful situation such as on a policy matter, the king consults his *purohita* too.

Counsel from the ministers was a must even in Vedic days. There was Vedic *sabhā* described as a "meeting place" in Vedic tradition.

---

113 *deśakālavidhānajñān bhartr̥kāryahitaiṣiṇaḥ* ।
nityamartheṣu sarveṣu rājan kurvīta mantriṇaḥ ॥ — ŚP LXXXIII.24

114 *kulīnān śīlasmpannāniṅgitajñānaniṣṭhurān* ।
deśakālavidhānajñān bhartr̥kāryahitaiṣiṇaḥ ॥ — Ibid. LXXXIII.8

Sabhā was replaced by the council of ministers. In Śānti-Parva the duties and importance of ministers and the method of their appointment are discussed in an elaborate manner. Thus ministers were considered as a cardinal element of the state.

KOŚA (TREASURY)

Kośa is an element of great importance in the body politic as all its undertakings ultimately depend upon finance.[115] It has been stated that through the decrease of treasury, the king's forces are reduced and army suffers deterioration.

> *aśaṅkamāno vacanamanasūyuridaṁ śr̥ṇu* ।
> *rājñaḥ kośakṣayādeva jāyate balasaṁkṣayaḥ* ॥ — ŚP CXXX.12

Hence, the king should replenish his treasury like one creating water in the forest, which is without water.[116] In Śānti-Parva it has been stated that stability of state depends upon nobility of blood, ministers of great wealth, knowledge as well as different kinds of forces.[117] The correlation of the king and his treasury is emphasized and it is mentioned that he should take care of seven limbs and *kośa* is one of them.[118] A rich treasury is possible only if the king is righteous and his administration is able. The origin of state also highlights on the importance of *kośa* in connection with the Pr̥thu and Manu tradition in the epic.

It is the duty of the king to increase the treasury because its richness helps him in emergency. According to Bhīṣma, it is one of the *upāya*s through which he can control his enemies. Therefore, all

---

115 ŚP XV.48.

116 *kośaṁ ca janayed rājā nirjalebhyo yathā jalam* । — ŚP CXXX.13, see also 130.14. Cf. Aristotle says: "There must be certain amount of revenue both for internal needs and for the purpose of war — *Politics*, Bk VII.8, p. 273

117 ŚP CXXI.42.

118 ŚP LXIX.64.

undertakings depend on *kośa* or finance.[119] Kauṭilya also stresses on the importance of it. In the lack of finance, army cannot be protected and maintained. The king's root is his *kośa*. Nīlakaṇṭha, a commentator on *Mahābhārata*, also testifies the same stand.[120]

The defence of the country ultimately rests upon its sound financial position. The sources of revenue are also discussed in the epic. Agriculture was one of the most important sources of income to the state. The king was enjoined to realize *ṣaḍbhāga* and *bali*. The king should do all the things by which the treasury gets enriched, many sources of income are discussed in Śānti-Parva, like cattle and forced labour.

JANAPADA (TERRITORY)

Janapada[121] is an essential element of the state because a king cannot rule over a barren land. The epic contains different terms for it such as *rāṣṭra*, *pura*[122] and *deśa*,[123] and all these terms are synonyms of each other according to *Amarakośa* and are interchangeably used for *janapada*. These terms not only refer to territory but also to population. It denotes the inhabited territory. In Śānti-Prava it is stated that state cannot exist unless the people are brave, hard working, followers of *dharma* and of good moral character. A piece of land inhabited by such virtuous and hardworking people enriches the state. Similarly, land should be very fertile. It should be covered with woods and watered by rivers, so it is the duty of the king to protect land[124] and people from external dangers. So that they may live a happy and prosperous life.

In Śānti-Parva it is stated again that king should give his attention

---

119 ŚP LXIX.64.

120 Ibid. CXXVIII.35, cf. ŚP CXXX, p. 282. See also Nīlakaṇṭha, *Śrīman Mahābhāratam*, p. 220.

121 ŚP LXIX.1, 10, 65.

122 Ibid. LXVII.2, 3, 5, 6.

123 Ibid. LXVIII.58.

124 *ātmano sarvato rakṣan rājan rakṣasva medinīm* I — ŚP LXXXIX.13 .

to this fact that beggars and dacoits must not reside in his territory, as they harass the people and cause trouble to them.[125] He should only allow such persons to reside in his state, who have compassion for all the *jīva*s and can contribute to its prosperity.[126] The king is called the heart (*hṛdayāṅga*) of his people, hence he should protect his kingdom with proper care.[127] Kauṭilya is also of the view that no territory deserves the name of a kingdom or country unless it is full of people.[128] Manu also stresses that *janapada* is an essential element for the formation of state.

It is right to say that the ancient concepts were very progressive because territory (*rāṣṭra*), populace (*prajā*), law (*dharma*) and authority (*daṇḍa*) are important factors not only well recognized, but also fully developed in classical traditions. They do contribute today, as much as they did centuries before Christ in India. As without a piece of land and population, a modern state cannot be defined, similarly, the king, minister and treasury were irrelevant to define sovereignty in the absence of *janapada* in the epic period.

DURGA (FORT)

It is another important constituent of the state, and was considered the strength of the sovereign. It was believed that with a well-equipped fort, a king could defend his country against enemy even stronger than himself. Being the chief means of defence, it was recognized that the forts should be fully equipped with all the necessities of life and other means of defence. We find detailed descriptions related to the selection of the place and construction of a fort in Śānti-Parva. In chapter 86 there is the description of *durga*s, how to make them, types and their importance. Śānti-Parva refers to six types of forts, namely, *dhanvan*, *mahīdurga*, *giridurga*, *manuṣyadurga*, *abdurga* and *vanadurga*:

---

125 Ibid. LXXXIX.13-14.

126 Ibid. LXXXIX.21.

127 ŚP LXVIII.58-59; LXIX.63.

128 *KA* Bk13, chap. 4.

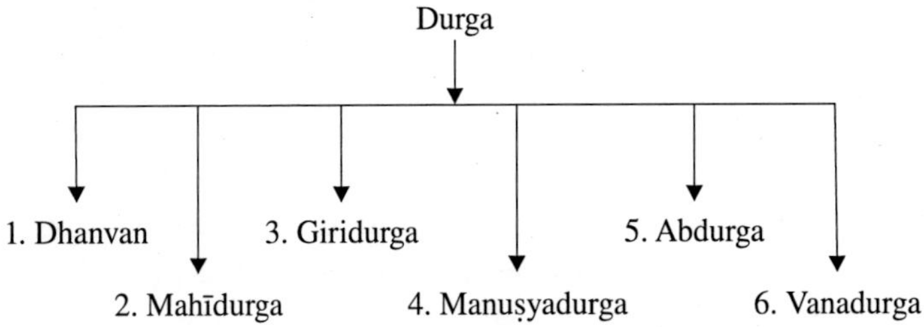

fig. 3.2: Types of *durgas*

dhanvadurgaṁ mahīdurgaṁ giridurgaṁ tathaiva ca ।
manuṣyadurgaṁ abdurgaṁ vanadurgaṁ ca tāni ṣaṭ ॥
— ŚP LXXXVI.5[129]

The forts were very useful for military purposes as well as the safety of the king. Śānti-Parva informs that a king even inferior to his enemy in military strength may harass the foe by taking shelter in a fort.[130] The first three types were built in desert, on the plain land and on the mountain respectively, the *manuṣyadurga* seems to be a fort of military, formed with the fourfold army at a particular place, which may be equated with the military cantonments, and the fifth and sixth types were built in the islands and forests respectively. Kauṭilya also gives a detailed technical account of fortification and he alludes only four types of forts but Manu mentions all the six types of forts.

The importance of the forts has also been highlighted by other political thinkers. According to Yājñavalkya, the saftey of the king, his subjects and treasury absolutely depends upon the erection of strong

---

129 Cf. "water-citadels, earth-citadels, hill-citadels human-citadels, mud-citadels, and the forest-citadels" — P.C. Roy, section LXXXVI, p. 187

Cf. Aristotle: " that the city and the territory should be connected with the sea, the defenders of the country, if they are to maintain themselves aginst an enemy, should be easily relieved both by land and by sea." — op. cit., p. 269.

130 *ekāṅgenāpi sambhūtaḥ śatrudurgamupāśritaḥ* ।
sarvam tāpayate deśamapi rājñaḥ samr̥ddhinaḥ ॥ — ŚP LVIII.18

forts.[131] The followers of the school of Ācārya Parāśara also consider *durgas* more important than *janapada*, with reason for their contention is that the fort is necessary for the deployment and protection of army as well as the protection of the treasury. This is also supported by Kauṭilya. It has been further observed by them that those forts, in comparison to *nagara* and citizens, serve more as an impregnable force and in emergency give shelter to everybody. The safety of the whole *rāṣṭra* depends on them.

In the epic it has been further stated that fort's construction is not enough but the defensive measures must be provided to the forts. If any fort is not useful, the king is instructed to destroy all the smaller forts in his kingdom. He should also cut down all the smaller trees, expect those that are called *caitya*.[132] Hence, there should also be the moats on all sides filled with water, dangerous fishes and aquatic animals, bushes and *triśūla* type devices in order to prevent the entry of foes.[133] In addition, towers should be built on the upper portions of walls and with a view to face the enemy, holes should be made into them for discharging arrows from a long distance. Beside the earlier defensive measures, the epic lays stress on providing stores, arsenals, military barracks, war instruments, cavalry, chariots and offices inside the forts.[134] It highlights the practical necessity of this element for the stability of the state.

Adequate steps are suggested to take guard against conflagration and espionage because these calamities cause a great loss to life and property and ultimately the state is weakened. The epic refers to many small kingdoms hence fortification of the city is essential both in theoretical and practical grounds. In order to watch the activities of the enemy and for using the missiles and firing shots at them, several small holes in fort walls should be made. Fuels, food grains, medicines

---

131 *YS* I.321.

132 ŚP LXIX.39, cf. Roy, ŚP CLIII.

133 Ibid. LXIX.41.

134 ŚP LXXXVII.6-12; *MatsyaP* 217.10-26; 227.24-25; *AgniP* 222.1-6; 227.19-20.

and weapons must be stored to meet the emergency.[135] The acrobats, dancers and singers during the peaceful time should be patronized but during the abnormal time their presence in the fort is considered risky, so at that time they should be expelled from the forts, so that the espionage may be checked and adequate defensive measures are taken.

Analogous to *durga*, Śānti-Parva refers to *pura*, a fortified capital city and the centre of administration. While *durga* is more associated with the military affairs and also with the defence of the country, *pura* is related to the capital of the state. The king resides in it, so it should be well fortified. It is the suitable place for consultation on the state affairs, and it should be built on a site where all provisions and amenities are available (*sarvasampata pradhāne*).[136] *Mahābhārata* refers to the forts which were well fortified such as Dvārakā in Saurāṣṭra, Hastināpura in the Kuru dynasty and Girivraja in Magadha *rāṣṭra*. So, it can be said that *durga* was, no doubt, a physical element without which the definition of state was not complete and convincing. Though this constituent of state has no relevance in the modern concept of sovereignty, Aristotle and Plato recognized its importance for the existence of city state in the classical Greek tradition. The Greek *polis* of historical times still shows the sense of "fortress". It denotes the meaning of "citadels, castles as well as stronghold".[137]

ALLIES (FRIENDS)

The significance and functional values of the *saptāṅga* theory of state cannot be understood unless the next element "ally" is examined.[138] The epic contains three important terms for an ally, namely, *mitra*, *suhr̥ta* and *sahāya*. *Suhr̥ta* is one who is a well-wisher and *sahāya* is one who

---

[135] *saṅkaṭadvārakāṇi syurucchavāsārthaṁ purasya ca* ।
teṣām ca dvāravad guptiḥ kāryā sarvātmanā bhavet ॥
— ŚP LXIX.44; LI.54-57

[136] ŚP LXXXVII.4.

[137] Benveniste Émile, *Indo-European Language and Society*, tr. Elizabeth Palmer, pp. 289-99.

[138] ŚP CXXXVIII.51, cf. Roy, CXL, p. 31.

helps or assists. But who is a real ally? According to the epic the real ally is one in whom may have confidence as in his father. So faith is the main characteristic to be found in a real friend or ally.[139] Then an important question comes, what is the necessity of an ally? It is stated in Śānti-Parva that a real friend is the one who protects and serves his counterpart even by sacrificing his life; so on account of this, a king should make his friends, as it is a condition for the prosperity of his state:

sarvasaṁgrahaṇe yukto nr̥po bhavati yaḥ sadā ।
utthanśīlo mitrāḍhyaḥ sa rājā rājasattamaḥ ॥
— ŚP CXVIII.27

The thinkers on the epic emphasize that king should also consider an ally as an organ of his body. By accepting the advice of an ally, the material prosperity is achieved and protection is secured.[140] Śukra, Br̥haspati, Vidura, Devala and Kaṇikā have speculated on the necessity of a *mitra* by narrating stories in the epic, and from internal evidences of the epic it is clear that the king and his ally should protect each other and must tender mutual help during critical times.[141] The importance of *mitra* as one of the seven organs of a state can best be qualified in the following words of Manu — "the king with land and gold cannot make as much progress as he can with the help of the dipendable friends".[142] Yājñavalkya also holds more or less the same view.[143] Kauṭilya also accepts the importance of *mitra* under the *maṇḍala* theory.[144] Bhīṣma says that the king must know four kinds of allies.

caturvidhāṁ mitrāṇi rājñāṁ rājan bhavantyut ।
sahārtho bhajamānaśca sahajaḥ kr̥trimastathā ॥
— ŚP LXXX.3

---

139 Udyoga-Parva XXXVI.35.

140 ŚP CXIX.19.

141 Ibid. LXXXI.10-13.

142 *Manu* VII.208, cf. Bühler, 1886, *The Laws of Manu*, p. 250.

143 *YS* 1.352.

144 *KA* VII.9.

> Those who have the same goal to achieve (*sahārtha*), those who come to seek shelter (*bhajamānaśca*), those who are natural friends (*sahajaḥ*) and those who are acquired by offering something to them (*kr̥trima*).

Beside these four, there is a fifth type also and that is *dharmātmā-mitra* (righteous friend) who follows the right path and does not favour his friends in immoral acts.[145] Who is the best friend? In the view of Bhīṣma, *bhajamānaśca* and *sahajaḥ* types are best allies, but the king should be always cautious of *kr̥trima* and *sahārtha* types,[146] because they remain as friends only for the fulfilment of their own interests.[147]

Nīlakaṇṭha is of the view that a foe becomes a friend and a friend becomes a foe.[148] A king with unstable mind cannot make friends, it is very difficult to win over persons having selfish motives and acting falsely, so it is necessary to be selfless and honest to the persons with whom friendship is desired. Then the next question arises: what should be the characteristics of a true friend? In chapter 162 of Śānti-Parva it has been emphatically stated that a king should make those persons as his friends who are of high birth, have wide knowledge, are experts in delivering speeches, handsome, honest, truthful, hardworking, brave, liberal, softspoken, followers of justice, gifted with persuading eloquence, expert in the science of knowledge, industrious and worthy of helping him in the time of adversity and sharing his sorrows and pleasure, fit to maintain secrecy, etc.[149]

Bhīṣma also presents a very exhaustive lists of demerits to be found in the persons with whom friendship should not be established, such are those who are greedy, cruel, lazy, non-followers of *dharma*, wicked, rigid and ungrateful. The story of "Gautama a Brāhmaṇa and Rājadharma Baka" reveals the fact that ungrateful persons are so dislike

145 ŚP LXXX.4-5.

146 ŚP LXXX.6.

147 ŚP LXXXI.3-4.

148 *Śrīman Mahābhāratam*, p. 140.

149 ŚP LXIX.16; CLXII.17-25; *AgniP* CCXXXIX.34-37; 40-43; *NK* IV.75-77.

that even the vultures do not like to eat their flesh. The ungrateful ally cannot gain fame in society, can never realize happiness and suffers in the hell.[150] Kauṭilya has described six types of friends in connection with the *saptāṅga* theory: (1) tradition, (2) permanent, (3) who could exercise restraint upon himself, (4) who is not of hostile attitude, (5) who is endowed with courage and ability to offer worthy advice, and (6) those, who could help in need. A friend of all these qualities is, indeed, a real friend.[151] The thinkers of *Mahābhārata* have a realistic approach in connection with the formation of allies. They are of the view that friendship and enemity are not permanent affairs, it is based on the self-motive. In Śānti-Parva, four elements find priority in the formation of a state. It has been further stated that residing in the city (*pura*), the king should increase his stores of rice and other grains but he should also enhance the number of his friends.[152] And it is also mentioned that among the seven elements, priority is given to the king (his own self), councillors, treasury, machinery (*daṇḍa*), friends, his provinces (*janapada*) and his capital (*pura*).[153] So an ally was an important constituent in *saptāṅga*s of the state. Not only in ancient India but even in present days, the game of power politics revolves around the different allies. Victory and defeat depend more or less on the role of allied powers. During the world wars, the axis and allied powers realized the relevance of forming an alliance with like-minded countries.

---

150 ŚP CLXVII.19-22.

151 *KA* VI.1.

152 ŚP LXXXVI.11, cf. LXXXVI, p. 188.

153 ŚP LXIX.62-63, cf. section LXIX, p. 154. Cf. according to Vidura, "if the king's treasury is empty, he obtains friends, councillors and servants, but he must be without deceitfulness, be active, grateful, intelligent and guiltless". — Udyoga XXXVIII.34. Cf. section XXXVIII, p. 833; actually, due to virtues of his friends, the king was successful in interstate relations streamlining administration as well as getting victory in war.

DAṆḌA (MILITARY)

Daṇḍa occupies an important place in the *saptāṅga* theory of state. In the Western political thought, it is related with sovereignty. It has been propounded as an element of state in Greek political thought, though Plato and Aristotle have discussed the necessity of chastisement in connection with state and justice. In ancient Indian political thought, this *daṇḍa* has been identified with the king. According to Manu, "*daṇḍa* is the one by which the kingdom can be governed". In *Mahābhārata*, the king is considered *daṇḍadhara*. Because of *daṇḍa* every caste (*varṇa*) performs its duty. And in the absence of *daṇḍa* there is confusion and anarchy. Brahmā realized the necessity of *daṇḍa* and in order to maintain law and order in the society, he composed *daṇḍanīti* (science of chastisement) to regulate the four orders and four *varṇa*s. But the king is not above the *daṇḍa*. Kauṭilya also accepts *daṇḍa* as a painful necessity. The king has to apply it properly and he must be careful and willing to inflict punishment on culprits. Every thinker of the epic, namely, Bṛhaspati, Vidura, Devala, Śukra, etc. recommends its proper application according to the intensity of crime. In the interstate relations, it stands for an army.

Its importance has been realized by thinkers in the field of judiciary, administration of treasury as well as in the sixfold policies and four *upāya*s. And it has been also stated that when the other three means fail to bring in the desired result, *daṇḍa* must be applied, the commendation of *daṇḍa* presupposes the theory that people obey law and the dictates of Śāstras due to the fear for the former (*daṇḍa*).[154] In *Mahābhārata*, it has also been stated that King Saṁvara of Ayodhyā had successfully protected his state from aggression by Pāñcālas.[155] The political aspirants lead military to war, hence the growing armed clashes enabled our ancient political *paṇḍita*s (thinkers) to assess the

---

154 Kane, 1965, op. cit., p. 22, cf. ŚP LIX.39, see also section LLX, p.123. In this verse *amātya* is on second place and *bala* denoting *daṇḍa* is on the fourth position and treasury (*kośa*) is the fifth and their characteristics are triple (*tribidhigaṁ*) — bad, middling and good. — ŚP LIX.39

155 Ādi XC.31-42.

relevance of *daṇḍa* as a cardinal element of state administration.

H.N. Sinha has also presented same views regarding the origin of the state based on the force theory. To him there were various foreign tribes who attacked the northern and western regions of ancient India, hence *daṇḍa* come into being. An army was organized and expedition was taken against them. Fearing *daṇḍa*, the ministers stick to respective duties and the robbers do not dare to loot the property. Kauṇapadanta considers the army superior to *kośa* on the ground that the latter cannot be protected without the former. Kauṭilya also accepts this view with some reservations. According to Kauṭilya, an army depends upon *kośa*. If the army is paid in time, there is no room for military revolt. The thinkers of the epic also inculcate the same view. They are complementary. In the educational scheme prescribed for the princes, the study of *daṇḍanīti* is imperative. About *daṇḍanīti* Kauṭliya, Manu and the epic have corresponding views. "He followed righteousness. He protected brāhmaṇas, he gave gifts to the deserving ones. He had a rich treasury but he did not care for depending states, he got deafeated by his enemies". In some internal evidences of the epic, priority has been given to *daṇḍa*. In one of the verses of Śānti-Parva, emphasis has been laid down on four elements of the state: *kośa*, *bala*, *mitra* and *daṇḍa*. The king is enjoined to take proper care of the above *aṅga*s, though the order of the precedence in enumerating the seven elements is not mentioned. Kṛpācārya advises Duryodhana to increase treasury and army for getting victory against Pāṇḍavas.[156] Manu also prescribed the same injunctions.[157] Even there is no importance to *durga* if there is no army; without the latter, the former cannot be protected. In Śānti-Parva it has also been stated that *daṇḍa* should not be more hard or should not be more simple, but it always should be according to crime.

mṛduhi rājā satataṁ laṅghyo bhavati sarvaśaḥ ।
tīkṣṇāccodvijate lokastasmādubhyamāśraya ॥ — ŚP LXVI.21

[156] Virāṭa XXVIII.11-12, cf. Virāṭa, section XXIX, p. 53.

[157] *Manu* VII.159, cf. Bühler, op. cit., p. 241.

And it is also said that *daṇḍa* is the one who governs on the whole world, and protects the subjects and all the animals. When protectors and arrangers of the are asleep, the rod of chastisement is awake. Because of this the wise have designated the rod of chastisement as righteous itself.[158] Its importance is also discussed in many Nītiśāstric texts. In ancient Indian tradition we find a great discussion on the topic. Many types of *daṇḍa* have been accepted at that time. But the purpose of all types of *daṇḍa* was same: to establish peace by doing justice in society. The predecessors of Kauṭilya and he himself have discussed the comparative and relative importance of different elements of the state in detail.[159] But the epic does not discuss this problem in this way. Kauṭilya and Manu, however, have arranged the seven elements in this order, viz. *swāmī, amātya, janapada, durga, kośa, daṇḍa* and *mitra*, and they are of the opinion that when calamities befall on and deterioration sets in, each of the seven elements, those that befall each preceding one, is more serious for the state than those of each succeeding one.[160] Among these, according to Kauṭilya, the king is the brain in the body politic and occupies most important place among the constituents.

Śānti-Parva furnishes a different view and does not regard any element as superior or inferior to each other. So, it does not arrange them in the traditional order. It has changed the sequence at one place, placing the *mitra* at the head, and the king at the end of the order.[161] The theorists of *Mahābhārata* further hold that there is an organic unity among different elements and they must work unanimously and harmoniously towards one ideal.

The modern state has only four elements — a piece of land, population, territory and the sovereignty — in comparison to and contrast with the seven components of state in Śānti-Parva. On the analysis of the organic theory, it clearly shows that it bears a close

---

[158] ŚP XV.2.8 (Bhandarkar Oriental Research Institute).

[159] *KA* VIII.1.

[160] Ibid.; *Manu* IX.225.

[161] ŚP CCCVIII.153-55.

resemblance to similar theories expounded by the Western thinkers.[162] In a narrow sense, the organism is based on the analogy between the individual and the state, because the king (*swāmī*) is called *śarīra* and *hr̥daya* (heart) of the people. He has to protect his own self. In the epic tradition people are related to *swāmī* in two ways — better half and children. Vidura's view is instructive in this context. Though the context is different, it establishes an analogy between individual and state. Hence the state in Śānti-Parva was defined as the integration of *swāmī*, *amātya*, *janapada*, *durga*, *kośa*, *daṇḍa* and *mitra* based on historical factors. These are important political institutions without which there is no possibility of a state.

Summarizing the above it is to say that absence of any one of these elements weakens the state. All must exist in combination. The state as speculated by the political thinkers of the epic is not the people (*janapada*), nor the government (*swāmī*, *amātya*, *bala*, *kośa* and *durga*), but all of them exist in combination.

---

162 From Plato to modern times, organism occupies an important place in the Western political thought. To quote, Coker, Hobbes holds, " public minister to be the nerves and the tenders of the state, the judges to be organs of will and money to be blood." — Sarkar, 1922, op. cit., p. 35.

According to R.H. Geldern (1942), "The king is Mount Meru, his right eye representing the sun, his left eye, the moon, his arms and legs the four cardinal points, the six lower heavens his pointed crown, the spine Indra's palace on the summit of Meru and his slippers the earth." — "Conception of State and Kingship in South East Asia".

4

Interstate Relations and Forms of Government

Interstate Relations

Mahābhārata is considered as the precious gem of ancient Indian political thought. It describes the functions and duties of the king, known as *rājadharma.* It has religious background and philosophical basis and has a concept of *dharma.* It also deals with the principles of social conduct, administration of civil and criminal laws and also the foreign policy, i.e. interstate relations. The study of the concept of the state in *Mahābhārata* remains incomplete sans the discussion of interstate relations. In this context, the thinkers of the epic have discussed the relevance of *mitra* under the *saptāṅga* theory of the state. Relation between *swāmī* and his *mitra* finds an important place in interstate relations.

In the context of *Mahābhārata*, interstate relations denote the meaning of foreign policy of the state towards another state or a sovereign ruler. Though the epic does not supply a systematic account, the ideas of the *maṇḍala* theory, institution of spies and ambassadors, consideration of sixfold policies and adaptation of four *upāya*s justify the theoretical and practical necessity of interstate relations in it.

Concept of Maṇḍala in Śānti-Parva

In ancient India, the concept of interstate relationship was conceived in the form of a *maṇḍala* (circle of states) which aimed at the maintenance of balance of power and consisted of twelve types of states (headed by twelve kings). According to the conception of *maṇḍala*, a king was to regard one's own kingdom as the centre of twelve concentric circles, the outer circle re-representing the kingdom situated away from one's own. A king's relation with all the kingdoms on the circumference of one circle was expected to be similar. He was to manipulate his relation with other states in such a way that foes and friends were so pitted around him that at no time he was rendered helpless. In the event of any invasion of his country, there were always rulers, to oppose the invasion for their own interest. So, the ancient Indian thinkers described and unanimously prescribed the formation of a *maṇḍala.*

Śānti-Parva throws light on the concept of *maṇḍala*. It consists of four sub-circles, each of which is constituted by three states as follows:

1. The state at the centre of the *maṇḍala*, the friend and the friend's friend (three states);
2. the enemy, his friend and his friend's friend (three states);
3. neutral state, its friend and its friend's friend (three states); and
4. intermediary state, its friend and its friend's friend (three states).

According to *Mahābhārata*, a *maṇḍala* consists of seventy-two elements as follows: each of the twelve constituent states of a *maṇḍala* has seven constituents (*saptāṅgas*) of a state, viz. *swāmī* (sovereign), *amātya* (ministers), *janapada* (land and population), *durga* or *pura* (fortress or a fortified capital), *kośa* (treasury), *daṇḍa* or *bala* (army) and *mitra* (allies). *Swāmī* being merged in the state and *mitra* "in the allies among the twelve kings",[1] only five constituents of a state exist. These five constituents, when multiplied by the twelve constituents of a *maṇḍala*, make a total of sixty. The twelve members of a *maṇḍala* if added to sixty, the total elements of a *maṇḍala* comes to seventy-two. *Arthaśāstra*,[2] *Manu-Smṛti*[3] and *Kāmandaka Nītisāra*[4] furnish a similar explanation of the seventy-

---

[1] Law, 1920, *Inter-State Relations in Ancient India*, p. 15.

[2] *Arthaśāstra*, p. 291.

[3] *Manu* VII.157.

[4] *NK* VII.157.

two constituents of a *maṇḍala*.

Classification of States and Six Expedients of Foreign Policy

Mahābhārata refers to the existence of a number of states in ancient India. Although international law and relationship as understood in the modern times cannot be said to have prevailed in ancient India, they are to be found, however, in a rudimentary form in *Mahābhārata*. *Mahābhārata* classifies the different states under four heads, viz.:

1. friendly states or allies (*mitra* or *suhṛd*),
2. inimical states (*ari* or *śatru*),
3. neutral states (*udāsīna*), and
4. intermediary states (*madhyastha* or *madhyagata*).[5]

This classification is based on the following kinds of relationship with the foreign states:

1. friendship (*mitratā*),
2. hostility (*vigraha* or *yuddha*),
3. neutrality (*udāsīnatā*), and
4. mediation (*madhyasthatā*).

These relationships are closely related with *ṣāḍguṇya* which was an essential art of diplomacy. When the measures of *sāma, dāna, daṇḍa* and *bheda* failed, the king had to follow a very judicious policy towards his enemy. Śānti-Parva asserts that the king's prosperity depends upon the proper implementation of the sixfold policy:

> *ṣāḍguṇyaṁ ca trivargaṁ ca trivargaparamaṁ tathā* ।
> *yo vetti puruṣavyāghra sa bhuṅgkte pṛthivīmimāṃ* ॥
> — ŚP LXIX.66

Then the question arises: what are the constituents of *ṣaḍguṇas*? Like Kauṭilya, *Mahābhārata* also describes and prescribes *ṣaḍguṇas*. The six expedients (*ṣāḍguṇya*) of foreign policy are: *sandhi*

---

[5] ŚP LXXXVI.21.

(alliance), *vigraha* (war), *yātra* or *yāna* (march of the army), *āsana* (neutrality), *saṁśraya* (seeking protection by a weak prince from a powerful king) and *dvaidhībhāva* (dual policy):

ṣāḍguṇyamiti yat proktaṁ tannibodha yudhiṣṭhira ।
sandhānāsanamityeva yātrāsandhānameva ca ॥

vigṛhyāsanamityeva yātrāṁ samparigṛhya ca ॥
dvaidhībhāvastathānyesāṁ saṁśryo 'tha parasya ca ॥
— ŚP LXIX.67-68[6]

Let us discuss these expedients in brief:

SANDHI (TREATY AND ALLIANCE)

This is intended to avert any confrontation and establish a friendly relation between two or more states. *Mahābhārata* says that a king should make peace with another when the latter is more powerful than him. When the king is in distress, he should also

---

[6] Commenting on the above verses Nīlakaṇṭha says:

sandhānāsanaṁ sandhiṁ kṛtvā 'vasthitiḥ yātrāsandhānaṁ yānam ॥
vigṛhya vairaṁ kṛtvā 'vasthānaṁ vigrahaḥ । *yātrāṁ samparigṛhya āsanaṁ śatrorbhyapradarśanārthaṁ yānaṁ pradarśya svasthāne 'vasthānam* । *dvaidhībhāvaḥ ubhayatra saṁdhikaraṇaṁ parasya anasyāśrayo durgādemahārājasya vā* ॥

— Nilakaṇṭha's commentary on ŚP LXIX.67-68

Cf. *ṣāḍguṇyasya prakṛtimaṇḍalaṁ yoniḥ* ॥1॥ *sandhivigrahāsanayāna-dvaidhibhāvāḥ ṣāḍguṇyamityācāryaḥ* ॥2॥ *dvaiguṇyamiti vātavyādhiḥ sandhivigrahābhyāṁ hi ṣāḍguṇyaṁ sampadyata iti* ॥3॥ *ṣāḍ-guṇyamevaitadavasthābhedāditi kauṭilyaḥ* ॥4॥

tatra paṇabandhaḥ sandhiḥ, apakāro vigrahaḥ, upekṣaṇamāsanam । *abhyuccayo yānaṁ, parārpaṇaṁ saṁśrayaḥ, sandhivigrahopādānaṁ dvaidhībhāva iti ṣaḍgunāḥ* ॥5॥ — *Arthaśāstra* (ed. G.P. Sastry), Bk. VII, chap. I.1-5

saṅdhiṁ ca vigrahaṁ caiva yānamāsanameva ca ।
dvaidhibhāvaṁ ca saṁśrayaṁ ca ṣaḍguṇāṁścintantyetsadā ॥
— *Manusmṛti* VII.160

do the same thing to protect his life.[7] When a person is afflicted by a stronger one, he should make peace even with enemy.[8] In Śalya-Parva, Kṛpācārya advised Duryodhana to make a treaty with the Pāṇḍavas because at that time the power of Pāṇḍavas was increasing and that of Kauravas was decreasing.[9] *Mahābhārata* says that self-preservation is the highest law and abnormal times have ethics of their own, *āpaddharma,* and end justifies means. He who, keeping in view his interests, makes a treaty with an enemy and opposes a friend, attains good results. But, after having entered into a treaty with a superior, he should exercise perpetual care and vigilance to protect his interest without being cheated by the superior.

According to Śānti-Parva, treaty is of three kinds, viz. *hīna* (bad), *madhyama* (middling) and *uttama* (good), made respectively because of fear (*bhaya*), respect (*satkāra*) and through gifts of wealth (*vitta*).

sandhiśca trividhābhikyo hīno madhyastathottamaḥ ।
bhayasatkāravittākhyaṁ kātsnryena parivarṇitam ॥
— ŚP LIX.37[10]

VIGRAHA (WAR)

In the ancient Indian works, the word *vigraha* has two meanings, viz. (1) the threat of war, and (2) the actual waging of war. Nīlakaṇṭha explains it as the posture, adopted after the declaration of hostility. Śānti-Parva says that war should be declared and waged against an inferior ruler when he is facing difficulties, but never against one, who

---

7 *balīnā saṁnikṛṣṭasya śatrorapi parigrahaḥ* ।
kārya ityāhurācāryā viṣame jīvitārthinā ॥ — ŚP CXXXVIII.45-46

8 *yadā pare ca balinaḥ svapakṣaścaiva durbalaḥ* ।
sārdhaṁ vidvaṁstadā kṣīṇaḥ paraiḥ sandhiṁ samāśrayet ॥
— Āśramavāsika VI.8

9 *hīyamānena vai sandhiḥ paryeṣṭavyaḥ samena vā* ।
vigraho vardhamānena matireṣā vṛhaspateḥ ॥ — Śalya IV.43

10 Commenting on the above *śloka*, Nīlakaṇṭha writes:
bhayena sandhiḥ hīnaḥ । *satkāreṇa madhyamaḥ* । *vittagrahaṇena uttamaḥ*।
tat trayaṁ sandhikāraṇaṁ varṇitam ॥

has self-respect and whose soldiers are happy and satisfied.[11] One, who does not follow this advice, attains neither kingdom nor happiness.[12]

YĀTRĀ OR YĀNA

Nīlakaṇṭha opines that *yātrā* consists in actual pursuit of direction of marching for a war.[13] Śukra defines it as the invasion with a view of attaining victory and defeating the enemy.[14] According to Manu, *yāna* is twofold: (i) marching alone against the foe, and (ii) attacking the foreign state with the aid of the allied powers.[15] Śānti-Parva, however, does not throw any further light on it.

ĀSANA

According to *Mahābhārata, āsana* stands for the posture of war, but no actual war, after showing one's readiness for marching against the enemy.[16] It is half-way to war by exhibiting some military movements. Thus, a king makes attempts to defeat his enemy. Vishwanatha says that *āsana* suggests that a king should assume the attitude of neutrality, known as *udāsīnatā* in the ancient Indian literature.[17] As stated by him, there are four main classes of neutrals in *Mahābhārata*. They are influenced by different motives and the neutrality is due to different reasons:

1. Neutrals whose position is bound to be affected by the results of the war.
2. Neutrals whose fortunes are practically unaffected by the course of the struggle.

---

11 ŚP CXL.44.

12 Ibid. CXXXIX.III.

13 *yātrāsandhānaṁ yānaṁ* । — Nīlakaṇṭha's commentary on Ibid. LXIX.67

14 *śatrunāśārtha gamanaṁ yānaṁ svābhīṣṭa siddhaye* । — *NŚ* IV.1068

15 *Manu* VII.165.

16 *vigrahyāsanamityeva yātrāṁ samparigṛhya ca* । — ŚP LXIX.68
Commenting on this verse Nīlakaṇṭha says:
śatroḥbhayapradarśanārthaṁ yānaṁ pradarśya svasthāne'vasthānaṁ ।

17 Viswanatha, 1925, *International Law in Ancient India*, p. 192.

3. Neutrals who may be affected by the war and who can, if they choose, change the course of the war by maintaining economic forces.
4. Neutrals, who are powerless to enter into the war, though their fortunes may be affected by the war.

On the basis of what *śloka*s in *Mahābhārata* this classification has been made is difficult to say. Viswanatha has not given the reference. He has made this classification on the basis of the Mitra's *War Philosophy: Ancient and Modern*.

SAṀŚRAYA

Saṁśraya can be defined as the act of seeking protection of a powerful monarch by a weak monarch to gain more strength. According to Nīlakaṇṭha, it means to seek protection of another king or to take shelter in forts.[18] N.N. Law says that when a sovereign is attacked by two powerful sovereigns, he should have recourse to *saṁśraya* with the nearer one or to have *kapāla saṁśraya* with both, telling each of them that unless he is shown mercy he will be ruined by the other.[19] Manu describes two types of *saṁśraya* thus:

> Twofold is said to be the nature of alliance with a more powerful ally, according as it is made by (a sovereign) highly pressed by his enemy at the time, or only as a pretext to intimidate his future and intending invaders.[20]

The states which followed this policy can be compared with modern protectorates. Although these states enjoy freedom, they have to acknowledge the authority of the state which has given them protection.[21]

---

18 *parasya anyasyāśrayo durgādermahārajasya vā* | — Commentary on *Mbh*, ŚP LIX.68

19 Law, 1934, "The Six Guṇas in the Kauṭilya", p. 451.

20 *Manu* VII.169.

21 Chatterjee, 1958, *International Law and Inter-State Relations in Ancient India*, p. 34.

DVAIDHĪBHĀVA OR THE DUAL COURSE OF ACTION

The term *dvaidhībhāva* has two meanings: (i) double standards or duplicity, apparently maintaining friendly relations with the enemy, and (ii) dividing the enemy's superior army and harassing him by attacking the smaller units of the army in isolation.[22] Manu uses the word in the latter sense. It means waging a war against one and making peace with another. Nīlakaṇṭha looks at it as *ubhayatra sandhikaraṇaṁ*, which can be interpreted as making treaties with both the parties, fighting with each other.[23]

The Fourfold Foreign Policy

The foreign policy is of four types: *sāma* (conciliation or negotiation), *dāna* (cession, persuasion, or making gifts), *bheda* (creating differences) and *daṇḍa* (war). According to Śukra,

> When two kings become friends and make mutual promises not to harm each other and help one another in distress, that policy is known as *sāma*.[24]
>
> When a king tells another king that everything belongs to him and gives away some villages to him or pays taxes (as tribute) to him or pleases him by any other means, the policy is known as *dāna*".[25]
>
> When a king weakens the army or allies of another king, takes shelter of a powerful king and lifts or raises a weak king, the policy is known as that of *bheda*.[26]
>
> When a king uses troubles to his enemy through the robbers, sweeps away his treasury and granary, watches his weak points to declare

---

22 Apte, *Students Sanskrit–English Dictionary*, SV Dvaidhībhāva, p. 267.

23 *dvaidhībhāva ubhayatra sandhikaraṇaṁ* ।
— Nīlakaṇṭha's commentary on Mbh, ŚP LXIX.67-68.

24 *susahāyyaṁ hi karttavyaṁ śatrav sāma prakīrtitam* । — Śukra IV.28

25 *mama sarva tavaivāsti dānaṁ mitre sajīvitam* ॥ — Śukra IV.25

26 *śatrusādhakahīnatvakaraṇātprabatāśrayāt* ।
taddhīnatojjīvanācca śatrubhedanamucyate ॥ — Śukra IV.30; see also *Arthaśāstra* VII.16, pp. 338.9, *Kāmandaka* XVII.8

war, threatens him with strong force and fights bravely against him, such a policy is known as *daṇḍa*.[27]

Śānti-Parva[28] also gives much importance to diplomacy for maintaining the balance of power in the interest of promotion of good and harmonious interstate relations. It also prefers "battle of wits" to the "battle of arms". War be regarded only as the last resort when all the *upāya*s have failed. The epic commends the victory achieved with the help of other *upāya*s and condemns the win achieved in a battle. Bhīṣma says that such a view was held by Bṛhaspati also. Manu, Yājñavalkya, Kāmandaka and Śukra to a large extent agree with *Mahābhārata* in allowing war as the last resort and, thus, display a high moral spirit and sense of responsibility. War was not only preached but was also practised as the last resort in *Mahābhārata*.

A king should be careful in using the policies of *sāma, dāna, daṇḍa* and *bheda*, because their proper application leads to the long-lasting happiness. As regards the application of these fourfold policies, the commentator Nīlakaṇṭha has clarified that one should follow the policies of *sāma* and *bheda* towards equals. The policy *dāna* should be adopted against a powerful and a superior king. The policy of *daṇḍa* should be used against a weaker and an inferior king. The latter should be killed in a war or made to pay taxes as tribute. In another context also, *Mahābhārata* says that when the enemy's army is strong, the policy of *sāma* should be used. If it does not serve the purpose, the policy of *dāna* should be followed. In Śānti-Parva, king has been advised to create dissension (*bheda*) in the army of his enemy.[29] Combining the policy of *dāna* with that of *bheda* would be worthy of praise; *bheda*, being the greatest enemy of an army, *dāna* be resorted to create *bheda* in the army of his enemy. *Mahābhārata* cites several examples where these policies were applied in practice.

---

27 Śukra IV.31-32; see also *Kāmandaka* XVII.8

28 ŚP XCIV (southern recension, G.P. edn).

29 ŚP CIII.17.

DIPLOMATIC AGENTS

In *Mahābhārata* the part played by the diplomatic agents in the field of diplomacy and foreign affairs has been realized. These agents are classified under two heads: (a) ambassadors (*dūta*), and (b) spies (*cara*).

Ambassadors

In Śānti-Parva[30] the term *dūta* has been used to denote what we call as ambassador today. Unlike the modern practice of stationing representatives, as permanent agents in foreign states, in *Mahābhārata* they were officers appointed for and sent on a special mission. The ambassador was an important agency for carrying out the interstate relationship. The relationship among the states depended more upon the working of diplomats.

The epic asserts that the king should appoint efficient persons as ambassadors. Those persons should be appointed as ambassadors who follow the *śīla* and are very efficient. They should be of high birth, capable and active.[31] The *dūta* was to be wise as he was to work among persons of different natures:

ajñāyamāne ca mate parasya, kiṁ syāt
samārabhyatamaṁ mataṁ vaḥ ।
tasmādito gacchatu dharmaśīlaḥ śuciḥ kulīnaḥ puruṣo
pramattaḥ ॥

dūtaḥ samarthaḥ praśamāya teṣāṁ, rājyārdhadānāya
yudhiṣṭhirasya ।
niśamya vākyaṁ tu janārdanasya dharmārthayuktaṁ
madhuraṁ samaṁ ca ॥
— Udyoga I.24-25

In *Mahābhārata*, there is a narrative in which sending of the priest of Drupada as ambassador to the Kaurava court shows that much care

30 Ibid. LXXXV.26.

31 *prājñā medhāvino dāntā dakṣāḥ sūrā bahuśrutāḥ* ।
kulīnaḥ satvasampannā yuktāḥ sarveṣu karmaṣu ॥ — ŚP 86.17

was given to the selection of an ambassador.[32] Similarly, the virtues and requisites of Sañjaya, *dūta* of Dhṛtarāṣṭra to the Pāṇḍavas, also reveal the same thing. According to Vidura, there should be eight virtues in a person who is appointed as an ambassador. He should be egoless, fearless, active, kind, pure hearted, honest, healthy and sweet in speech.

Functions of an Ambassador: The main functions of an ambassador were to deliver the message correctly as entrusted to him, to make or break alliances or treaties, to declare war or make peace, to study the geographical position, and strong points, military strength and financial condition of a foreign state and to gather the greatest possible information. He was thus primarily concerned with the vital issues of the foreign policy of a state. Ambassadors had to perform very delicate and dangerous duties. *Mahābhārata* is conspicuously silent about the different kinds of ambassadors, while Kauṭilya classified them under three heads: (1) *niḥsṛṣṭārtha*, (2) *parimitārtha* or *mitārtha*, and (3) *śāsana-vāhaka.* This threefold classification of ambassadors by Kauṭilya holds good even in modern times. It is based on the country to which the ambassador is assigned; his duties and the types of functions he has to discharge. Further, *Mahābhārata* emphasizes the sacredness and inviolability of ambassadors. It lays down salutary regulations in connection with the behaviour to be meted out to them. An envoy should be respected and treated courteously even if he conveys an unpleasant message because he is merely the mouthpiece of the king who deputes him. He should never be killed. The murderer of an ambassador goes to hell along with his ministers.[33] And he suffers the sin equivalent to that gained by abortion.[34] The golden rule of immunity and privileges of the ambassadors was generally observed except once in the case of Kṛṣṇa and that too not because Kṛṣṇa was

---

32 Udyoga IV.26, V.18.

33 ŚP LXXXV.26-27.

34 *na tu hanyānnṛpo jātu dūtaṁ kasyāñcidāpadi* ।
dūtasya hantā nirayamāviśet sacivaiḥ saḥ ॥

yathoktavādinaṁ dūtaṁ kṣatradharmarato nṛpaḥ ।
yo hanyāt pitarastasya bhrūṇahatyāmavāpnuyuḥ ॥ — ŚP LXXXV.26-27

an envoy, but because he was the backbone of the Pāṇḍavas whom the Kauravas regarded as their greatest enemies.

Spies

In India, the system of espionage is as old as *Ṛgveda*. *Mahābhārata* says that it was a permanent and prominent feature of a state and was one of the eight limbs of the army. As spies were the "eyes of the kings"[35] they were appointed by the ruler to collect information about the internal affairs and administration of his kingdom as well as foreign states. Ancient Indian states were inclined to regard the spies as highly indispensable and their work was considered to be of utmost importance. Hence, they were scattered throughout his own kingdom and also foreign states. Manu, Kauṭilya, Śukra and Somadeva Sūri also hold the same view. Secrecy was the characteristic feature which distinguished them from the envoys. If found out and detected, the spies could be ill-treated and even killed by the foreign state. Spies should therefore be so clever as not to be detected or identified by others. *Mahābhārata* gives a list of persons who could be entrusted with this risky job, such as brāhmaṇas, hypocrites, *siddha*s, persons capable of doing impersonation, posing as blind and deaf depending on the situation and be as cunning as possible.[36] The most important condition was to examine them thoroughly before their appointment and to appoint them so secretly that they could not recognize one another to avoid any conspiracy among the spies themselves. Bhīṣma himself employed such persons as spies. Regarding their types, the epic refers *vahiścaraḥ*[37] or those who went to other states to gather information. This shows that there were some other spies perhaps known as the *antaścaraḥ* who worked inside the state and tried to find out the enemy's agent or the people's attitude towards the king. The spies were

---

35 *yadā paśyati cāreṇa sarvabhūtāni bhūmipaḥ* ।
kṣemaṁ ca kṛtvā vrajati tadā bhavati bhāskaraḥ ॥ — ŚP LXVIII.43

36 *praṇidhīṁśca tataḥ kuryājjaḍāndhabadhirākṛtīn* ।
puṁsaḥ parīkṣitān prājñān kṣutpipāsāśramakṣamān ॥ — ŚP LXIX.8

37 Virāṭa XXIV.5-6.

classified into different classes such as the *pāṣaṇḍāḥ*, *tāpasāḥ*, fool, deaf and blind.[38] There are several instances to prove the existence of an efficient and active intelligence department or the system of espionage in *Mahābhārata.*

To conclude it can be said that *Mahābhārata* is silent on the means to be employed by the spies to create trouble in other states. Kauṭilya, on the other hand, permits any and every means for the spies, moral or immoral. He says that they should create dissensions in the foreign states, indulge their army chiefs in love-affairs with young ladies and afterwards cause animosity among them. They should give poison to them by saying that "this is a medicine which would make his beloved devoted to him". They should disguise themselves as palmists and arouse the ambition of becoming a king in the chief and high officers of the enemy state and make them unloyal to their king. In war time, they should, distribute wine or liquor, mixed with poison to the important military officers of the enemy king.

It will be appropriate to say that interstate relations in the epic were well developed. The importance of the *maṇḍala* theory, sixfold policies, and four *upāya*s were the theoretical foundations of interstate relations. The way, the thinkers of the epic applied the above, reflects its practical justification, though there was low practice and high principles.

Types and Forms of Government

Classification of states is a controversial topic. Some writers on political science classify the forms of state. But this is wrong; there can be no form for the state. All states are alike in their nature and all are comprised of the same essential elements — population, territory, organization and unity. As Garner says:

> In their legal character, in their essence and in their primary ends and purpose, all states are essentially alike and cannot, therefore, be differentiated one from the another in the same way as natural organism, physical objects or chemical elements may be

[38] ŚP CXXXVIII.40.

distinguished.[39]

Differences in population and territory do not make any difference in their status of statehood. A distinction is, no doubt, sometimes made between city state, a nation state and an empire. But this distinction has no practical value in political science, for classification.

All states are sovereign and all sovereign states are equal. Accordingly it is illogical to classify the equals. But the states do differ in organization. The organization of the state is its government and it is through the instrument of the government that the state formulates, expresses and realizes its purpose. The purpose of every state is the same — the well-being of its people — and the form of the government is the expression of the way in which the purpose of the state is realized. This involves the problem of determining in whose hands is vested the legal authority of the state, to what extent it is made use of, what are the instrumentalities or organs employed in its use? And what rules and procedures are followed by such organs in performing their functions?

These differences are wide and matter a good deal in differentiating the organization of one state from another. The form of the government is, therefore, the actual basis of division. Gettell said:

> Since states manifest their existence only through their government and since no other basis can they be properly distinguished the classification of the government, in essence, is classification of states.[40]

CLASSIFICATION OF GOVERNMENT IN MAHĀBHĀRATA

What were the different types of states existing during the period of *Mahābhārata*? Ancient constitutional writers hardly discuss this issue. This is probably due to them having flourished in an age when monarchy had become the prevailing form of government. *Mahābhārata* generally refers to three types of states, viz. monarchy, anarchy and *gaṇarājya* (*fig.* 4.1).

---

39 Garner, 1928, *Political Science and Government*, p. 240.

40 Gettell, 1949, *Political Science*, pp. 191-92.

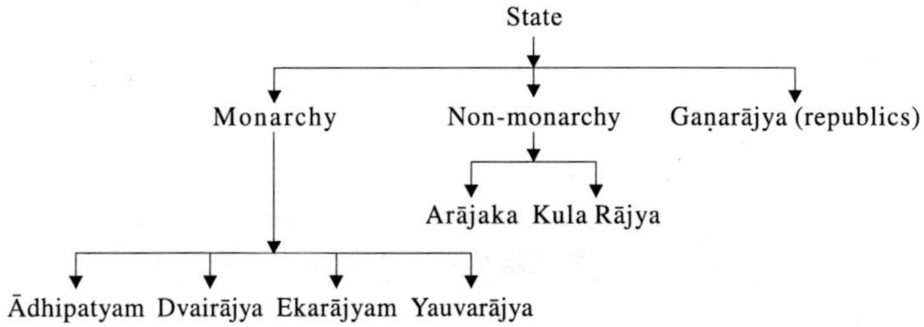

fig. 4.1: Types of states in *Mahābhārata*

Monarchical States

Monarchy was the most prevalent type of government, and this was based on the gradation of the rules and the number of the rulers.[41] Epic discusses many things regarding it. In this type, sovereign power lies in the hands of an individual who is regarded as the supreme head of the state. Several subtypes of the monarchical states are referred to, and the biggest type was the *sārvabhauma*. Yayāti, Dambodbhava and Bharata have been mentioned as *sārvabhauma* kings. But as a matter of fact, they were the kings of a small part of Indian territory. The concept *sārvabhauma* was never materialized.

Ādhipatyam type of the state was that sovereignty of which was accepted by other states which also offers tributes to the sovereign king. Such states retained their internal autonomy. The Kuru's had established such a state.[42]

Next one is the *dvairājya*, in this type there is rivalry between two kings who jointly rule[43] it, hence *Ācārāṅgasūtra* instructs the *bhikṣu*s not to visit such a state where there is trouble and insecurity.[44]

---

41 *rājā bhojo virāṭa samrāṭ kṣatriyo bhūpatirnr̥paḥ* ।
ya ebhiḥ stūyate śabdaiḥ kastaṁ nārcitumarhati ॥ — ŚP LXVIII.54

For details, vide Bhandarkar, 1929, *Some Aspects of Ancient Hindu Polity*, pp. 90-125.

42 Ādi CIII.1.

43 *KA* VIII.2.

44 *Ācārāṅgasūtra* 2.3.1.10, quoted by Jayaswal, 1967, *Hindu Polity*, p. 84.

Mahābhārata furnishes an example of this type such as the state Avantī which was ruled jointly by two brothers named Vinda and Anuvinda.[45] *Mahābhārata* does not refer to it directly, but it is said at three places. There are also other evidences to prove the existence of *dvairājya*. We are informed by the Greek historians that at the time of Alexander's invasion, the kingdom of Pāṭala was being ruled jointly by two kings, who belonged to the different dynasties.[46]

Kauṭilya was also familiar of this type of the state, it can be known from his *Arthaśāstra* wherein he says that the rule of a country by two kings perishes owing to mutual hatred, partiality and rivalry.[47] Kālidāsa in his *Mālavikāgnimitram* hints at the existence of such states by mentioning Yajñasena and Mādhavasena, two brothers as the joint rulers.[48] Nepal had two kings as late as the seventh century of the Christian era. Nepal was under such a constitution. Simultaneous inscriptions of the kings of Licchavi family and the Ṭhākurī family are found at the same capital and the dates prove that the two dynasties were ruling simultaneously.[49]

N.N. Law, however, does not believe in their prevalence in ancient India. To him this "cannot be a normal form of the government".[50] As regards the *dvairājya* in *Mahābhārata*, he says:

> The two chapters of *Mahābhārata* mention the compound *vindānuvindam* of Avantī. There is nothing else in the chapters to show that they were the joint kings and did not rule over separate territories within the country of Avantī.[51]

---

45 Udyoga CLXIII.6, Droṇa LII.17.

46 McCrindle, 1896, *The Invasion of India by Alexander the Great*, p. 296.

47 *dvairājyavairājyayordvairājyamanyonyapakṣadveṣānurāgābhyāṁ parasparsaṁgharṣeṇa vā vinaśyati* || —*KA* (ed. Shamasastry, 1919) VIII, p. 325

48 *Mālavikāgnimitram,* pp. 100-01.

49 Jayaswal, 1967, *Hindu Polity*, pp. 96-97.

50 Law, 1925 "Technical Hindu Constitutions", *IHQ*, 1(1): 394.

51 Udyoga CLXIII.6, Droṇa LII.17.

This view of Law is not in keeping with the verse of Udyoga-Parva, wherein it has been clearly described as the two kings of Avantī (*avantyau mahipālau*). The conjecture of separate territories within Avantī appears fanciful, since *Mahābhārata* makes no reference to the division of the country.

N.N. Law differs from Jayaswal and others as regards the significance of the Napalese inscriptions. He agrees with Fleet, who opines that:

> We have two separate families, ruling contemporaneously mostly on equal terms, but each preserving certain distinctive characteristics of its own . . . it seems pretty clear that the Licchavi *kula* or Sūryavaṁśī family and the Ṭhākurī family, of the territory to the west of it.[52]

In the present state of our knowledge it is difficult to say the final words on these epigraphic evidences. But keeping in view the literary evidences furnished by *Mahābhārata* and also by many other resources, N.N. Law's view seems to be untenable.

Next one is *ekarājyaṁ*; this is opposite to *dvairājyaṁ*, in which the state is not divided among many brothers and they are not made as joint rulers. It is ruled by a single person, Vidura has advised Dhṛtarāṣtra not to divide the state between his sons and Pāṇḍavas but to coronate Yudhiṣṭhira for the establishment of *ekarājyaṁ*.

Yauvarājya is another type of the monarchical state in which the prince had the upper hands in administrative affairs. The king, wishing to retire from active life, coronates the crown prince on the throne, handing over all the administrative charges, hence, such a type of state is known as *yauvarājya*. Duṣyanta has been referred to having coronated his crown prince Bharata as *yauvarājya*, and so was done by Śāntanu in the case of his son Bhīṣma.[53] These are the major types of monarchical state.

---

[52] Quoted by Law, 1925, "Technical Hindu Constitutions", *IHQ*. 1(1): 394-95.

[53] Ādi LXIX.44, LXXXIX.19, XCIV.38.

Anarchical States

Śānti-Parva also refers to anarchical states. The existence of the non-monarchical states in ancient India has been brought to light by many scholars, with K.P. Jayaswal as the pioneer in this field. They come to the conclusion that along with monarchy other types of governments also were known to the ancient Indians. The information about non-monarchies varies in inverse ratio from that of the monarchies. Due to scanty or little information, we have to depend only on the causal references to them, scattered throughout *Mahābhārata*. In Śānti-Parva the following types of non-monarchical states have been referred:

Arājaka Rājya: The *arājaka* state is that where there is no ruling authority. It is a kingless state which is a curse to people as they are without a protector, hence they face many difficulties. After the death of King Vicitravīrya, the Kuru country had become an *arājaka* state, which resulted in sufferings for the people. As stated:

> *arājakeṣu rāṣṭreṣu dharmo na vyavatiṣṭhate* ।
> *parasparaṁ ca khādanti sarvathā dhigarājakam* ॥
> — ŚP LXVII.3

By many other scholars this type of *rājya* is denoted as anarchy and to others, a type of non-monarchical government. Most prominent among the holders of the latter view is Jayaswal, who interprets the word as, "non-ruler state".[54] And calls it an "idealistic constitution"[55] the ideal of which was that "law was to be taken as ruler and there should be no man ruler". The basis of the state was considered to be a mutual agreement or social contract between the citizens. Jayaswal takes this opinion on the basis of Śānti-Parva[56] and *Ācārāṅgasūtra*. To Jayaswal, *matsya-nyāya* is a distinct term which is used to denote anarchy; hence, *arājaka* should be interpreted as a form of government. Jayaswal is followed by some other scholars.[57] But the evidences from

[54] Jayaswal, 1967, *Hindu Polity*, p. 97, fn 1.

[55] Ibid., p. 97.

[56] ŚP LIX.13-77, LXVII.4,17-20.

[57] Vajpai, vs 1998, *Hindu Rājyaśāstra*, p.181; Kapoor, 1958, *Dharma*

Mahābhārata goes against Jayaswal. The description of the chaotic and deplorable condition of *arājaka rājya*[58] leaves no doubt that anarchy is the possible and correct interpretation of the word. This conclusion is also corroborated by *Rāmāyaṇa*, *Manu-Smṛti* and *Arthaśāstra*.

That is why Śānti-Parva goes to the extent by saying that there is no evil greater than anarchy and one should not live in such a state.[59] Thus it becomes clear that the *arājaka rājya* means anarchy and has definitely no connection with a particular type of constitution or non-monarchical state.

Kula-Rājya: Another type of non-monarchical state in Śānti-Parva is *kula-rājya*[60] (rule of the families). Kauṭilya also gives hints about the existence of such states.[61] In Śānti-Parva Bhīṣma says that in such a state, greed and jealousy lead to mutual destruction.[62]

Gaṇarājya

The third type of state which Śānti-Parva refers is *gaṇarājya.*[63] Many modern scholars, especially Western, have presented their view that in ancient India there was the prevalence of only the monarchical type of states. But after studying our literature and inscriptions we come to know that there were other types of states which were not ruled by the king. *Avadānaśataka* (Bauddha text) also informs us about two types of states: (i) monarchical (*rājādhīna*), and (ii) *gaṇarājya* (*gaṇādhīna*). This *gaṇarājya* was totally different from the monarchical state in its structure and functions. *Ācārāṅgasūtra* also mentions different types of states. *Aṣṭādhyāyī* of Pāṇini also talks about republican institutions like *pūgas*, *vrātas* and *saṅghas*. Thus we find that history of republics is

---

Nirpekṣa Prācīna Bhārata ki Prajātantrātmaka Paramparāyeṁ, pp. 59-63.

58 ŚP LIX, LXVII.

59 *nārājakeṣu rāṣṭreṣu vyastavyamiti rocaye* | — ŚP LXVII.5

60 *gaṇānāṁ ca kulānāṁ ca rājñāṁ bharatasattama* || — ŚP CVII.10

61 *kulasya vā bhavedrājyaṁ kulasaṁgho hi durjayaḥ* || — *Arthaśāstra* I.17.55

62 ŚP CVII.10-11.

63 ŚP CVII.10.

saved in our literature and inscriptions which started from the Buddha and Pāṇinian period to the Gupta period.

Republics in Śānti-Parva: *Mahābhārata* also provides the link to the great and long history of these *gaṇarājyas* (republics). "Republics" is the modern political English term which is generally used in the place of ancient *gaṇarājya*. The study of *Mahābhārata* reveals the fact that it generally refers to three types of states, viz. monarchy, anarchy and *gaṇarājya*. Monarchy was the most prevalent type of government but a great deal of discussion is also found about *gaṇarājya* in it.

Mahābhārata along with *Khila Harivaṁśa* offers highly valuable information about the republican tenets. We found the whole chapter (107) in which the republic is discussed in a proper way. In a conversation between Bhīṣma and Yudhiṣṭhira both advantages and disadvantages of the republics have been recounted. After listening to all words of wisdom that Bhīṣma spoke about the political concepts such as the duties of the four *varṇa*s, the qualities of the ministers, the idea of of *ṣāḍguṇya*, the disposition of army and so on, King Yudhiṣṭhira requests Bhīṣma to explain to him the conduct of republics. He would like to know how republics thrive and remain united, how they endeavour to conquer their enemies and achieve friendly relations with others:

yathā gaṇāḥ pravardhante na bhidyante ca bhārata ।
arīṁśca vijigīṣante suhṛdaḥ prāpnuvanti ca ॥
— ŚP CVII.7

Yudhiṣṭhira had heard that republics are destroyed because of internal dissension and he feels it is very difficult to keep deliberations in the presence of many people. Hence he appeals to Bhīṣma to tell the matters to him:

bhedamūlo vināśo hi gaṇānāmupalakṣaye ।
mantrasaṁvaraṇaṁ duḥkhaṁ bahūnāmiti me matiḥ ॥
— ŚP CVII.8

Bhīṣma has given a detailed reply to Yudhiṣṭhira regarding the nature of the republics and the dangers that confront them. He says that the greed and intolerance among the citizens are the two enemies in the republican state and republican society just as those on the part of a prince in princely state:

gaṇānāṁ ca kulānāṁ ca rājñāṁ bharatasattama ।
vairasandīpanāvetau lobhāmarṣau narādhipa ॥
— ŚP CVII.9

Both these factors — greed and anger (intolerance) — destroy wealth and strength. They torment each other by means of spies, secret deliberations, use of force, giving of gifts, sowing dissensions, destruction of power and wealth, causing fear, etc. Even if the *gaṇa*s are united, they can be easily divided by giving of gifts (or bribes). Once they are split up, their harmony comes to an end and they submit to the enemy through fear:

tatrādānena bhidyante gaṇāḥ saṁghātavr̥ttayaḥ ।
bhinnā vimanasaḥ sarve gacchantyarivaśaṁ bhayāt ॥
— ŚP CVII.13

The *gaṇa*s are destroyed through differences and they can be very easily vanquished by the enemies. Hence they should constantly endeavour to preserve their unity. Once their strength and valour are united, the *gaṇa*s can acquire wealth very easily. Even outsiders try to cultivate friendship with them, fearing for their unity:

bhede gaṇā vineśurhi bhinnāstu sujayāḥ paraiḥ ।
tasmāt saṁghātayogena prayateran gaṇāḥ sadā ॥
— ŚP CVII.14, see also X.15

Bhīṣma also states how *gaṇa*s can achieve prosperity. They will prosper, if their members respect learned people, serve each other and refrain from cheating each other. The foremost of *gaṇa*s will prosper, if they establish sound dealings as laid down in the scriptures and behave according to them. They will also flourish, if they restrain their sons and brothers from going astray, are themselves well-disciplined and respect those who possess discipline:

putrān bhrātr̥n nigr̥haṇanto vinayantaś ca tān sadā ।
vinītāṁśca pragr̥haṇanto vivardhante gaṇottamāḥ ॥
— ŚP CVII.18

The *gaṇa*s will achieve all-round progress, provided they are keen on employing spies and having secret deliberations and on enriching the treasury:

cāramantravidhāneṣu kośasaṁnicayeṣu ca ।
nityayuktā mahābāho vardhante sarvato gaṇāḥ ॥
— ŚP CVII.19

Bhīṣma tells that the members of *gaṇa*s who are wealthy, brave, adept in the use of arms and proficient in scripture save their *gaṇa*s whenever the latter are deluded in any calamities.

dravyavantaśca śūrāśca śastrajñāḥ śāstrapāragāḥ ।
kr̥cchrāsvāpatsu sammūḍhān gaṇāḥ santārayanti te ॥
— ŚP CVII.21

Anger, dissension, fear, punishment, arrest and killing are the factors that reduce the strength of *gaṇa*s and makes them accessible to the enemies:

krodho bhedo bhayaṁ daṇḍaḥ karṣaṇaṁ nigraho vadhaḥ ।
nayatyarivaśaṁ sadyo gaṇān bharatasattama ॥

tasmānmānayitavyāste gaṇamukhyāḥ vadhaḥ ।
lokayātrā samāyattā bhūyasī teṣu pārthiva ॥
— ŚP CVII.22-23

Hence Bhīṣma states that the leaders of the *gaṇa*s should be mainly respected, since all the worldly dealings almost depend on them.[64] So it becomes clear that to protect *gaṇa*s unity is the most important factor and also tells that if the *gaṇa*s are subdued by the enemies, it is solely due to their dissensions and faults; hence unity has been said to be the greatest support of the *gaṇa*s; without unity, they will be nowhere:

bhedāccaiva pradānācca bhidyante ripubhirgaṇāḥ ।
tasmāt saṁghātamevāhurgaṇānāṁ śaraṇaṁ mahat ॥
— ŚP CVII.32

Thus we find the description of the *gaṇa*s with their structure and functions in Śānti-Parva. Sabhā, Ādi and Āraṇya *parva*s also mention

---

[64] ŚP CVII.16-23.

the republics of Yaudheyas, Kṣūdrakas, Mālavas,[65] Vasatis, Śibis, Trigartta, Ambasṭhas, Uḍumbaras, Kāśmīra, Madras, Kekayas, Prasthālas, Utsava-saṁketas[66] and Pāñcālas. These names in different *parvas* of *Mahābhārata* show the clear existence of *gaṇarājyas*.

The word *gaṇa* has been a riddle for the modern scholars, who have interpreted it variously. To Fleet, it means "tribes";[67] F.W. Thomas interprets the word as the "governing body" or "the senate"[68] and to Hopkins as "corporations of every sort"[69] and according to N.N. Ghosh as "local corporations". Literally the word *gaṇa*, taken as a verb, means to count, to number or to enumerate.

While taken in the sense of noun, it denotes an assembly or group. Keeping in view the context of its use and its characteristics, its best explanation will be "the rule of many", which is evidently a form of non-monarchy. And it stands for a type of non-monarchical state and is proved also by the internal evidence of *Mahābhārata* as it informs that Arjuna defeated several *gaṇas*.

Some scholars differ as regards the form of non-monarchy which it denotes. Some hold that *gaṇas* were aristocracies or oligarchies probably on the grounds that in *gaṇas* power was vested not in the whole body of the citizens but in a small aristocratic class. It would be, however, better to translate the word as republics. *Mahābhārata* hints at a trend of ultra-republicanism by saying that there were kings in every house, who were interested in their own welfare.[70] It further says that all the members of *gaṇa* had equal rights and share in the affairs of state. To brief it can be said that *Mahābhārata* also refers to

---

65 Āraṇya CCLIV.19-20.

66 Sabhā XXIV.1.

67 *JRAS*, 1915, pp.138-40.

68 Ibid., p. 524.

69 "Social and Military Position of the Ruling Class in Ancient India", p. 82.

70 *gṛhe gṛhe hi rājānaḥ svasya priyaṁkarāḥ* I — *Mbh* Sabhā XV.2; see also, ŚP CCCXX.149.

republics and in such a republican state power was exercised not by individual, but by many as organized on the *kula* basis.

ARISTOTLE'S CLASSIFICATION OF GOVERNMENT

Aristotle is the first one who has presented the suitable and valuable classification of the state. He also borrowed from Plato and Socrates. He said:

> Every form of the government or administration must contain a supreme power over the whole state, and this supreme power must necessarily be in the hands of one person, or a few or many, and when either of these apply their power for the common good, such sates are well governed: but when the interest of the one, the few or the many who enjoy this power is alone consulted then ill; . . . we usually call a state which is governed by one person for the common good, a kingdom or monarchy; one that is governed by more than one, but by the few only an aristocracy; when the citizens at large govern for the public good, it is called a state (or policy) . . . now the corruption attending to each of these government are these, a kingdom may degenerate into tyranny, an aristocracy into an oligarchy; and a state (or policy) into democracy. Now a tyranny is a monarchy where good of the one man only is the object of government, an oligarchy considers only the rich, and democracy only for the poor, but neither of them have the common good of view.[71]

Aristotle classification is based on two principles:

1. The number of persons who exercise supreme power, and
2. the ends they serve.

Applying the first principle, Aristotle said if the supreme power is vested in one single person it is monarchy. If it is the rule of a few, it is aristocracy, and if the supreme power is vested in many, it is polity.

Aristotle, then proceeds to distinguish between what he calls the "normal" and the "preverted" form of the government basing his conclusion on the ends which the ruler serves. A normal state is

---

[71] *The Politics of Aristotle* (every man's Library), pp. 78-79.

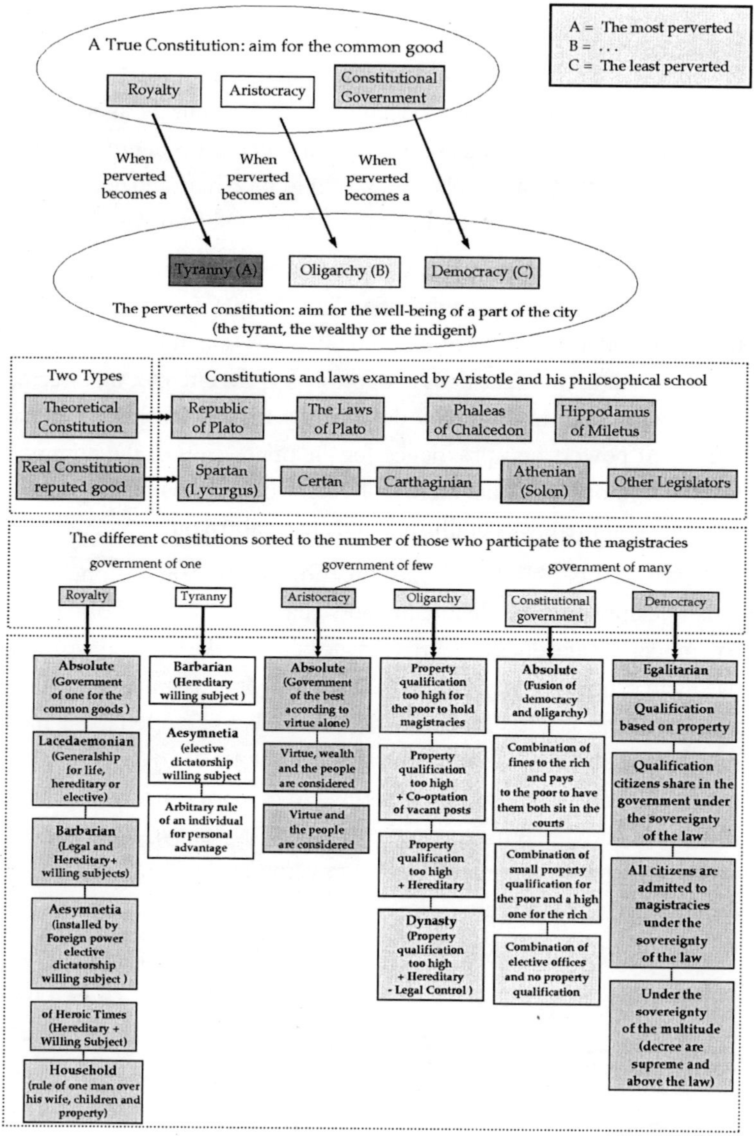

Source: Aristotle, *Politics*, Bk II, chaps. 7-14 of Bk III and chaps. 4-10 of Bk IV.

fig. 4.2: Forms of government according to Aristotle

that which always aims at the good of the community as a whole. It becomes perverted when the rulers/ruler become(s) selfish and they or he exercise(s) power vested in them or him for their or his own benefits rather than the benefits of the community as a whole. Monarchy, aristocracy and polity are the normal forms of government. In their preverted form they become tyranny, oligarchy and democracy. Aristotle's classification can be easily understood from *fig*. 4.2.

Tyranny, Aristotle said, was the degenerated form of monarchy, oligarchy as the degenerated shape of aristocracy and democracy as the degenerated form of polity. Tyranny allows the monarch to have arbitrary control over the lives and fortunes of the citizens, all directed to his own good. In oligarchy the wealthy ruled for selfish end and used their powers and previleges for the oppression of the common people. Democracy meant mere mob rule, wherein the interest of none was safe and there was confusion and chaos all-round.

Two points about this classification deserve attention. First, Aristotle draws a clear distinction between aristocracy and oligarchy. But modern usage does not differentiate between the two and we often use them synonymously. Second, democracy for Aristotle has not the same meaning as it has for us. He regarded it as a perverted form, mob rule, whereas we regard democracy as the best form of government. The perverted form of democracy according to modern use is mobocracy. Moreover, the modern sociologists have clearly shown that there is no government of the many, that all governments are government of the few, or, in fact oligarchies.[72]

Nowhere in the world do the people or even substantial number of them rule. In all states exercise of the government is left to a few hands, while the determination of policy is actually in the hands of yet similar minority, the political leaders.

Conclusion

By the analysis of both the views of Aristotle and *Mahābhārata*, we

[72] MacIver, 1946, *The Web of Government*, p. 149.

reach a conclusion that they differ in their ideas, because Aristotle's division is based on two principles: normal (monarchy, aristocracy and polity) and perverted (tyranny, oligarchy and democracy) which is quite different from *Mahābhārata*'s classification of state, because *Mahābhārata* refers to only normal types of classification. *Mahābhārata* does not refer to perverted types of classification. It had no idea about a democratic state. It only prefers monarchical type of states, but in some places it throws light on the republics in the form of *gaṇarājya,* according to scholars. Though *Mahābhārata* does not agree with modern classification, it has its own importance in the field of political science. So we find that Aristotle's classification is more relevant according to modern theorists. In spite of this, Aristotle's classification has been subjected to severe criticism. It is argued that his classification is not based on any scientific principle as it emaphasizes quantitative rather than qualitative aspects. John Burgess has rightly said that Aristotle's classification is organic or spiritual rather than numerical.[73]

Moreover, Aristotle's classification does not embrace modern form of government like a constitutional monarchy, unitary and federal governments, parliamentary and presidential types. The city state of Aristotle, as Seely says, does not fit in with modern country states. Perhaps Aristotle could not conceive, at the time when he flourished, the various forms into which a government might develop.

---

[73] Kapur, 1950, *Principles of Political Science*, pp. 228-30.

5

Judiciary and Ethical Concepts

Judiciary

THE administration of justice, the chief task of the judiciary, comprised the third organ of the government machinery. The welfare of citizens greatly depends upon the speedy and impartial justice. Lord James Bryce has aptly remarked that there is no better test of excellence of a government than the efficiency of its judicial system. The judiciary is the guardian of the rights of the man and it protects these rights from all possibilities of individual and public encroachments.

The feeling in an average citizen that he can rely on the certain and prompt administration of justice maximizes his liberty. If there is no adequate provision for the administration of justice, the liberty of the people is jeopardized, for there is no definite means which should ascertain and decide rights, punish crimes and protect the innocent from injury and usurpation, "if the law be dishonestly administered", says Bryce, "the salt has lost its flavour, if it be weakly and fitfully enforced, the guarantees of order fail, for it is more by the certainty than by sovereignty of punishment that offenders are repressed. If the lamp of justice goes out in darkness, how great is that darkness".[1]

In ancient polity the executive and the judicial functions were combined. The early monarch was the fountain of justice. But afterwards came to be realized that justice could not be secured if the judicial system was centred on one person. The concentration of power to interpret and administer justice in the same hands has always

---

[1] Bryce, 1921, *Modern Democracies*, vol. II, p. 284.

historically been associated with tyranny.[2] Every citizen needs the amplest protection against the danger of capricious interpretation of law. The modern state is, accordingly, inconceivable without a separate judicial organ functioning independently and impartially.

Justice has an important place in the life of the citizens. By understanding its importance in life it has been taken as a subject of debate in both *Mahābhārata* and Western tradition, to find out their idea of justice and of the judicial system. It is considered that political thoughts generally came into existence by the major efforts of the Western scholars, mainly with the works of Aristotle and Plato. They have presented their views on justice, in a systematic way. So first we will discuss here the concept of justice according to Plato and Aristotle. Both are considered as the pioneer scholars of the Western thought. After that we will discuss about these concepts in *Mahābhārata*.

JUSTICE ACCORDING TO PLATO AND ARISTOTLE

Plato in his book *Republic* has given the idea of justice. This book is considered as "A Justice" by many scholars. This became proved by the words of Harmon, "The republic represents Plato's search for justice, its definition and full content".[3] Justice in Plato means very nearly what we mean by morality.[4] As said by the scholars that *Republic* is the consideration of justice and this justice is the central of Plato's thinking.[5] Justice is not used by Plato in the sense of law. What is Plato's intent of justice? To clarify this, many scholars have presented their views.

Foster: "Plato's sense of justice is that a lot of our morality."[6]

Barker: "Justice is the component of the goodness and it is not

---

2 Laski, 1925, *A Grammar of Politics*, p. 129.

3 Harmon, 1964, *Political Thought: From Plato to the Present*, p. 31.

4 Foster, 1941, *Masters of Political Thought*, vol. 1, p. 36.

5 Ibid.

6 Barker, 1960, *Greek Political Theory*, p. 153.

different from goodness."[7]

C.H. Mcllwain: "Each individual should do his own appointed work in contenment. This in Plato's eye is justice."[8]

Plato defines justice in these words "man should complete those works, which were desired by him, according to the social aims, that is justice. To him, justice is the part of human virtue."[9] Human virtue is the combination of the wisdom, courage, temperance and justice. The presence of all these is the necessity of the state. Wisdom for king, courage for soldiers and temperance for manufacturers.

According to him, justice is non-interference, and is the principle of specialization, it is the principle of the social unit, and he defines two types of justice: social and individual, but at last he argues that they are not different from each other. Justice for Plato is, at once, a part of human virtue and bond which joins men together in status. It is an identical quality which makes man good and social. This identification is the first and fundamental principle of Plato's political philosophy.

In conclusion, Plato's definition of justice is that which is having and doing of what is one's own. A just man is a man just in the right place, doing his best and giving precise equivalent of what he has received. This applies both in the individual and universal levels.[10]

To Aristotle, the good in the sphere of *Politics* is justice, and justice consists in what tends to promote the common interest.[11] To him, "justice will necessarily imply an equality". To clarify the form of justice, he has presented two divisions in his book *Nicomachean Ethics*.Aristotle's idea of justice is clearly depicted in *fig*. 5.1 and Table 5.1.

---

7 Barker, 1960, *Greek Political Theory*, p. 153.

8 Mcllwain, 1932, *The Growth of Political Thought in West*, p. 30.

9 Foster, 1941, *Masters of Political Thought*, vol. 1, p. 37.

10 Plato, 1984, *Republic*, tr. Robin Waterfield, Oxford: Oxford University Press.

11 Aristotle, *Politics*, p. 129.

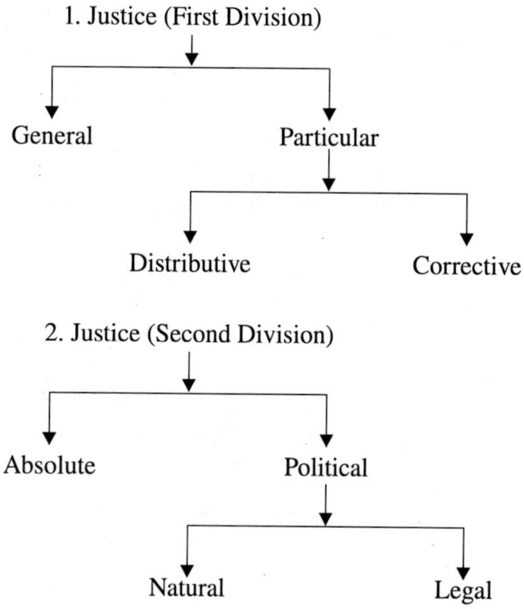

fig. 5.1: Types of justice

Aristotle agreed with Plato, though not for Plato's reason, that justice was the greatest and most inclusive of all human excellences.[12] It was the most inclusive because it was the most social. Implicitly Aristotle, like Plato, defines justice as the principle which ensures that society will run harmoniously and which guarantees attainment of the human excellence. He knows that there is a subtle connection between justice and homonoia, the spirit of unity, but thinks that Plato sacrificed too much on the altar of social unity. If unity is carried so far that it becomes sheer uniformity, the *polis* will cease to be a *polis* and will revert to the condition of a family. A *polis* to be a *polis* must allow and indeed encourage human variety, although the variety will be incompatible with justice unless it is a veriety tempered by homonoia.[13] It must be recognized that men differ in temperament and in talent, in taste and in opinion; but it must also be recognized that unless they

[12] *Nichomachean Ethics* 1130a.

[13] *Politics* 1261a; cf. *Nichomachean Ethics* II79B.

Table 5.1: Types of Justice

Name	*Information*
Justice General	It is related with moral properties and goodness. It also includes virtues and righteousness.
Justice Particular	It is related with the specific form of goodness. Which decides what is appropriate and what is inappropriate.
Justice Distributive	A just distribution of offices among a number of different persons will involve a consideration of the personal merits of each person.
Justice Corrective	Corrective justice restores a position of fairness or equality which has been disturbed.
Absolute or Complete Justice	Complete justice is the whole of moral virtue from the point of view of one's relation to others.
Justice Political	Political justice finds place among those who live simple life for the freedom and because of this they are connected to each other.
Justice Natural	It is same in every situation and cannot be changed.
Justice Legal	It is dependent on both written and produced laws. It is quite different in each and every state.

agree basically upon certain ideals and values society will not long hold together. In so far as they differ it must be by agreement to do so.

On political or social justice what Aristotle says is highly complex and not without its ambiguities. He thinks that it is nearly always "just" to be law abiding, since a large part of "justice" must consist in the respect for the law assuming that the law does satisfactorily embody the city's values and ideals. But he admits that to be law abiding in an unjust *polis* would by no means "just", but the odds would be against it, since most men will not be "just" unless they have been conditioned to be so by good education, good institution and good laws.[14]

Aristotle is aware that law and justice are not interchangeable terms but he is not wholly clear about the difference. He recognizes the principle of equity or fairness which may not comply strictly with

[14] *Politics* 1287-a-b; cf. *Nichomachean Ethics* 1179b.

law. He realizes that justice must penetrate beyond action to intention and therefore must not punish accidental or unintended injury. He knows, too, that complete justice must be able to deal with special or "hard" cases which the law, being wholly generalized, cannot always do. He is not prepared, however, to give full recognition to the idea of the universal or "natural" moral law or to a "natural justice" which is above the laws of any particular state. He has already accepted the idea of justice as the giving to every man what is "due"; and he has himself called justice the greatest virtue because it alone is social and seeks the good of other men.[15] Aristotle's concept of justice is more scientific and well organized than Plato. Thus "justice" in the modern term was first used by Western scholars. Now it is necessary to discuss judiciary in Indian context especially in Śānti-Parva to find out the form of judicial system. What was the concept of justice, its definition, judicial authorities and what was the major role of the judicial system in the society?

JUDICIARY IN MAHĀBHĀRATA

The growth of the state activities and establishment of extensive empires necessitated the growth and the development of adjudication authorities in ancient India. Hence, the courts and judges came into existence.[16] Śānti-Parva also throws light on the judicial system. The accounts of *Mahābhārata* alludes to the need of a judiciary in order to reform the criminals and not to suppress criminals, though, it aims at the eradication of crimes.

The thinkers of *Mahābhārata* laid down certain norms to be followed by the officers-in-charge of judicial system with a view to impart true justice to the people. They are firm that there should not be any delay in imparting justice to the people. They advocate that there should not be any delay in imparting justice to the parties, otherwise

---

15 *Nichomachean Ethics,* 1130a-1133b.

16 The word, adjudication authorities stands for judiciary or for those persons who act as judges in court, cf. *The Concise Oxford Dictionary*, p. 12.

many evils may come into existence.[17] The epic regards *dharma* as the root of the state, hence the enforcement of law is necessary for its existence. The *daṇḍa* is coercive but an effective power given to the king for regulating the life of the subjects.

In *Mahābhārata* it has been asserted that king got prosperity if he inflicts punishments after examining the cases and finding out the real offenders.[18] In Śānti-Parva it is clearly stated that while imparting justice, the king must be impartial to all who have violated the existing *dharma* (rules) of the state or country. He should not show any type of favour while sitting at the seat of justice, either to his parents, brothers, wives and *purohita* or even the judges or lawyers in case they are not interpreting *dharma* in accordance with the spirit of *dharma* and Śāstras. Kauṭilya and Manu had also similar thinking and ideologies in this connection.[19] For hearing charges and defences in judicial suits, the king should always appoint wise persons endowed with the knowledge of worldly affairs, for the state really depends on a proper administration:

> *śrotuṁ caiva nyased rājā prājñān sarvārthadarśinaḥ* ।
> *vyavahāreṣu satataṁ tatra rājyaṁ pratiṣṭhitam* ॥
> — ŚP LXIX.28

We found many references in Śānti-Parva and Āraṇyaka-Parva of the epic alluding the cases of guilty sons who could not escape punishment under the existing rule (*dharma*). King Janaka of Mithilā and Sagara of Ayodhyā did not show any soft corner for their sons in inflicting punishment upon their progeny because they have broken the law of the soil.[20]

In *Mahābhārata* it is asserted that the administration of justice is

[17] *nityamudyatadaṇḍaḥ syādācaredapramādataḥ* ।
loke cāyavyayau dr̥ṣṭvā br̥hadvr̥kṣamivāsravat ॥ — ŚP CXX.9

[18] Udyoga XXXIII.86.

[19] *yathā putrāstathā pautrā draṣṭavyāste na saṁśayaḥ* ।
bhaktiścaiṣāṁ na kartavyā vyavahāre pradarṣite ॥ — ŚP LXIX.27

[20] ŚP LXXV.8-9.

not merely a matter of public order, but is a sacred and religious duty of the king. This is clear in Śānti-Parva, which declares that by the proper administration of justice, the king will not merely obtain the goodwill of his subjects but would attain the heaven, and that in miscarriage of justice he will not merely lose the goodwill of his subjects, but also incur punishment for sin.

Śānti-Parva while referring to the administration of justice mentions many a time *dharma* and *daṇḍa*. In order to know the judicial system, it is imperative to know about the concept of *dharma*. *Dharma* is a very comprehensive term. Though it is translated into English as religion, it does not convey the complete and true meaning. *Dharma* stands for a way, a path of life and a mode of conduct. The root of *dharma* is *dhṛ* which connotes the meaning to hold or support, but it has been used in different senses in the epic, namely, duty and righteousness. It also stands for the law of the land as well as morality.

Dharma also means the law or the ordinance and stands for the moral concepts which are to be protected and preserved by the king. The king is the protector of *dharma* and it is his duty to enforce its observance by the people. If any of the *varṇa*s violates righteousness, the king is to inflicit punishment accordingly. Hence, it stands for ethical values, duties, good works, religious virtues, the universal truth, divine justice, conventions, social and individual duties and international law.

Judiciary was committed to *dharma* in epic tradition, though it should not be understood in the present sense of committed judiciary. The king was the regulator of *dharma*, he was not above *dharma*, hence it becomes clear that *dharma* was the root of justice in *Mahābhārata*. Even the judges were subject to the provisions of *dharma* and for delaying justice, they were liable to be punished under the judicial procedure established by *dharma*. Establishment of *dharma* has been proclaimed to be an important function of the state in the epic which goes to the extent of saying that it is for the course of *dharma* that sovereignty exists. For the realization of this function, a state is given the right to exercise *daṇḍa* (coercion). *Daṇḍa* was regarded to be capable of restraining the natural turbulence and depravity of men, which led them to violate different rules and regulations. It was *daṇḍa* which made them follow *dharma*. In the absence of this chaos prevailed and people did not perform their duties properly.[21]

Śānti-Parva has instructed the king to act according to the injunction of *dharma*. But where from does it originate?[22] It does not refer to sources of *dharma* in a systematic manner, but there are several scattered references which throw considerable light on the topic. There are four types of sources of *dharma*, such as *śruti*, *smṛti*, *sadācāra* and *pariṣad*. The thinkers of the epic allude to the Vedas as the sources of law (*dharma*). In Śānti-Parva, the law approved by the Vedas has been identified with Vedokta and Vedāntādhigata *dharma*.[23] In Śānti-Parva *dharma* is described as threefold — the Vedas, the Smṛti and Siṣṭās.[24] There is another ground which suggested Vedas as the source of *dharma*. In Udyoga-Parva, a reference has come to *niyoga vidhi* and Kṛṣṇa refers to the authority of Vedas as the source of *dharma*.[25] The expressions *vaidikaṁ, ityehā-vaidikī sthiti, ityeṣā śruyuyate śrutiḥ* reveal the fact.[26] These things become more clear and apparent when the epic regards *daṇḍa* as *vedātmā* and *vedapratyaya* (enjoined by Vedas) and on this basis asserts that *dharma* originated from Vedas (*vedaprasūta-dharma*).[27] Moreover on many controversial matters, the thinkers present the views of the *veda itiveda-vido-viduḥ*.[28]

In all early societies, the custom was regarded as the supreme

---

21 ŚP XV.41-45.

22 Ibid. CCLI.1-4.

23 *vedoktāścaiva ye dharmā vedāntādhigatāśca ye* |
tān sarvān samprapaśyāmi vardānāt tavācyuta || — ŚP LIV.19

24 *tataḥ sadharmaṁ vedoktaṁ tathā śāstroktameva ca* |
śiṣṭācīrṇaṁ ca dharmaṁ ca vividhaṁ cintya cetasā || — ŚP CCCLIV.6

25 Udyoga CXXXVIII.7; cf. ŚP CCCLIV.6 and Anuśāsana CXLI.65.

26 ŚP LXXVII.10, LXXX.9,16.

27 ŚP CXXI.49-52.

28 ŚP LXXVII.13.

force and was obeyed. There was no concept of government, and no authority like government was evolved at that time so there was no existence of formal laws. A.S. Altekar and N.C. Sen Gupta are of the same view when they discuss the comparative ideas on *dharma*. Even in the unwritten constitution of England, customs and conventions have been obeyed by the people and they are considered as part of British Constitution. In the same way, the rules of *dharma* and Śāstras were based on customs, traditions and conventions, which were accepted by the society and of late became the spirit of ancient India.

Mahābhārata also regards the Dharmaśāstras as a source of law and instructs the king to act according to their injunctions. The original code of Brahmā and the composite work by the Citraśikhaṇḍinaḥ are referred to as containing matters related to *dharma*. Though these are the sources of *dharma*, the epic regards that it must be bound on injunctions of the Vedas.[29] In Āraṇyaka-Parva it is mentioned that the good conduct (*sadācāra*) is another source of *dharma* if it is not appeared to the rules made by Śruti and Smṛti. *Dharma* originates from good customs.

According to P.V. Kane the import of words *ācāra* or *sadācāra* has been shifting from age to age commentators. In early traditions like Purāṇic and Arthaśāstric, the good conduct has been identified by the terms *śīla* and *caritra*.[30] At the same time the custom was the supreme force and was obeyed, and there wasn't given any significance to government-like authority. So no formal law had come into existence. Sociability and imitation gave rise to the similarity of conduct, and the latter to custom. Though, we know that *sadācāra* is considered as a source of *dharma*, then the question arises is that whether all the conducts done by good persons to be followed or to be considered as the source of law.[31] According to the thinkers of the epic only the good conducts are to be followed and bad conducts of good persons should

29 ŚP CCLII.9-10.

30 Kane, 1965, *History of Dharmaśāstra*, vol. III, p. 875.

31 ŚP CCLII.6.

not be considered as the source of *dharma*. For instance, Paraśurāma had killed his mother on his father's order, but such actions of the great ones should not be followed. Though *sadācāra* is said to be a source of *dharma*, it is difficult to define it because a custom that may be good under certain circumstances, may be bad under others. From one narrative we got the reference on it — Sage Viśvāmitra who knew well that eating the flesh of dog is not a good conduct, but in a critical situation his conscience allowed him to partake it in order to save his life from starvation. In order to prove his act and viewpoint, he gave the example of Sage Agastya who ate the flesh of Vātāpī.[32]

The central point is that *dharma* is not to be considered as a rigid principle of life, it is flexible as it takes shapes according to the place and time factors. It is to be inferred from the conduct of the good persons.[33] It would not be out of place to mention that even the formal constitution of the present time is flexible to meet the demands and needs of emerging situations. If the conducts were against the teachings of the Vedas, should them be followed? For example, Yudhiṣṭhira's proposal to Drupada to marry off his daughter to five Pāṇḍavas, though it was against the law. This proposal was not acceptable to Drupada, the father of Draupadī because it was repugnant to Vedas and customs, but the former argued that *dharma* is subtle and cannot be scrutinized. This is an interesting example of a custom being followed against Vedic and social opposition (*lokavedaviruddha*).[34]

In the comprehensive code of Brahmā, the nature of custom has been discussed.[35] In order to know the essence of the custom it is relevant to deal with *kula, jāti, śreṇī* and *deśa-dharma*, as these were described

---

32 *yathā vai brāhmaṇaḥ sīdannyājyamapi yājayet* ।
abhojyānnāni cāśnīyāt tathedaṁ nātra saṁśayaḥ ॥ — ŚP CXXX.21

lokaṣaṁgrahasaṁyuktaṁ vidhatrā vihitaṁ purā ।
sukṣadharmārthaniyataṁ satāṁ caritamuttamaṁ ॥ — Ibid. CCLII.6

33 Ibid. CXL.18-19.

34 Ādi CLXXXVII.26-28.

35 ŚP CCLXI.17.

in the comprehensive code of Brahmā. References to these sources of law are mentioned in the epic as well as in the code of Manu.[36]

The epic refers to King Kekaya in whose reign the subjects practised their respective *kula-dharma*. At that time *kula-dharma* was an important matter in religious rituals. According to that *kula-dharma* it was the *dharma* (practice) among the Kurus to coronate the eldest son as the king. The violation of this *kula-dharma* by the sons of Dhṛtarāṣṭra was sharply criticized by Sage Vyāsa.[37] It has been discussed in the context of the law of succession of the king.

In the same way, *jāti-dharma* consisted of customs and practices peculiar of different castes and sub-castes. It describes the *dharma* of different *varṇa*s. According to *jāti-dharma*, there was no interference of anyone in another's business, but to remain to one's respective platform. Similarly, the *śreṇī-dharma* was formulated and followed by the guilds of merchants and other professional and industrial organizations.[38] They were attached to their own guilds and trade conventions. In setting their disputes, the judiciary had to take *jāti-dharma*, *śreṇī-dharma* and *kula-dharma* into account. And other one was *deśa-dharma* which was the custom of a particular place. According to *Mahābhārata*, *dharma* is changeable and it takes its forms according to the time and place factors.[39]

The epic allowed judges to interpret the disputes according to one's *deśa-dharma*. It is a custom of a particular place not for the whole country. So it is not necessary to follow the same law throughout the country. It seems that it is the *deśa-dharma*, which is responsible for great variations in Hindu law in different regions. In ancient Indian system it has been asserted that if there is a conflict between the three sources of *dharma* a council of learned bodies or persons is made to decide on the dispute. This council is technically known as *pariṣad*. It

---

36 ŚP LIX.71, LXXVIII.19, Manu I.118.

37 Udyoga CXLVI.29, Bhīṣma IV.6.

38 ŚP XXXVII.14.

39 Ibid. XXXVII.8.

was only an ad hoc body, to remove conflicts (*vipratipatti*) and doubt (*saṁśaya*) if there was any difficulty in making a genuine verdict. It has been called *dharma-saṁśaya.*[40] But here another issue emerges: who is able to decide on the matter and what should be the number of persons in the council? Different views have been given by different authorities. Gautama is of the opinion that one or three persons constituted the council while Baudhāyana thinks that such matters should be decided by a council of five or ten members. Vasiṣṭha is in favour of either three or ten while Manu suggests the number as advanced by the last-mentioned *dharmasūtrakāra*. Śānti-Parva also refers to the same number of the members of *pariṣad* as suggested by Vasiṣṭha and Manu. It is stated:

> *daśa vā vedaśāstrajñāstrayo vā dharmapāṭhakāḥ* ।
> *yad brūyuḥ kārya utpanne sa dharmo dharmaśaṁśaye* ॥
> — ŚP XXXVI.20

It means that the number of persons should be three or ten and these persons should be well versed in the Vedic and scriptural studies. For example, in *Mahābhārata, pariṣad* (council) was convened at that time to decide a doubtful matter and that was the marriage of Pāṇḍavas with Draupadī. The *pariṣad* consisted of five members, namely, Dhṛṣṭadyumna, Yudhiṣṭhira, Drupada, Kuntī as well as Vyāsa. First, according to Drupada, it was against the Vedic and social tradition:

> *adharmo 'yaṁ mama mato viruddho lokavedayoḥ* ।
> *na hyekā vidyate patnī bahunāṁ dvijasattama* ॥
> — Ādi CXCV.7; see also 9 and 10

After hearing the view of Drupada, Dhṛṣṭadyumna, Yudhiṣṭhira and Kuntī,[41] Vyāsa approved the view of Yudhiṣṭhira that a woman may be married with many persons:

> *tato dvaipāyanstasmai narendrāya mahātmane* ।
> *ācakhyau tad yathā dharmo bahūnāmekapatnitā* ॥
> — Ādi CXCV.23

---

40 ŚP XXXVII.15.

41 Ādi CLIX.10-22.

To conclude, it can be said that *pariṣad* is not a source of *dharma* in the same sense in which we take *śruti, smṛti* and *sadācāra*. It is only a machinery to decide doubtful matters and to give verdict on the same.

Orgainzations of Judiciary

For the development of state and establishment of systematic empires, it was required the organization of judicial agencies to work on behalf of the king. Hence the courts and judges came into existence. From the reference in *Mahābhārata* we are convinced that there existed a well-established judicial system to delve into many challenges faced by the then society. At that time courts were considered to be the main institutions to impart justice to the people, but the epic does not furnish more details on them. Kauṭilya has referred to two types of law — (1) *vyavahāra*, and (2) *kaṇṭakośadhana*, which respectively represent the present civil and criminal laws.

Śānti-Parva also refers to these two types of laws. So, it may be inferred that it intends to refer to two types of courts after the names of these two types of law. These were established at the headquarters of different administrative units. Some writers refer to many types of courts which were instituted by the popular bodies not by state and the main function of this type of courts was to decide on the internal disputes arose in the organizations. Yājñavalkya and Bṛhaspati refer to this type of courts as *śreṇī*, *pūga* and *kula*.[42]

The epic does not present a systematic organization of judiciary, though mention has been made of *prāḍa-vivāka*[43] in Śānti-Parva, which may be equated with the Chief Justice of the present time, who was a prominent person in the field of judicial administration, who examined, cross-examined, investigated the whole matters and pronounced a decision. He was the judicial officer appointed by the

---

42 Altekar, 1977, *State and Government in Ancient India*, p. 251.

43 ŚP CCLIX.14-15, cf. both Jayaswal and Saletore are of the view that Chief Justice was not only a head of the justice below the king, but a minister of law (*dharma*) and a legal advisor to the king. Jayaswal, 1967, *Hindu Polity*, p. 316.

king. However, no specific qualification is mentioned for the post of Chief Justice in the epic. Yet merit and virtues were always given priority in the appointment of judges. There were many judges, besides the Chief Justice, to administer justice in different courts established by the state. Epic refers to the qualification of judges, Dhṛtarāṣṭra has advised Yudhiṣṭhira to appoint such person as judges who are reliable and have purity of ideas.[44] They must be well versed in the Vedic and scriptural studies.[45] The same view advanced by the epic is given by Āpastamba that before appointing the judges the persons, family background, wisdom and clarity in thinking and their outlook towards *dharma* should be taken into account. So the person who was qualified but anti-Vedic was not to be appointed as judges. Sometimes the judges were designated as *puruṣa* to advise the king whenever asked on legal matters. If they did not follow they became sinners and were punished by Varuṇa.

At that time king was considered to be the supreme head of the judicial administration. Generally, he was seen in *sabhā-maṇḍapa* surrounded by the priest and ministers for imparting justice. The term *sabhā* is used in the sense of a court, though on this *sabhā* Ludwig and Zimmer differ from each other. According to Ludwig, *sabhā* denotes a "court" while Zimmer thinks it in the sense of a court deciding the local suits.[46] In this connection Kauṭilya also says that the king must spend everyday about a couple of hours in adjudication.[47] The epic considers *daṇḍa* as the *naikanayanaḥ*,[48] having many eyes in which many instruments are employed for the perception of the truth, i.e. many persons are required for imparting true justice to the parties. Hence, the king was assisted by many persons, namely, the priest, the

---

44 Āśrama X.1-2.

45 ŚP XXXVII.15.

46 Ghoshal, 1957, *Studies in Indian History and Culture*, p. 357.

47 *KA* 1.16.

48 ŚP CXXI.15.

*sabhya*s and ministers. Manu is also of the same opinion.[49] The king was the highest court of appeal and his decision was final and should be obeyed.

In the organization of judiciary, *purohita*, also played an important role and was the king's chief advisor. He had to be well versed in Śāstras. The offenders may be released if they go to the *purohita* and promise that they will never commit the offences in future.[50] *Purohita* has to acquaint himself with the current and outdated practices in society. There are also references of *sabhya*s (jurors) in the epic, who acted as assistants to the king and judges. Sabhā-Parva also throws some light on their qualifications and duties in connection with Draupadī's case of assault by Duḥśāsana in the court of Kauravas.[51] It is the duty of the *purohita* to express their views on legal matters without any hesitation, otherwise there would be the violation of *dharma*.[52] Kauṭilya also throws proper light in the same connection. It reveals a more or less full-fledged and well-developed judiciary. The most important feature of the judicial organization was the system of jury. Even the king and Chief Justice could not begin the trial of the case, if they were not assisted by a panel of three, five or seven jurors. The epic refers to the brāhmaṇas as *sabhya*s.[53]

CODE CONDUCT OF JUDGES

In the epic the code of conducts of the judges are described. The thinkers of the epic are of the view that even the judges are not free from passions or greed so it may be possible for them to take bribe from the parties upsetting the whole judicial system. So, it is stated in Āśrama-Parva that the king must set spies on them to find out the

---

49 *Manu* VIII.1.

50 ŚP CCLIX.14-15.

51 Sabhā V.70.

52 Ibid. LXI.52.

53 Ibid. LX.30.

evils in the functioning of the judiciary, if any.[54] They must be severely punished; even death penalty should be given to them if they found involved in the serious offences like accepting bribe, for uttering harsh words, making false justice and committing immoral acts.[55] Character and morality of the judges were important things as far as judiciary was concerned. Kauṭilya also prescribes the same thing.[56]

LEGAL PROCEDURE

In the epic, there is no systematic and satisfactory account of legal procedure. But there are some references by which it has been assumed that justice was administered at different levels. From *Arthaśāstra* and also other inscriptional and literary sources, we come to know that in the past some legal procedures were adopted for ensuring justice. In this connection, the observation of Megasthenes is incorrect that in the absence of formal laws, justice is impossible. Saletore has criticized the narrow view of Megasthenes. On the other hand, Sarkar gives priority to the evidences of archaeological and inscriptional sources to examine the crime and nature of punishment in legal proceedings during the epic period. Dreeakmeir is very critical of Sarkar's approach and considers his views as mere commentaries. U.N. Ghoshal and B.C. Law are very critical of the readings of rock edicts and pillars during Aśoka's time. To them, some terms noticeable in the rock edicts are not authentic in connection with the legal preceedings and they are not helpful to corroborate the literary sources because they carry different meanings.[57]

Śānti, Udyoga and Virāṭa Parvas mention a disputed case which was to be examined and argued. It has also been stated that there was a practice of summoning the defendant as well as of taking oath

---

54 Āśrama X.1.

55 Ibid.

56 *KA* III.20.

57 Law, 1984, "The Chain of Justice".

during legal proceedings. A party had to produce witness(es)[58] at the time of procedure. There was the process of oath and it was essential in legal proceedings. It has been stated that the concerned party had to take oath either before a jar of water or fire to speak the truth. In the violation of this rule and in the case of non-compliance, he was to be punished by Varuṇa. In Ādi-Parva, it is mentioned that a witness should not remain silent knowing the facts as it also results in grave consequences to him in both the worlds.[59]

DAṆḌA (PUNISHMENT) IN THEORY AND PRACTICE

It is the duty of the king to hold *daṇḍa* (the science of chastisement or the rod) and punish the culprits. As *guru* is the Śāstā for pupils, the king is to evil-doers.[60] Though the king is known as *daṇḍadhara,* it is not possible for all kings to use it properly. The king should be the knower of all types of punishments and should be knowlegeable and wise, because with little knowledge he cannot protect his subjects. The people cannot be persuaded to follow the right path, if the king has not controlled himself. In Śānti-Parva it is stated that it is the king's duty to be always ready to inflict punishment upon the culprits:

> *nityamudyatadaṇḍaḥ syādācāredapramādataḥ* ।
> *loke cāyavyayav dr̥ṣṭvā br̥hadvr̥kṣamivāstravat* ॥
> — ŚP CXX.9

It means that the king should always have the rod of punishment uplifted in his hands. He should always levy taxes carefully after examining the incomes and expenses of his subjects, like men going to a full-grown *palmyra* for drawing juice.

If the king does not perform his duty properly he causes destruction to the society. The king must inflict punishment even on his parents,

---

58 N.C. Sen Gupta refers to torture also while P.V. Kane, in the light of ancient judicial system, suggests some remedies for the poor functioning of present judiciary, vol. 3, chap. 14.

59 Ādi LXXVII.16-17.

60 ŚP CXXI.56-57, CCLIX.29.

gurus, *purohita* and *tāpasa*s if they break *dharma*:

> *mātā pitā ca bhrātā ca bhāryā caiva purohitaḥ* ।
> *nādaṇḍyo vidyate rājño yaḥ svadharme na tiṣṭhati* ॥
> — ŚP CXXI.60

So, the epic opines that king should inflict *daṇḍa* properly upon the culprits.[61] This mode of his conduct has been regarded as his highest duty. But how can a king inflict *daṇḍa* properly? It is possible only when he performs all his duties according to the injunctions of the law. So, he must inflict punishment without any hesitation or consideration and such a king never falls but remains always prosperous.

There are various types of *daṇḍa* in the epic. In Śānti-Parva two kinds of *daṇḍa* and in another place four types of *daṇḍa* have been mentioned.[62] It may be assumed that these are the corporal and non-corporal punishments. The four kinds of punishment are as follows:

1. *Dhigdaṇḍa* (admonition)
2. *Vāgadaṇḍa* (severe reproof)
3. *Ādānadaṇḍa* (imposition of fine)
4. *Vadhadaṇḍa* (capital punishment)

But all these kinds also come within the fold of corporal and non-corporal punishments.[63] Śānti-Parva mentions words *śārīrapāda* (torture) and *śāstradaṇḍa*.[64] Except brāhmaṇas, the corporal punishment was to be inflicted upon all the offenders of all *varṇa*s. At some place it refers the works of *daṇḍa* as to cut, to pierce, to break, to tear and to kill.[65]

In the epic the term "mutilation" is referred to many times as a kind of punishment to be inflicted on the culprits. For example,

---

61 Anuśāsana CXXXVIII.51.

62 ŚP LVIII.10.

63 Ibid. CCLIX.11-15.

64 Ibid. LVI.31-33.

65 Ibid. CXXI.18.

in Śānti-Parva the term *virūpakaraṇa* (stands for disfiguring) and *vyaṅgyatā* (stands for the body) are the two terms denoting mutilation. It is prescribed for the offence of robbery. Kauṭilya also recommends the same types of punishment. It is stated that Likhita inflicted this punishment himself by cutting his hand. Those who have committed sins should be put on the *sūlī* and so also those who have done robbery. For example, Sage Aṇimāṇḍavya[66] was punished with this type of the punishment. It was the practice of the republican form of government in the epic. In the administration of Andhaka-Vṛṣṇi this type of punishment was inflicted on those who violated its order on prohibition.[67]

Śānti-Parva refers to the term *citrabadhaṁ* which seems to be a kind of death penalty.[68] Kauṭilya also refers to it.[69] The epic is in favour of light punishment too.[70] Both *Manu-Smṛti* and *Mahābhārata* instruct the king to inflict death penalty on the violators, except a brāhmaṇa.[71]

Hiraṇya-daṇda is another term used for the economic punishment. The king is enjoined to impose this punishment on those who don't follow the existing *dharma*. It increases the *kośa* (treasury) of the king and restrains the persons from committing offences. This punishment is for all the *varṇa*s but it is inflicted upon the vaiśyas as they earn more wealth and are in the habit of hoarding it. It is imposed on those persons who do not follow the *daśa-dharma*[72] (ten rules of morality). The epic does not give the proper account of facts regarding economic punishment. While Kauṭilya refers to at least 350 different rates of fines. According to Śānti-Parva, the *arthadaṇḍa* was to be imposed by courts upon the culprits and the king was the higher authority to reduce or increase the punishment. In the same *parva*, it is mentioned

66 Ādi LVII.77.

67 Mausala II.18-20.

68 ŚP LXXXVI.21.

69 *KA* IV.11.

70 ŚP CLX.69.

71 ŚP CCLIX.

72 ŚP XV.9.

that the city courts had the rights to impose such fines.[73]

We also find the description of capital punishments in the epic. The dialogue between King Dyumatsena and Prince Satyavān throws light on the question of capital punishment. This type of punishment was inflicted upon those offenders who committed crimes of the most serious nature. The persons who state the state's property or inflict injuries on brāhmaṇas should be killed. The judges who accepted bribe from the parties also got capital punishment.[74] The epic recommends death penalty to be inflicted upon those who rebel against the state.[75] The dialogue between the King Dyumatsena and Prince Satyavān is relevant for the modern judiciary. The prince is in favour of giving forgiveness to the culprit, if he goes to the *purohita* and promises to reform himself. He urges the cause of natural justice and advocates the removal of death penalty on the humanitarian ground. But King Dyumatsena supports the method of finishing the culprits by giving them proper punishment. To Dyumatsena, good kings feel ashamed when they see the evil-doers in the state, hence, they must given punishment to teach the lesson to the rest of offenders. But according to Prince Satyavān robbery should be eliminated and robbers must be persuaded to follow righteousness.

Their agreement, disagreement regarding the modes and methods of punishment are not only an interesting account but also relevant to the present time. The former Chief Justice of India P.N. Bhagvati in his judgement cited the extracts from Śānti-Parva in order to sustain his verdict that capital punishment stands against human rights.[76]

From the above it can be said the king was the final authority of appeal from lower courts, though his decision was based on *dharma*. The king was the main appointing authority of the judges. The relation

---

[73] ŚP LXIX.25.

[74] Āśrama X.24.

[75] ŚP LVII.5.

[76] Bachan Singh, Sher Singh and others vs State of Punjab and others, Aug. 1982.

between the judges was always normal and king administered the law and justice with the cooperation of *prāḍa-vivāka*. All his judgements were under the command of *dharma*.

The judicial system in *Mahābhārata* was committed to *dharma*, as said in Śānti-Parva that the king was totally under the command of *dharma*. It refers to the law and morality. After discussion on justice, we reach the conclusion that Western concept of justice was related with individuality; in contrast, this form of justice is for all the society members and it is not limited to individuality as mentioned in *Mahābhārata*.

There is confusion among the Western scholars that judiciary or the concept of justice is the result of the efforts of the Western scholars. But this is not true, because by the literary and historical survey it becomes clear that judiciary is the result of early monarchial system as discussed in *Mahābhārata*. In the West, the aim of justice is to establish a combination of unity, goodness and virtues. It has divided Justice into many branches, where the important one is distributive justice. According to this branch of justice, preference will be given on the basis of the personal merits of each person.

In *Mahābhārata* there is no distributive type of justice; there is only the concept of *dharma*, which enforces men to act according to the rules, which are made by the society. The epic regards *dharma* as the root of the state, hence the enforcement of law is necessary for its existence. So *daṇḍa* (the coercive but an effective power) is given to the king for regulating the life of the subjects. The epic concerns with justice for all the *varṇa*s and *āśrama*s. In the West "to do your act according to your situation" is the key concept of justice. The theory of justice of Plato and Aristotle is that of fascism, and is considered as the biggest shock to liberal assumptions. In this, public peace and order are only in a normal sense, not related with morality and dependent upon totalitarianism, so rejected by the modern liberal society. Though their idea of justice cannot be neglected as it has its own importance. Judiciary in *Mahābhārata* is connected with morality and there the main concern of justice was also related with public peace and order.

Hence it can be said that concept of justice in *Mahābhārata* is slightly similar to the liberal theory. Plato had differentiated the law from justice, but in *Mahābhārata* both law and justice are interconnected.

Ethical Concepts

Ethics as a subject begins with the works of Aristotle. In its original form, this subject is concerned with the question of virtue (Greek *aretē*) of character (*ēthos*), or in other words having excellent and well-chosen habits. The acquisition of an excellent character is in turn aimed at living well and eudemonia, a Greek word often translated as well-being or happiness.[77] In other words, ethics is a systematic study of how individuals should best live.

This study was originally coupled with the closely related study of politics, including law-making. Politics has an effect on how people are brought up, which therefore addresses the same question of how people should live, from the standpoint of the community. The original Aristotelian and Socratic answers to the question of how best to live was to live the life of philosophy and contemplation. Three Aristotelian ethical works survive today which are considered to be either by Aristotle, or from relatively soon after:

- *Nicomachean Ethics*, the most popular
- *Eudemian Ethics*
- *Magna Moralia*

Nicomachean Ethics has received the most scholarly attention, and is the most easily available to the public in many different translations and editions. Aristotle's *Politics* is often regarded as the sequel to the *Ethics*; Aristotle's *Ethics* states that the good of the individual is subordinate to the good of the city state or *polis*. Aristotle believed that ethical knowledge is not only a theoretical knowledge, but rather that a person must have "experience of the actions in life" and have been

---

77 *Nicomachean Ethics*, tr. T.H. Irwin, Introduction, Indianapolis: Hackett Publishing Co., 1999, p. xv.

"brought up in fine habits" to become good.[78] For a person to become virtuous, he can't simply study what virtue is, but must actually do virtuous things. To Aristotle, "we are not studying in order to know what virtue is, but to come good, for otherwise there would be no profit in it".[79]

Aristotelian *Ethics* explicitly aims to begin with approximate but uncontroversial starting points. Aristotle's starting point is that everything humans do is aimed at some good, with some good higher than others. The highest human good that people aim at, he said, is generally referred to as happiness.

Aristotle asserted that popular accounts about what life would be happy divide into three most common types: a life dedicated to vulgar pleasure; a life dedicated to fame and honour; and a life dedicated to contemplation. To judge these, Aristotle uses his method of trying to define the natural function of a human in action. A human's function must include the ability to use reason (*logos*), because this is an essential attribute of being human. A person that does this is the happiest because he is fulfilling his purpose or nature as found in the rational soul.

The question of how to be happy therefore becomes a question of which activities of the human soul represent the highest excellence in using reason. Aristotle proposed that we could accept it when people say that the soul can be divided into three parts: the nutritive soul (plants, animals and humans), the perceptive soul (animals and humans) and the rational soul (humans only).

Aristotle believed that every ethical virtue or positive character trait can be described as a pleasant intermediate activity, between a painful excess and a painful deficiency. But seeing what is most pleasant and most painful in truth is not something everyone can easily do, especially if they are badly brought up and not experienced. Another way Aristotle describes each of the moral virtues is as a correct aiming

---

78 *NE* 1095a3 and b5.

79 *NE* 2.2.

at what is beautiful.

For example, courageous (or literally manly) action is a mean between the painful activities of fear and rash overconfidence. Too much fear or too little confidence leads to cowardice, and too little fear or too much confidence can lead to rash, foolish choices. But courage is also described as an ability to rationally choose the beautiful, which in some cases can be a beautiful death.

Aristotle distinguishes virtue and vice in their true sense as stable dispositions about what they would consciously choose between perceived pleasant and painful options. Dispositions to feel emotions are distinguished by Aristotle as something other than virtues or vices, although they can also be seen as a mean between two extremes, and these are also to some extent a result of upbringing and habituation. Two examples of such dispositions would be modesty or a tendency to feel shame,[80] and righteous indignation (*nemesis*), which is a balanced feeling of sympathetic pain concerning the undeserved pleasures and pains of others.[81] Exactly which habitual dispositions are virtues or vices and which only concern emotions differ between the different works which have survived, but the basic examples are consistent, as is the basis for distinguishing them in principle.

Some people, despite their perceptions and habits concerning what they think is beautiful and pleasant, act on the basis of emotions, even though it is not what they choose. This is not vice according to Aristotle's definition, but *akrasia*, sometimes called weakness of will or lack of self-mastery in English translations. In English, the person who would choose the virtuous option but does not, is sometimes translated as "incontinent" in opposition to having vice or being "vicious".

One apparent emotion is separated from the others and not treated as an emotion by Aristotle, and this is *thumos*, the spiritedness which is the cause of anger. Aristotle, like Plato in his Socratic dialogues, treats *thumos* as an important and positive part of the human soul, which

---

80 *NE* IV.9.

81 *EE* III.vii. Also see *MM*.

helps a well brought-up young person to become virtuous. *Thumos* is not an emotion (*pathos*) according to Aristotle because it tries to follow the leadership of the rational part of the soul which makes conscious decisions. The true emotions, on the other hand, are able to distort rational thinking and dominate it.

Aristotle has described how people become virtuous by performing virtuous actions, which they might not have chosen themselves when young. They must develop proper habits during childhood and this usually requires help from teachers, parents and law makers. A good community is normally required for the development of good people. Virtue in the highest sense, in an adult who has been brought up well, will not just involve good personal habits such as courage and temperance, but also friendship and justice and intellectual virtue.

ETHICS IN ŚĀNTI-PARVA

Ancient Indian thinkers did not clearly mark the sphere of law, religion and ethics. In *Mahābhārata* the same tendency is noticeable, although there are many discussions about the rules of moral conduct and their applicability to the various stations in life. Śānti-Parva lacks a precise and specific terminology for ethics. It does not deal with the modern concept of ethics, but many terms which are used in *Mahābhārata* are analogous to it, only in meaning. In *Mahābhārata*, however, words *dharma*, *nīti*, *ācāra* and *sadācāra* can be interpreted as words denoting ethics. The epic does not believe in the absolute uniformity and universality of the moral standards which change in accordance with time, place, circumstances and other similar factors. In *Mahābhārata*, *dharma* and *ācāra* are deemed to be mutually complementary and interdependent.

The word *dharma*, with a very comprehensive import, can be traced back to the Vedic literature, wherein it denotes law and custom.[82] In *Mahābhārata* it has been used in different senses. When it is said that a particular person should do a particular act because it is his *dharma* (duty). In Śānti-Parva Bhīṣma gives instructions to Yudhiṣṭhira that

---

82 *Ṛgveda*, I.22.18.

he should perform his duty according to *dharma*.[83] The word *dharma* means righteousness and duty. *Rājadharma* (duties of the rulers), *prajā-dharma* (duties of the subjects) and *mitra-dharma* (duties of a friend) are the few examples of the use of this term. But the most used term is *rājadharma*, because whole Śānti-Parva gives instructions about *rājadharma*. *Rājadharma* is the greatest one among all the *dharmas* as stated in Śānti-Parva.[84]

Whatever be the meaning of the word *dharma* it does not matter but it always imposes the certain limitations on human conduct. Ethics does the same thing. As written by Sukthankar, it has, at its basis, a "belief in conservation of moral values" and it "presupposes an eternal moral order".[85]

Varying Interpretation of "Dharma"

There is no particular English word for *dharma* which conveys the exact sense. Due to its pervasiveness and untranslatability it has been interpreted by many modern scholars.

B.G. Tilak by providing an ethical interpretation of *dharma* says that it implies the "path leading to next worldly happiness". According to him "Ethics may be given the name of *dharma*".[86] E.W. Hopkins says that it means "ethical good usage" and it implies in itself a code of conduct to avoid all crimes such as murder, adultery, theft.[87] According to J.S. Makenzie the term *dharma* covers not only conduct but the whole conglomeration of forms of conduct that were established. To Bhagvan Das (1959) it is an ethico-religious conception, which comprises "religion, rites, modesty and specific property functions, etc. . . . but above all the duty, incumbent on man . . . in the situation,

---

83 ŚP LVII.16.

84 *rājñāṁ vai paramo dharmaḥ iti dharmavido viduḥ* । — ŚP LVI.2
Cf. *sarvasya jīvalokasya rājadharmaḥ parāyaṇam* ॥ — Ibid. LVI.3

85 On the meaning of *Mahābhārata*, p. 80.

86 *Śrīmadbhagavadgītā Rhasya* (English tr. B.S. Sukthankar), vol. I, p. 88.

87 Hopkins, 1924, *Ethics of India*, p. 92.

he may be in".[88] According to S. Radhakrishnan *dharma* is stable and it is capable of having satisfaction to the people and helps them in the attainment of happiness and salvation. To him, its end is the welfare of all creations.[89] P.V. Kane (1965) defines it as the "code of conduct".[90]

To H.N. Sinha (1938),

> *Dharma* may bear the interpretation of customs and usage, both scared and secular in society.[91]

According to J.J. Anjaria (1935) it stands for social law, duty, custom and religion.[92] It is the only principle which holds together the whole world, physical as well as moral. Hence the word *dharma* comes to mean, first the cosmic ordrer and second the law governing human society.[93] V. Raghavan remarks:

> The scope of *dharma* is universal and incorporates even the personal habits of hygiene, details of courteous behaviour and moral endowments, duties of kings and administration of justice and the seeking of *summum bonum*, spiritual realization.[94]

To quote G.H. Mees, *dharma* is the "fundamental motive force in the life of man as a social being".[95] According to him, it is signified Vedic *ṛta*, the ethical duty, virtue, good works, religious duty and justice, the ideal, the god or absolute truth, divine justice, convention, a code of customs and traditions, international law, and comprises between the actual and normal law.[96]

---

88 Das, 1959, *The Science of Social Organisation*, p. 7.

89 Radhakrishnan, 1931, *Indian Philosophy*, vol. I, pp. 505-56.

90 Kane, 1941, *History of Dharmaśāstra*, vol. 2, p. 2.

91 Sinha, 1938, *Sovereignty in Ancient Indian Polity*, p. 27.

92 Anjaria, 1935, *Nature and Grounds of Political Obligations in Hindu State*, p. 147.

93 Ibid., p. 150.

94 Raghavan, 1998, *The Indian Heritage*, Introduction, p. 39.

95 Mees, 1935, *Dharma and Society*, preface, p. xii.

96 Ibid., p. viii.

From the above interpretations it becomes clear that many scholars have tried to interpret the term *dharma* from different angles and there is nothing by which these meanings can be rejected. The most acceptable interpretation is produced by the epic itself. On the basis of its derivation, *Mahābhārata* explains *dharma* as:

dhāraṇād dharmamityāhūrdharmo dhārayate prajāḥ ।
yat syād dhāraṇasaṁyuktaṁ sa dharma iti niścayaḥ ॥
— Karṇa LXIX.58

Which bears society (people, by establishing order). For the proper functioning of social life of any human being, there is the need of some certain rules and regulations and are necessary. The fundamental requirements, by prescribing certain duties and principles of morality, for improving the general behaviour of man.

SOURCES OF DHARMA

The most important sources of *dharma*, prescribed by ancient Indian works, are Śruti (the Vedas), Smṛti (Dharmaśāstra works), *sadācāra* (conduct of the noble people) and *ātma-tuṣṭi* (self-satisfaction). According to Vasiṣṭha the Vedas and Smṛtis are more important than the conduct of noble men, which should be relied upon only in their absence.[97] Yājñavalkya, who also has mentioned the first three sources mentioned earlier but he also refers another one source, desire (born of proper intension) as the fourth source.[98]

Śānti-Parva also refers to the Vedas, Smṛtis and *sadācāra*.[99] In Śānti-Parva regarding the relative importance of Śruti and Smṛti it has been stated that duties have been laid down for the respective ages according to the powers of human beings in the respective ages.

---

[97] *Vasiṣṭha Dharmasūtra* I.4-6.

[98] *śrutiḥ smṛtiḥ sadācāraḥ svasya ca priyamātmanaḥ* ।
samyak saṅkalpajaḥ kāmo dharmamūlamidaṁ smṛtam ॥
— *Yāñjyavalkyasmṛti* I.7

[99] *tataḥ sa dharmaṁ vedoktaṁ tathā śāstroktameva ca* ।
śiṣṭācīrṇaṁ ca dharmaṁ ca trividhaṁ cintya cetasā ॥ — ŚP CCCLIII.6

Therefore, all the declarations in the Vedas do not apply equally in all the ages. To say that the Vedas are true is only a popular form of speech which is indulged only for satisfaction. The origination of Smr̥ti is from Śrutis whose scope again is very wide. If the Vedas have the authority for everything, then authority would attach to the Smr̥tis also because the latter was dependent on the former. If the Śrutis and Smr̥tis contradict each other then how can either be authoritative.[100] Another interesting information from Śānti-Parva is that if there is some doubt regarding *dharma*, then three or ten persons who are well versed in Vedic and scriptural studies should be asked to decide on the matter. As stated:

> *daśa vā vedaśāstrajñāstrayo vā dharmapāṭhakāḥ* ।
> *yad bruyuḥ kārya utpanne sa dharmo dharmasaṁśaye* ॥
> — ŚP XXXVI.20

FORMS OF DHARMA

Dharma has been classified in more than one way. Thus, on the basis of its sources it has been classified under the heads of Śrauta, i.e. Vedic *dharma* and Smārta, i.e. *dharma* based on Smr̥tis, and *śiṣṭācaraṇa* (conduct of noble men).[101] In Śānti-Parva *dharma* is again classified in threefolds,[102] namely:

1. *Deśa-Dharma*: *Dharma* for a particular country or place
2. *Jāti-Dharma*: *Dharma* for a particular caste
3. *Kula-Dharma*: *Dharma* or tradition belonging to one's own

---

[100] *anye kr̥tayuge dharmāstretāyāṁ dvāpare pare* ।
anye kaliyuge dharmā yathāśakti kr̥tā iva ॥

āmnāyavacanaṁ satyamityayaṁ lokasaṁgrahaḥ ।
āmnāyebyaḥ punarvedāḥ prasr̥tāḥ sarvatomukhāḥ ॥

te cet sarvapramāṇaṁ vai pramāṇaṁ hytra vidyate ।
pramāṇe 'pyapramāṇena viruddhe śāstratā kutaḥ ॥ — Ibid. CCLX.8-10

[101] *śrutidharma iti hyeke netyāhurapare janāḥ* । — Ibid. CIX.13

[102] *deśajātikulānāṁ ca dharmajño'smi janārdana* । — ŚP LIV.20, see also Bhīṣma III.55

family.

Mitākṣarā also produced a comprehensive classification of *dharma*; according to it *dharma* is sixfold.[103]

These *dharmas* are also discussed in Śānti-Parva. And it can be classified under two heads, viz. *sāmānya* - or *sādhāraṇa* (or *nitya*) *dharma* (universal moral code) and *viśiṣṭa-dharma* (the specific moral code), e.g. *varṇa-dharma* (the code conduct of different *varṇas*) *āśrama-dharma* (code of conduct for the different *varṇas*), *guṇa-dharma* (the code conduct prescribed for one, holding a particular office), *naimittika-dharma* (the acts done with special purpose, e.g. expiatory rites), *yuga-dharma* (code of conduct of the different *yugas*) and *āpaddharma* (the morality of the times of distress). The description of these *dharmas* is as follows:

Sādhāraṇa-Dharma (*Universal Moral Code*)

Sādhāraṇa-dharma means the moral code which is common for all the human beings. This universal code consists of the moral virtues to be observed by everybody, to whatever caste or creed, he or she may belong. There are many important examples of morality in the whole *Mahābhārata*. The important properties of these is recognized and emphasized by all religions. Some important moral virtues are given below:

Satya (*truthfulness*): According to *Mahābhārata, satya* is the fundamental necessity for the moral life. It is considered as the highest duty and nothing is greater than this.[104] *Satya* is the basis of all things and it has the property to make people prosperous if they act according to it. Its importance lies in the belief that it has the capability to purify mind.[105]

---

103 *dharmaśabdaḥ ṣaḍvidhasmārtadharmaviṣayaḥ* ǀ *tadyathā varṇadharmaḥ āśramadharmaḥ varṇāśramadharmaḥ guṇadharmaḥ nimittadharmeśceti* ǁ — *Mitākṣarā* of Yājñavalkya, ed. S.S. Setlur, Madras, 1912, I.1

104 *nāsti satyasamo dharmo na satyād vidyate param* ǀ — Ādi LXXIV.105

105 *manaḥ satyena śuddhyati* ǀ — *Manu* V.109

In Śānti-Parva, Bhr̥gu describes the merits of *satya* and condemns *asatya*. According to him:

> Truth is Brahmā; truth is penance; it is the truth which creates all creatures. Truth sustains the entire universe and it is with the help of truth that one goes to heaven. And untruth is only another shape of darkness. It is darkness that leads downwards. Those who are possessed by darkness, cannot see the bright regions of heaven. It also has been said that heaven is light and hell is darkness. The creatures living in this world may obtain heaven and hell. In this world truth and untruth bring on contrary indications, such as righteousness and unrighteousness, light and darkness, pleasure and pain. Amongst these "truth is righteousness; righteousness is light" and light is happiness, likewise untruth is unrighteousness; unrighteousness is darkness; and darkness is sorrow or misery.

As stated:

satyaṁ brahma tapaḥ satyaṁ satyaṁ visr̥jate prajāḥ |
satyena dhāryate lokaḥ svargaṁ satyena gacchati ||

anr̥taṁ tamaso rūpaṁ tamasā nīyate hyadhaḥ |
tamograstā na paśyanti prakāśaṁ tamasā "vr̥tāḥ ||

svargaḥ prakāśā ityāhurnarakaṁ tama eva ca |
satyānr̥taṁ tadubhayaṁ prāpyate jagatīcaraiḥ ||

tatrāpyevaṁvidhā loke vr̥tti satyānr̥te bhavet |
dharmādharmau prakāśaśca tamo duḥkhaṁ sukhaṁ tathā ||

tatra yat satyaṁ sa dharmo yo dharmaḥ sa prakāśo yaḥ prakāśastat sukhamiti |
tatra yadanr̥taṁ so'dharmo yo'dhaprmastat tamo yat tamastadduḥkhamiti ||

—ŚP CXC.1-5

In *Mahābhārata* there are many examples of untruth being given preference over truth. In Ādi-Parva and Śānti-Parva it is described that shelter of falsehood is allowed only when one's life is in risk on the occasion of marriage, for the protection of wealth to maintain the dignity of *dharma*, when the assets have been taken away along with ladies, for the sake of preceptor:

na narmayuktaṁ vacanaṁ hinasti na strīṣu rājanna vivāhakāle ।
na gurvarthaṁ nātmano jīvitārththaṁ pañcānṛtānyāhur pātakāni ॥
— Ādi LXXXII.16-17, see also ŚP CLXV.5-6

Truth assumes the colour of untruth, when truth is dissociated from righteousness. Maharṣi Gautama allows untruth when it is urgently needed for the protection of good people's life and restricts it when it is about to be used as the protector of the wicked persons.[106] He is of the view that an infant, old man, idiot, insane, angry and a frightened man cannot be considered a sinner even if he speaks lie.[107] Manu is also in favour of sweet truth and not in support of a pleasing untruth.[108] In short, it can be said that in all situations truth is always superior to that of untruth, but sometimes it is permissible to indulge in falsehood.

Ahiṁsā: In modern day it is defined as non-violence. According to ancient Indians it is a practice of love, which aims not to hurt anybody by any means such as *manasā, vācā, karmaṇā*. To think always good for others also comes under its criteria. *Mahābhārata* also emphasizes it in many places. As stated in Ādi and Śānti-Parva, respectively:

ahiṁsā paramo dharmaḥ sarvaprāṇabhṛtāṁ vara ।
— Ādi XI.13
na bhūtānāmahiṁsāyājyāyān dharmāsti kaścana ॥
— ŚP CCLXII

Brahmacarya: It is a discipline to control over the sense-organs. When one leads life with celibacy, self-discipline and continence, dedicated to higher pursuits, one overcomes all difficulties.[109]

---

106 Gautama XIII.

107 Gautama V.

108 *Manu* IV.138.

109 *ye tapaśca tapsyanti kaumārabrahmacāriṇaḥ* ।

Dama: In the epic the virtue which is a means to control over the sense-organs has also been emphasized. The importance of this virtue is discussed in *Bhagavadgītā*, a section of *Mahābhārata*. There in Kṛṣṇa tells Arjuna that sense-organs should be completely checked.[110] Even the attachments towards their objects should be abandoned.

While describing the attributes of *sthitaprajña* and *guṇātīta*, the ideal man of *Gītā*, this moral virtue is described.[111] One should draw his sense-organs from the worldly objects like a tortoise that draws in its limbs. Vidura compares the human body with a *ratha* (chariot), *sattva* (living principle) being its charioteer, sense-organs as horses and *buddhi* (intellect) as reins. One who does not make control over these horses can never be free from the bondage of birth and death.[112]

Kṣamā (*forgiveness*): One who possessed with this power is praiseworthy. One should forgive only deserving persons, never to the bad and wicked people.[113] Yudhiṣṭhira also speaks about *dharma*. According to him, everyone should have this virtue *kṣamā;* because of this virtue one becomes victorious. Giving the reference of Kaśyapa, he says that forgiveness is *dharma*, sacrifice (*yajña*), the Vedas, knowledge, the brāhmaṇa, truth (*satya*), penance (*tapas*) and purity (*śauca*). This universe is combined together because of the concept of forgiveness. He is indeed a wise man, who forgives even those who

---

vidyāvedavratasnātā durgāṇyatitaranti te ॥ — ŚP CX.14

110 Bhīṣma XXVI.14.

111 Ibid. XXVI.

112 *rathaḥ śarīraṁ bhūtānāṁ satvamāhustu sārathiṁ* ।
indriyāṇī hayānāhuḥ karmabuddhistu raśmayaḥ ॥

teṣāṁ hayānāṁ yo vegaṁ dhāvatāmanudhāvati ।
sa tu saṁsāracakre'smiścakravat parivartate ॥
— Strī VII.13-14

Cf. *ātmanaṁ rathinaṁ viddhi śarīraṁ rathameva ca* ।
buddhiṁ tu sārathiṁ viddhi manaḥ pragrahmeva ca ॥
— *Kaṭhopaniṣad* I.III.3

113 ŚP CVIII.30.

insulted and rebuked him. One who has the quality of forgiveness (*kṣamā*) attains *Brahman*. He receives honour here and acquires a state of blessedness hereafter. Hence it is the most important virtue.[114]

Śīla: Next most important virtue is *śīla* which means good behaviour. The importance of *śīla* lies in the belief that *dharma, satya, vṛtta* (conduct) are dependent upon it. As stated in Śānti-Parva:

> *dharmaḥ satyaṁ tathā vṛttaṁ balaṁ caiva tathāpyaham* ।
> *śīlamūlā mahāprājña sadā nāstyatra saṁsayaḥ* ॥
> — ŚP CXXIV.62

For instance, it is described in the narrative of Prahlāda, who was devoid of all the virtues because he gave away his character as a boon to Indra, who approached the former in the disguise of a brāhmaṇa.[115] There are many other important virtues like *madhura vacana, śaraṇāgata-rakṣā* (protecting a suppliant) and *atithi sevā.*

Gautama Dharmasūtra VIII.20-21, *Manusmṛti* VI.20-21, *Arthaśāstra*[116] and *Śukranītisāra* III.1 also mention these virtues.

In Śānti-Parva CX Yudhiṣṭhira requests Bhīṣma to describe the ways of how to overcome difficulties and adversities. In reply Bhīṣma refers to some moral virtues and says that persons who are free from difficulties and calamities are those who are self-controlled (*saṁyatātmano*), who are not involved in the objects of sense-organs (*viṣayān nigrahyanti*), who are not proud (*dambhannacaranti*), who are not jealous of others prosperity (*parariyā na tapayante*), who do not commit sins (*pāpaṁ na kurvanti*), who speak truth (*vadantīha satyāni*), who do not do to others what is disagreeable to themselves, i.e. who treat others in the way they want themselves to be treated (*yeṣām ātmasamo loko*)[117] and in whom the *sattva guṇa* is dominant.

---

114 Vana XXIX.13-14.

115 ŚP CXXIV.

116 *Arthaśāstra* (tr. R. Shamasastry, 5th edn), p. 10.

117 *na tatpareṣu kurvīta jānannapriyamātmanaḥ* ।
— ŚP CCLIX.20

Viśiṣṭa-Dharma

Viśiṣṭa-dharma stands for *dharma*, specifically laid down for the dfferent persons or groups of persons.

Varṇa-Dharma

From very ancient times we found that the Hindu society was made up of four types of *varṇa*s (castes). Puruṣa-Sūkta of *R̥gveda* X.90.12 is an evidence to this classification. These four *varṇa*s are: brāhmaṇa, kṣatriya, vaiśya and śūdra. According to *Bhagavadgītā*, specific duties of four *varṇa*s have been described in the whole section of *Mahābhārata*, with their characteristics.[118]

The duties of brāhmaṇas are also described in the epic.[119] According to the epic they should observe fasts, attend religious discourses, follow the injunctions of Vedas, have control over their sense-organs, etc. In *Bhagavadgītā*, Kr̥ṣna describes the duties of brāhmaṇas. These are peace, self-restraint, religious austerities, straightforwardness, knowledge and should be of *āstīkya buddhi*:

śamo damastapaḥ śaucaṁ kṣāntirrājavameva ca ।
jñānaṁ vijñānamāstikyaṁ brahmakarma svabhājam ॥
— Bhīṣma XLII.42

The inherent duties of kṣatriyas are bravery, brilliance, courage, intentness and generosity:

śaurya tejo dhr̥tirdākṣyaṁ yuddhe cāpyapalāyanam ।
dānamīśvarabhāvaśca kṣātraṁkarma svabhāvajam ॥
— Bhīṣma XLII.43

In Śānti-Parva, R̥ṣi Mārkaṇḍeya opines that studying Vedas, protecting the subjects, performing sacrifices and dying in the battlefield are the main responsibilities of the kṣatriyas:

kṣatrajaṁ sevate karma vedādhyayanasaṁgataḥ ।

---

118 *brāhmaṇakṣatriyaviśāṁ śūdrāṇāṁ ca paraṁtapaḥ* ।
karmāṇi pravibhaktāni svabhāvaprabhavair guṇaḥ ॥— Bhīṣma XLII.41

119 ŚP LX.8-12.

dānādānaratiryastu sa vai kṣatriya uccayte ||
— ŚP CLXXXIX.5

In the same way the duties of vaiśyas are also described in the epic. Epic connects the duties of the vaiśyas with agriculture, honest trade and cattle rearing. *Kṛṣi, gorakṣya* and *vāṇijya* are the main duties mentioned in Bhīṣma-Parva.[120]

Specific duties of śūdras[121] consisted in attending upon the three higher *varṇa*s in accordance with their position, as they have their origin from the feet of the Virāṭa-Puruṣa, the supreme man or *Brahman*.[122] In Bhīṣma-Parva it is mentioned that serving higher castes is the inherent duty of the śūdras:

paricaryātmakaṁ karma śūdrasyāpi svabhāvajam ||
— Bhīṣma XLII.44

For him, moral virtues, control over the sense-organs, hospitality towards others and righteous conduct are also prescribed in Anuśāsana and Śānti-Parva.[123] *Mahābhārata* emphatically says that one should do his ordained duties properly and sincerely, because who performs his duties properly get victorious and leads to heaven.[124] Mārkaṇḍeya narrates the story of the dutiful hunter (*dharma-vyādha*) of Mithilā, who discoursed on the principle of *dharma* to a brāhmaṇa, named Kuśika. There the hunter says that glory can be earned by sticking to the code prescribed for the

---

120 *kṛṣigaurakṣyavāṇijyaṁ vaiśyakarma svabhāvajam* || — Bhīṣma XLII.44

121 *sarvabhakṣaratirnityaṁ sarvakarmakaro'śuciḥ* |
tyaktavedastvanācāraḥ sa vai śūdra iti smṛtaḥ || — ŚP CLXXXIX.7

122 *Ṛgveda* X.90; ŚP LXXII.4-5.

123 *śūdradharmaḥ paro nityaṁ śuśrūṣā ca dvijātiṣu* ||
sa śūdraḥ saṁśitatapāḥ satyavādī jitendriyaḥ |
śuśrūṣaratithiṁ prāptaṁ tapaḥ saṁcinute mahat ||
nityaṁ sa hi śubhācāro devatādvijapūjakaḥ |
śūdro dharmaphalairiṣṭaḥ samprayujyeta buddhimāna ||
— Anuśāsana CXLI.57-59, see also Bhīṣma LXXXIX.7

124 Ibid. ŚP CXCI.6.

different *varṇas*.[125] Describing the *dharma* of the all *varṇas* Kṛṣṇa in Bhīṣma-Parva says that "one's own *dharma*, even is defective, is better than the *dharmas* of others". Then the next most important *dharma* is *āśrama-dharma*. The description of this is as follows.

Āśrama-Dharma

In ancient Indian tradition four types of *āśramas* are described: *brahmacaryāśrama, gṛhasthāśrama, vānaprasthāśrama* and *saṁnyāsāśrama*. They are connected with the fourfold *puruṣārthas* (goals of life). The *āśramas* are ladders to reach *Brahmaloka*.[126] Proper observation of *āśrama-dharma* helps one to overcome all sorts of calamities and difficulties.[127]

In Śānti-Parva Bharadvāja asked Bhṛgu to describe him the four modes of life that were formerly laid by brāhmaṇas, also the practices enjoined by them. Then Bhṛgu tells him about the four *āśramas* in these words:

> *pūrvameva bhagavatā brahmaṇā lokahitamanutiṣṭhatā*
> *dharmasaṁrakṣaṇārthamāśramāścatvāro 'bhinirdiṣṭā* ।
> *tatra gurukulavāsameva prathamamāśramamudāharanti* ॥
> — ŚP CXCI.8

This means in the days of yore, the divine *Brahman*, for the behoof of the world, and for the protection of righteousness, laid down four modes of life.

Then he describes these *āśramas*.

Brahmacaryāśrama: According to him the *brahmacaryāśrama* means that *brahmacārin* was to live in the house of the *guru* (preceptor) and respect him. In this mode of life he should have his soul cleansed by purity of conduct, by Vedic rites and by restraints, and vows and humility. He should adore the morning and evening twilights the sun, his

---

125 Ibid. Vana CCII.

126 *catuṣpadi hi niḥśreṇī brahmaṇyeṣā pratiṣṭhitā* ।
etāmāruhya nīḥśreṇīṁ brahmaloke mahīyate ॥ — ŚP CCXLII.15

127 Ibid. CX.2.

own consecrated hearth and the gods. He should shake off procastination and idleness. He should purify his soul by saluting his preceptor by studying the Vedas. He should perform his ablutions thrice.[128]

Gṛhasthāśrama is the second *āśrama*, after *brahmacaryāśrama*. One should pay *guru-dakṣiṇā* (preceptor's fee) and then marry to lead the life of a householder and a worldly man.[129] Śānti-Parva establishes the superiority of this *āśrama* over others by calling it their foundation:

> *taddhi sarvāśramāṇāṁ mūlamudāharanti* ।— ŚP CXCI.10
>
> *śāstradṛṣṭaḥ paro dharmaḥ sthito gārhasthyamāśritaḥ* ॥
> — ŚP XXIII.2

In this *āśrama,* a *gṛhastha* should realize the *trivarga* consisting of *dharma, artha* and *kāma*. It is the period in which one can pay back the debts that one owed to gods, guests, dependents and ancestors by performing sacrifices, by studying Vedas, performing the rites of *śrāddha* and by doing good to others. As stated in Śānti-Parva:

> *samāvṛttānāṁ sadācārāṇāṁ sahadharmacaryaphalārthinā gṛhāśramo vidhīyate* । *dharmārthakāmāvāptirhyatra tri-vargasādhanamapekṣyāgarhitena karmaṇā dhanānyādāya svādhyāyopalabdhaprakarṣeṇa vā brahmarṣinirmitena vā adrisāragatena vā* । *havyakavyaniyamābhyāsadaivataprasādopa-labdhena vā dhanena gṛhastho gārhasthyaṁ vartayet* ।[130]
>
> Those who having completed their residence in the preceptor's abode return home, who are of pious conduct, who desire the fruits of a virtuous course of behaviour with spouse in their company, have this mode of life ordained for them. In it virtue, wealth, and pleasure,

128 ŚP CXCI.8: *samyag yatra śaucasaṁskāraniyamavrataviniyatātmā ubhe saṁdhye bhāskarāgnidaivatānyupasthāya vihāya tandryālasye gurora-bhivādanavedābhyāsaśravaṇapavitrīkṛtāntarātmā triṣavaṇamupaspṛśya brahmacaryāgniparicaraṇaguruśuśrūṣānityabhikṣābhaikṣyādi sarva-niveditāntarātmā guruvacananirdeśānuṣṭhānāpratikūlo guruprasāda-labdhasvādhyāyatatparaḥ syāt* ॥

129 Anuśāsana CXLI.37.

130 ŚP CXCI.10.

> may all be obtained. It is (thus) suited to the cultivation of the triple aggregate. Acquiring wealth by irreprochable acts, or with wealth of high efficay which is obtained from recitation of the Vedas, or living upon such means as are utilized by the regenerate *ṛṣi*s, or with the produce of mountains and mines, or with the wealth represented by the offerings made in sacrifices and on the termination of vows and other observances, and those made unto dieties, the householder should lead this mode of life.

Vānaprasthāśrama: In this *āśrama*, one leads the life of a forest dweller. It is the life of contemplation and of gradual withdrawal from worldly ties.[131] According to Śānti-Parva, after passing through *brahmacaryāśrama* and *gṛhasthāśrama*, one should leave for the forest, with or without his wife[132] in his old age when his hairs become grey and when the grandchildren are born.[133] He should sleep on bare ground, worship gods, perform sacrifices, practice celibacy and self-control, forgiveness, purity and eat roots and fruits. He should wear the clothes made from the animal skin and bark of the trees.[134] One should follow strictly the rules prescribed for this stage, because the person who, with controlled soul, follows such duties, consumes all his sins like fire and acquires blissful regions for themselves which are so difficult to attain. As stated:

> *yastvetāṁ niyataścaryāṁ brahmarṣivihitāṁ caret sa dahedagnivaddoṣān jayellokāṁśca durjayān* ||
>
> —ŚP CXCII.2

Saṁnyāsāśrama: After the *vānaprasthāśrama*, one has to enter the *saṁnyāsāśrama*. In Śānti-Parva *saṁnyāsī* is called as *parivrājaka*. Bhṛgu describes the conducts of *parivrājaka*s that they should allineate

---

131 ŚP CXCII.1.

132 ŚP LXI.3-4.

133 *gṛhasthastu yadā paśyed valīpalitamātmanaḥ* |
apatyasyaiva cāpatyaṁ vanameva tadā śrayeta ||
tṛtīyamāyuṣo bhāgaṁ vānaprasthāśrame vaset || — Ibid., CCXLIV.4-5

134 ŚP CXCII.1.

themselves from attachment to the sacred fire, wealth, wife and children, and robes, seats, beds and such other objects of enjoyment, and snapping the fetters of affection, they walk about, keeping an equal eye on a clump of earth or rock or gold.[135] It is also said that a *saṁnyāsī* should always be free from anger (*roṣa*), delusion and ignorance (*moha*) and should practise *yama*[136] and *niyama* consisting of *satya* (truth), *ahiṁsā* (non-violence), *asteya* (non-stealing), *brahmacarya* (discipline and celibacy), *aparigraha*, *śauca* (purity), *santoṣa* (contentment), *svādhyāya* and *īśvara-praṇidhāna* (devotion to God).[137] By leading such a restrained and disciplined life, one attains salvation according to *Mahābhārata*.[138] So it specifies that *dharma* is the essence of all conducts.

Thus, in *Mahābhārata*, ethics has been deemed to be a normative science dealing with the conduct of human being. In Śānti-Parva some confusion is created when Yudhiṣṭhira asks a question to Bhīṣma whether *dharma* (ethics) and *rājya* (politics) are two different things?

> *dharmacaryā ca rājyaṁ ca nityameva virudhyate* ।
> *evaṁ muhyati me cetaścintayānasya nityaśaḥ* ॥
> — ŚP XXXVII.37.4

In answer to this question Bhīṣma replies that all the *dharma*s are contained in *rājadharma*,[139] both are same. *Rājya* (politics) is the theoretical aspect and *dharma* (ethics) is the practical aspect. Hence, it can be said that they are closely connected and interdependent. Politics creates the atmosphere wherein one can persue the goals of life as laid down by ethics. The ethics of *Mahābhārata* aims at putting proper checks and limitations on an unrestricted course of life with the view

---

135 Ibid. CXCII.3.

136 Ibid. CCXLIV.

137 *yameṣu ahiṁsāsatyāsteyabrahmacaryāparigrahāravyeṣu cāt-śauca saṁtoṣatapaḥ svādhyāyeśvarapraṇidhānākhyeṣu niyameṣu svaśāstreti* ॥
— Nīlakaṇṭha's commentary on ŚP CCXLIV. 30

138 ŚP chap. CCXLV specially the *śloka*s 21-36.

139 *trivargo hi samāsakto rājadharmeṣu kaurava* । — ŚP LVI.4

to maintain peace and order in the society and leading to the general welfare. The purpose of *dharma* is not only to establish peace and order in the society, but who follows it gets the final goal (salvation) for what he desires.

Ethics, as concieved in *Mahābhārata*, aims at salvation, purification and uplift of the individual soul for realizing its true nature as the essence of the universal soul. The goal of liberation is the absolute in which the liberated souls merge. At some places, it regards the attainment of heaven as the final goal of human life and as the end of ethics. *Mahābhārata* repeatedly says that one can realize the ultimate goal by following the above-mentioned moral code, by properly performing one's ordained duties without thinking of, and caring for, the fruits derived therefrom. It advocated renunciation of inaction and not the renunciation of action. It is described as *niṣkāma-karma* (detached action). Otherwise, in the situation of delusion (attached action or *sakāma karma*), emancipation is not possible.[140] So *niṣkāma karma* is the bedrock of the ethics as conceived in Śānti-Parva.[141]

In the Western conception, there is no such a connection between ethics and politics. According to Aristotle the aim of ethics is the highest human good what they aim, but generally refers to happiness. From the above accounts it clear that Aristotle's *Ethics* aims only at how to live happily (or related with the good of the individual). Aristotle's *Ethics* states that the good of the individual is subordinate to the good of the city state. But there is no interconnection between ethics and state (politics). To Plato ethics and politics are not separate branches of learning. Plato's problem was to realize virtue. For this, he made politics subservient to ethics and his state, guided by moral standards, was to help the individual in the realization of the life of virtue. The state itself has the moral purpose. It could not abandon moral standards, for it could alone make its citizens moral.

140 *tatra cet sampramuhyeta dharme rājarṣisevite* |
loksaya saṁsthā na bhavet sarvaṁ ca vyākulībhaveta || — Ibid. LVI.6

141 Jauhari, 1968, *Politics and Ethics in Ancient India*, p. 56.

Aristotle differs from Plato. He gave to politics the character of an independent science by distinguishing it from ethics without drawing a clear-cut line of demarcation between the two. His politics is triological being a combination of ethics, because it aimed at virtue; economics, because it dealt with the science of the satisfactory management of the household; and politics, which is the science of the state. According to him, man is a social and political being. He has to live in the state for realizing his highest self. The functions of the state are not merely to protect its people from enemies, prevent them from violating each other's rights and to prevent them if they do so; it is to realize the moral ends also. He regards state as a moral and spiritual entity and, hence, emphasizes the necessity of its membership for the attainment of good life. So according to him there is no co-interring relation between ethics and politics. The actual states of Greece were neither ethical association nor were guided by ethical standards. In them ignorance masqueraded as wisdom and selfishness guided the actions of statesmen and individuals. So their thinking about ethics and politics is quite different from that of *Mahābhārata*, because *Mahābhārata* establishes their co-interrelation and interdependency. According to *Mahābhārata* politics and ethics have same end — the attainment of *mokṣa*. This is quite different from the main thinking of the West, because there politics and ethics (in combination) do not deal with salvation.

It is necessary to say that in some contexts both *Mahābhārata* and the views of the West are quite different from each other. But in some contexts their ideologies are similar.

Conclusion

Mahābhārata gives a comprehensive account of Indian political thought, the highest watermark being reached in Śānti-Parva, known as "Rājadharmānuśāsana Parva". The study of *Mahābhārata* reveals that it is the core text of Indian polity. It is a gold mine for the researchers and scholars. Śānti-Parva has an abundant material related to political ideas and institutions. The challenge of the present work was to find out the political ideas in Śānti-Parva vis-à-vis the political ideas of the West.

Each of the foregoing chapters has been concerned with some aspect of political development in the epic tradition. It is desirable to look upon certain points which have emerged in the present study. Though *Mahābhārata* appears to be posting different patterns of thought, a careful attempt to synthesize them reveals some unity of purpose among them.

While working on *Mahābhārata*, we have come across many difficulties such as the uncertainty of its authorship, the date of events as well as composition. These defects, however, do not lessen the importance of the work, especially when one bears in mind the vast time factor, the changes, editions and redactions it had undergone in different ages, resulting in the voluminous size it has attained.

There is a widespread belief among scholars that the Western thought is the foundation of political thoughts, and the modern political system is the result of their efforts. Political science mainly focuses on the study of state and government. The state, its stages of development and its function are the main concerns of politics. To understand politics, it is a the painful necessity to know the idea of liberalism.

Liberalism on political side promotes democracy, and it is concerned with fulfilling the needs and aspirations of ordinary people. It is also concerned with the concept of a welfare state. Liberalism is one idea committed to freedom as a method and policy in government, as an organizing principle in society and a way for organizing the doctrine of liberty.

In ancient India, political science was known by several terms like *daṇḍanīti, arthaśāstra, nītiśāstra, rājanītiśāstra* and *rājadharma.* These terms were used to denote what we call politics today. In Śānti-Parva, the term *daṇḍanīti* is used in the sense of politics. According to Śānti-Parva *daṇḍanīti* was necessary for the establishment of peace, prosperity, happiness and welfare of people and the society. The fundamentals of politics were related with the state.

Theoretical aspect of the state includes it origin, evolution and function. It is very complicated, because it is related to *dharma.* The area of *dharma* is very wide and it is a core point of discussion in *Mahābhārata*. Because of its enormity it was not possible to describe the whole ideas of *dharma* in Śānti-Parva. Accordingly, it was concentrating only on *rājadharma*, which was the greatest of all *dharma*s, as far as Śānti-Parva was concerned. It is not erroneous to say that all the *dharma*s find their refuge in *rājadharma*. Practical aspect of the state includes the principles and applications of the state and its institutions.

The state (*rājya*) was conceived to be an entity of beneficial institutions which were primarily brought into being for the welfare of its citizens. To be more precise, the state was the guardian of *dharma* which was an embodiment of justice. It is clear from the contents of the treatise dealing with the state that its scope is very wide. Salvation is regarded as its ultimate aim. This proves that according to Śānti-Parva, the end purpose of politics was ethical.

The state, denoted by terms *rājya, rāṣṭra* and *janapada* in Śānti-Parva, consists of seven elements, and they are regarded as the political institutions. They are *swāmī* (king), *amātya* (minister, i.e. officers of a state), *janapada* (population), *durga* or *pura* (fort or fortified capital), *mitra* (allies), *kośa* (treasury) and *daṇḍa* (army). These institutions were very important for the proper functioning of the state.

The maintenance of law and order (*dharma* of respective *varṇas*) was the king's primary responsibility and it had been vested with the permanent authority wielding *daṇḍa*, he was an appointing authority of *purohita* and other ministers. Law was enshrined in religious texts and customary uses. That was only to enforce according to *deśa-dharma* and *rājadharma*. Finally the king was under the moral obligation to visit *āśramas* and *tāpasas* enquire about their welfare.

Coming to the next constituent of the state, it is observed that a king was assisted in the task of administration by a council of ministers. It was constituted of *mantrins* who were qualified, skilled, virtuous and possessed sufficient knowledge of the state affairs. Śānti-Parva no doubt alludes to a political organization well developed on certain norms. Administration was constituted of *amātyas* and *sacivas*. It also included *mantrins*. They were the executive heads of the state's administration.

The capital was the power centre of the state and it finds the next important institution of the state. Being invariably, fortified both by natural and artificial means, it was known as *durga* or *pura* and it was distinguished from the rest of the country which was termed as *rāṣṭra*. *Daṇḍa* occupies an important place in *saptāṅga* theory of state. Its importance has been realized in the field of judiciary, administration of treasury as well as in the sixfold policies and four *upāyas*. It is considered as the cardinal element of state.

Allies commanded an important position though Śānti-Prava does not focus on the *maṇḍala* theory, yet the application of sixfold policies as well as four *upāyas* supports one's thinking that political thinkers of ancient India propounded such principles to minimize the chances of war and establish peace. In this context the aim of the composition of Śānti-Parva was to ensure peace and order in the society for what the whole world is struggling.

Though, all these political institutions (seven constituents) have no relevance in modern politics, they have their own significance in their times when they were established. In modern politics four constituents like state, population, territory and sovereignty are referred, they are different in their functions and activities in modern time, while we found some indication of seven constituents in the modern constituents.

The study of the concept of the state in *Mahābhārata* remains incomplete unless the interstate relations are discussed. In this context, the thinkers of the epic have discussed the relevance of *mitra* under the *saptāṅga* theory of state. The relation between *swāmī* and *mitra* finds an important place in interstate relations. In the context of *Mahābhārata*, interstate relations denote the meaning of foreign policy of the state towards another state or a sovereign ruler. Although international law and international relationship as conceived in our times cannot be said to have prevailed in ancient India, in *Mahābhārata* they are found in a rudimentary form. It classifies different states under four heads, viz. friendly states or allies (*suhr̥d* or *mitra*), inimical states (*śatru* or *ari*), neutral states (*udāsīna*) and intermediary (*madhyastha* or *madhyagata*) states. This classification is based on the following kinds of relationship with the foreign states: hostility, neutrality, meditation and friendship. *Mahābhārata,* like other ancient works, prescribes the *ṣāḍguṇya*s, the six expedients of foreign policy, such as *sandhi, vigraha, āsana, saṁśaya* and *dvaidhībhāva*. The fourfold foreign policy, consisting of *sāma, dāna, daṇḍa* and *bheda* are also described in the epic.

The concept of *maṇḍala*, the circles of state, is discussed in the epic. Like *Arthaśāstra*, *Manu-Smr̥ti* and *Nītiśāstra*, the epic holds the view that *maṇḍala* consists of seventy-two elements. *Mahābhārata* also discusses about the diplomatic agents and these have been classified under two heads, viz. ambassadors (*dūta*) and spies (*cara*). Concept of stationing the envoys in foreign countries in *Mahābhārata* is just opposite to the modern concept. In modern day they are placed in foreign countries as permanent agents while during the time of *Mahābhārata* they were only temporary officers and the concept was in rudimentary form. They had to perform manifold functions but they were concerned mainly with the vital questions of foreign policy. Since they had to perform important duties, they had to be highly qualified. *Mahābhārata* mainly emphasizes on the sacredness and inviolability of ambassadors.

Spies, however, were a prominent and permanent feature of the state. They were to be appointed by the ruler to collect information about the internal affairs and the administration of his kingdom as well as foreign states. Ancient Indian states were inclined to regard the spies as highly indispensable and their work was considered to be of utmost importance. Hence, they were scattered throughout the kingdom and also in foreign states. Manu, Kauṭilya, Śukra and Somadeva Sūri also endorse this practice. Secrecy was the characteristic feature which distinguished them from the modern envoys. They could be roughly handled, if found out. *Mahābhārata* gives a list of persons, who could be assigned this risky task. According to it the prosperiety of the enemy was a cause of concern and his misfortunes were of happiness to a king. Hence, a king should resort to all means, righteous and unrighteous to put his enemy down. But an audit of evidence shows that the place of morality in the foreign affairs varies in inverse ratio from that of its place in the internal affairs of state.

When we talk about the forms of government we found that in *Mahābhārata* monarchy was the most popular form of government, but sometimes it also gives the examples of non-monarchical states. Several types of monarchical states are referred, the biggest type was *sārvabhauma*. Yayāti, Dambodha and Bharata have been mentioned as *sārvabhauma* kings. There were many other states like *ādhipatyam* and *dvairājya*. *Ādhipatyam* type of state's sovereignty was accepted by other states, which also offerred tributes to the sovereign king. Such states retained their internal autonomy. The Kurus had established such a state. In *dvairājya* there is rivalry between two kings who jointly rule. *Mahābhārata* furnishes Avantī as an example of this type of state which was ruled jointly by two brothers named Vinda and Anuvinda. *Mahābhārata* does not refer to it directly, but it is said at three places. There are also other evidences to prove the existence of *dvairājaya*.

We are informed by the Greek historians that at the time of Alexander's invasion, the kingdom of the Pāṭala was being ruled jointly by two kings, who belonged to two different dynasties. Next type of state was *ekarājyaṁ* and this is opposite to *dvairājyaṁ*, in which the state was not divided among many brothers and they were not made as joint rulers. It was ruled by a single person. Vidura had advised Dhṛtarāṣṭra not to divide the state between his sons and Pāṇḍavas but to coronate Yudhiṣṭhira for the establishment of *ekarājyaṁ*. *Yauvarājya* is another type of the monarchical state in which the prince had the upper hands in administrative affairs.

Śānti-Parva also refers to anarchical types of state. The existence of the non-monarchical states in ancient India has been brought to light by many scholars, being K.P. Jayaswal the pioneer. They come to the conclusion that along with monarchy other types of governments were also known to the ancient Indians. The information about non-monarchies varies in inverse ratio to that of the monarchies. Due to scanty or little information, we have to depend on the casual references to them, scattered throughout *Mahābhārata*. In Śānti-Parva the following types of non-monarchical states have been mentioned:

Arājaka state is that where there is no ruling authority. Another type of non-monarchical state is *kula-rājya* (rule of the families). Kauṭilya also hints at the existence of such states. In Śānti-Parva, Bhīṣma says that in such a type of state, greed and jealousy lead to its destruction.

Gaṇa-rājya is another non-monarchical type of state. *Mahābhārata* also provides the link to know the great and long history of these *gaṇa-rājya*s (republics). Republics is the modern political term which is generally used in the place of ancient *gaṇa-rājya*. Bhīṣma has given details about *gaṇa-rājya*: about their functions, structures and their concept of morality.

The word *gaṇa* has been a riddle for the scholars, who have interpreted it variously. To Fleet, it means "tribes", F.W. Thomas interprets the word as the "governing body" or "the senate" and to

Hopkins it is "corporations of every sort" and for N.N. Ghosh, "local corporations". Literally the word *gaṇa*, taken as a verb, means to count, to number or to enumerate.

While taken in the sense of a noun, it denotes an assembly or group. Keeping in view the context of its use and its characteristics, its best explanation will be "the rule of many", which is evidently a form of non-monarchy. And it stands for a type of non-monarchical state as proved also by the internal evidences of *Mahābhārata*. *Mahābhārata* informs that Arjuna defeated several *gaṇa*s.

Though *Mahābhārata* does not deal with all types of non-monarchical states and their morals in explicit terms, casually it refers to the relation between *gaṇa* and *saṅgha-rājya*. From such passages it is easy to infer that the place of morals in non-monarchies was as important as in monarchies. Sometimes it was emphasized more in the former than in the latter, because in the case of the former the existence and security of a state depended upon the morality of the people as a whole whereas in the latter, mostly it was upon the morality of the king. Thus it says that the members of *gaṇa* should avoid greed, ignorance, jealousy, *krodha* and *bheda*. They should respect their elders and women. But the state affairs, in practice, were sometimes, specially during the decadent periods, just the contrary theory. *Gaṇa*s were in fact the seats of the evils mentioned above. Even a great diplomat Kr̥ṣṇa is found complaining to Nārada that he was the target of severe and unhealthy criticism, also hard word and abuses. Dissatisfaction and party politics were quite dominant. Thus it actually fell short of the ideal status even among the non-monarchical states.

On account of judiciary, *Mahābhārata* was committed to *dharma*. The thinkers of *Mahābhārata* laid down certain norms to be followed by the officers in-charge of the judicial system with a view to impart true justice to the people. They ensured that there was no delay in delivering justice to the people. They believed that delay in ensuring justice would give many evils to creep into the society. The epic regards *dharma* as the root of the state, hence the enforcement of law is necessary for its existence. The *daṇḍa* is the coercive but an effective power given to the king for regulating the life of the subjects. In *Mahābhārata* it has been asserted that the king gets prosperity if he inflicts punishments after examining the cases and finding out the real offenders.[1] In Śānti-Parva it is clearly stated that at the time of imparting justice, the king must be impartial to all who have violated the existing *dharma* of the state or country.

Śānti-Parva while referring to the administration of justice mentions many a time *dharma* and *daṇḍa*. In order to know the judicial system, it is imperative to know about the concept of *dharma*. *Dharma* is a comprehensive term. Though it is translated into English as religion, it does not convey a complete and true meaning. *Dharma* stands for a way, a path of life and a mode of conduct. The root of *dharma* is *dhṛ* which connotes the meaning to hold or support, but it has been used in different senses in epic — duty and righteousness. It also stands for law of the land as well as morality. And it should be regarded as the embodiment of all those rules and means which prevent evil from the world, particularly evil in human life.

The king was the regulator of *dharma*, but he was not above *dharma*, hence it is clear that *dharma* was the root of justice in *Mahābhārata*. Even the judges were subject to the provisions of *dharma* and for delaying justice, they were liable to be punished under the judicial procedure established by *dharma*. Establishment of *dharma* has been proclaimed to be an important function of the state in the epic which goes to the extent of saying that it is for the course of *dharma* that sovereignty exists. For the realization of this function, a state is given the right to exercise *daṇḍa* (coercion). *Daṇḍa* was regarded capable of restraining the natural turbulence and depravity of men, which led them to violate different rules and regulations. It was *daṇḍa* which made them follow *dharma*. In the absence of it chaos prevailed and people did not perform their duties properly.

The epic does not present a systematic organizational structure of judiciary, though mention has been made of *prāḍa-vivāka* in Śānti-

1 Udyoga XXXIII.86.

Parva, which may be equated with the Chief Justice of present time, who was a prominent person in the field of judicial administration, who examined, cross-examined, investigated the whole matters and pronounced a decision. He was the judicial officer appointed by the king. However, no specific qualification is mentioned regarding the post of Chief Justice in the epic. Yet merit and virtues were always given priority in the appointment of judges. There were many judges, besides the Chief Justice, to administered justice in different courts established by the state. The epic refers to the qualification of judges: Dhṛtarāṣṭra advises Yudhiṣṭhira to appoint such persons as judges who are reliable and have purity of ideas. The king was considered to be the supreme head of the judicial administration; generally, he was seen in *sabhā-maṇḍapa* surrounded by the priest and ministers for imparting justice. In the organization of judiciary, *purohita*, also played an important role and was the king's chief adviser. He had to be well-versed in Śāstric knowledge. As *guru* is the *śāstā* for pupils, so is the king to evil-doers. Though the king is known as *daṇḍadhara*, it is not possible for all kings to use it properly.

In the epic the term "mutilation" is referred to many times as a kind of punishment to the culprits. For example, in Śānti-Parva the term *virūpakaraṇa* which stands for disfiguring and *vyaṅgyatā* which stands for body are the two terms denoting mutilation. It is prescribed for the offence of robbery. King was the final authority of appeal from lower courts, though his dicision was depended on *dharma*. The king was the main appointing authority of the judges. The relation between the judges was always normal and king administered the law and justice with the cooperation of *prāḍa-vivāka*. His all judgements were under the command of *dharma*. Judiciary was committed to *dharma* in epic tradition, though it should not be understood in the present sense of committed judiciary.

Ancient Indian thinkers did not clearly demarcate the areas of law, religion and ethics. In *Mahābhārata* the same tendency is noteworthy. *Mahābhārata* lacks a precise and particular term for ethics. In *Mahābhārata*, the words *dharma*, *nīti*, *ācāra* and *sadācāra* are used to define the term ethics. The epic itself does not believe in the absolute uniformity and universality of moral standards, which change according to time. Hence, in the epic *dharma* has been classified under the following heads: *sāmānya-dharma* (universal moral code), *āśrama-dharma* (code of conduct for different *āśrama*s, i.e. stages of life), *varṇa-dharma* (code of conduct of the different *varṇa*s), *guṇa-dharma* (code of conduct prescribed for one), *naimittika-dharma* (acts done with a special purpose, e.g. expiatory rites), *yuga-dharma* (code of conduct for the different *yuga*s) and *āpaddharma* (morality at the time of distress).

In *Mahābhārata*, ethics has been deemed to be a normative science dealing with the conduct of human beings, living in the society. End of ethics in epic is the realization of salvation, the ultimate goal of human life. Thus, according to *Mahābhārata*, politics and ethics have a common end, the attainment of salvation.

The social and political life of the people was grounded on *dharma*, which was embodied not only on the entire set of ethical virtues but also on various rules of outward conduct applicable to an individual at any specific time and place. It can be said briefly that politics (state) and ethics (*dharma*) in Śānti-Parva have one and the same end, the attainment of *mokṣa*. Politics creates an environment where one can pursue the goal laid down by ethics. Both are thus complementary and interconnected.

It is concluded that *Mahābhārata* is considered as the precious gem of Indian political thought, it is the oldest one which informs about the political institutions, i.e. state, government, etc. and also about the principles and ideas of politics. It informs about the duties of a king, known as *rājadharma*, which is not discussed in any other text in such a form and in depth.

Therefore, it is a little effort from my side to find the political ideas and principles discussed in Śānti-Parva. Śānti-Parva is the largest *parva* among the eighteen *parva*s of *Mahābhārata*, which comprises one-sixth of the total content of *Mahābhārata*. Because of its length and time factor, many may opt not to read all the *śloka*s deeply and seriously. This book may help them in finding out the nuances of politics in *Mahābhārata.* If the epic is read by scholars deeply and seriously, they can unearth a lot of political ideas. This modest and little effort, I hope, will initiate the scholars for further researches in this area.

Thus this study is extremely relevant for all concerned vis-à-vis the state, government and people of India at large. This study will help academicians, researchers and others for taking necessary steps for the larger interest of the society.

Bibliography

Primary Sources

DIRECT

Mahābhārata, ed. V.S. Sukthankar et al., 19 vols, Poona: Bhandarkar Oriental Reasearch Institute (BORI), 1933-66.

Mahābhārata, ed. with the commentary of Nīlakaṇṭha Nīla, Pune: Chitrashala Press, 1956.

Mahābhārata, ed. with the commentary of Nīlakaṇṭha Nīla, 6 vols, ed. R. Kinjawadekar, New Delhi: Oriental Books Reprint Corp., repr. 1979.

Mahābhārata, tr. M.N. Dutt, Delhi: Parimal Publications, repr. 1994.

Mahābhārata, ed. Pandit Ramanarayana Dutt Shastri Pandey (6 vols in Hindi and Sanskrit), Gorakhpur: Gita Press, 1956-59.

Mahābhārata, Śānti-Parva (fifth part), Gorakhpur: Geeta Press, 1956.

Mahābhārata, in 6 vols, Citraśāla Press, vol.1 (1929); vol. 2 (1930); vol. 3 (1931); vol. 4 (1931); vol. 5 (1932); vol. 6 (1933).

Mahābhārata, Śānti-Parva (1st part), ed. P.D. Sātvalekar, Pāradī: Svādhyāya Maṇḍala, 1971.

Mahābhārata, ed. V.S. Sukthankar et al., 4 vols, BORI, Poona, 1971-75.

Mahābhārata, tr. J.A.B. Van Buitenen, 3 vols, University of Chicago, 1973-78.

Mahābhārata, tr. K.M. Ganguli, 12 vols, New Delhi: Munshiram Manoharlal, 1981 (first published 1833-96).

INDIRECT

Agni Purāṇa, Bombay: Venkteshvara Press (n.d.).

Āpastamba Dharma-Sūtra, ed. A. Chinnaswami Shastry, Banaras, 1932.

Arthaśāstra of Kauṭilya, ed. R. Shamashastry, Mysore: Government Branch

Press, 1919.

Āśvalāyana Gṛhyasūtra, ed. A.F. Stenjlar, Lipzig, 1864.

Baudhāyana Dharmasūtra, ed. L. Srinivasacharya, Mysore, 1907.

Bhagavadgītā, ed. and tr. S. Radhakrishanan, London: Ruskin House, 1953.

Bhāgavata Purāṇa, Gorakhpur: Gita Press, 2000.

Gautama Dharmasūtra, ed. L. Srinivasacharya, Mysore, 1917.

Kāmandaka Nītisāra, Ānandāśrama Series, No. 136, 1958.

Kāmandakīya Nītisāra, ed. J.P. Misra, Bombay: Venkateshvara Press, vs 2009.

Kīrātārjunīyam, Bombay: Nirṇaya Sāgara Press, 1829.

Kauṭilya Arthaśāstara, ed. V. Gairola, Varanasi, 1962.

Mahābhārata Nāmānukramaṇikā, Gorakhpur: Gita Press.

Manusmṛti, Ganganath Jha (The Laws of Manu with Bhāṣya of Medhātithi), Calcutta: University of Calcutta, 1924.

Rājadharma Prakāśa, ed. V.S.S. Agnihotri, Sangamnera, 1930.

Rāmāyaṇa of Vālmīki, Kāśī: Pandit Pustakālaya, 1951.

——— ed. & tr. Chandramani Vidyalankara, Dehradun, 1953.

Śukra Nītisāra, ed. & tr. G.P. Shastry, Shamli, Muzaffarnagar: Hindu Jagat Karyalaya, vs 1998.

——— ed. & comm. J.V. Bhattacharya, Calcutta, 1882.

Vāyu Purāṇa, Ānandāśrama Series, 1905.

Yājñavalkyasmṛti, ed. J.R. Gharpure, Bombay, 1914.

——— ed. S.S. Sellur, Madras, 1912.

Secondary Sources

Abhayankar, K.V., 1944, "The Date and Time of the Bhārata War: A New Approach on Astronomical Considerations", *ABORI*, XXV: 116-36.

Agrawala, Vasudeva Saran, 1967, *Pāṇini Kālīna Bhāratavarṣa*, Varanasi.

Aiyangar, K.V. Rangaswami, 1916, *Consideration on Some Aspects of Ancient Indian Polity*, Madras: University Printers.

———, 1936, *Some Aspects of Ancient Indian Polity*, Madras.

———, 1941, *Rājadharma*, Adyar: Adyar Library.

———, 1949, *Aspects of the Social and Political System of Manusmriti*, Lucknow.

Aiyer, K.S. Rangaswami, 1938, "Warfare in Ancient India", *The Aryan Path*, IX: 502-07.

Aiyer, P.R. Chidambaram, 1946, "So-called Geographical and Astronomical Evidence to the Mahābhārata Problem", *Journal of Ganga Nath Jha Research Institute*, IV: 35-44.

Aiyer, P.S. Sivaswami, 1935, *Evolution of Hindu Moral Ideals*, Calcutta: University of Calcutta.

Altekar, A.S., 1943, "Ancient Indian Polity and Modern Constitutional Problems", *Bhartiya Vidya*, 10.

Altekar, A.S. (ed.), 1946, *Proceedings and Transaction of All India Oriental Conference, Twelfth Session*, Banares: Banaras Hindu University.

———, 1948, *Prācīna Bhāratīya Śāsana Paddhati,* Allahabad: Leader Press.

———, 1977, *State and Government in Ancient India,* Delhi: Orient Book Distributors.

Anderson, E.R. and A.S. Johnson, 1930-67, *Encyclopaedia of the Social Sciences*, London: Macmillan Publishers.

Anjaria, J.J., 1935, *Nature and Grounds of Political Obligation in Hindu State*, London: Longmans Green.

Appadurai, A., 1954, *The Substance of Politics*, 7th edn, New Delhi: Oxford University Press.

Aristotle, 1984, *Politics*, BK VII, 4, Chicago: Universiry of Chicago.

Athavale, V.B., 1945, "The Exact Date of the Kuru War", *Journal of Ganga Nath Jha Research Institute*, III: 11-25.

———, 1947, "The Co-ordination of Bhārata Events from the Exile of the Pāṇḍavas to the Death of Bhīṣma by Determining the Tithi of the each Important Event", *Journal of Ganga Nath Jha Research Institute,* IV: 125-58.

———, 1947, "Date of Kuru War", *Journal of Ganga Nath Jha Research Institute,* IV: 293-33.

Bandyopadhyaya, N.C., 1927a, *Development of Hindu Polity and Political Theories,* Pt I, Calcutta: 15 College Square.

———, 1927b, *Kauṭilya, or, An Exposition of His Social, Ideal and Political Theory*, Calcutta: R. Combray.

Barker, Ernest, 1960, *Greek Political Theory: Plato and His Predecessors*,

London: Methuen & Co.

Belavalkar, S.K., 1948, "The Origin and Functions of the State According to Rājadharma Parva", *The Annals of the Bhandarkar Oriental Research Institute*, 29: 293-301.

Benerji, Suresh Chandra, 1972, *Smṛti Material in the Mahābhārata*, Calcutta.

Bhambhari, C.P., 1959, *Substances of Hindu Polity*, Meerut: International Publishing House.

Bhandarkar, D.R., 1929, *Some Aspects of Ancient Indian Polity,* Banaras: Banaras Hindu University.

Bhasam, A.L., 1954, *The Wonder that Was India*, London: Sidgwick and Jackson.

Bhasin, R.V., 2007, *Mahabharata*, Delhi: National Publications.

Bhattacharaya, A.N., 1972, *Dharma–Adharma and Morality in Mahābhārata*, Delhi: S.S. Publishers.

Bhattacharya, H.D., 1937, "The Meaning of Dharma", *Proceedings and Transactions of Ninth All-India Oriental Conference*, pp. 640-57.

Bhattacharaya, P., 1984, *The Secret of Mahābhārata*, Aurangabad: Parimal Prakashan.

Bhattacarya, Sukhamaya, 1966, *Mahābhāratakālīna Samāja*, Allahabad.

Bhattacharya, T., 1950, "The Date of the Bhārata War", *Journal of Ganga Nath Jha Research Institute*, 8: 1-76.

———, 1951, "Date of Bhārata War", *Journal of Ganga Nath Jha Research Institute*, 8: 315-35.

Bluntschli, Johann Kaspar, 2000, *The Theory of the State*, 6th edn, Ontario: Kitchener.

Bob, J., 1987, *State Theory*, Cambridge: Polity Press.

Brockington, J., 1998, *The Sanskrit Epics*, Leiden: E.J. Brill.

Bryce, James, 1921, *Modern Democracies*, New York: Macmillan.

Buddha Prakash, vs 2014, "Mahābhārata: Ek Aitihāsika Adhyayana", *Nāgarī Pracāriṇī Patrikā*, IV: 269-92.

Bühler, Georg, 1879, *The Sacred Laws of the Aryans*, 2 vols, Asian Educational Services.

———, 1886, *The Laws of Manu*, Oxford: Clarendon Press.

Burgess, J.W., 1891, *Political Science and Comparative Constitutional Law*, vol.

1, Oxford: Ginn & Co.

Chaitanya, Krishna, 1985, *The Mahābhārata: A Literary Study*, New Delhi: Clarion Books.

Chakravarti, C., 1923, *A Study in Hindu Social Polity,* Calcutta.

Chakravarti, P.C., 1941, *The Art of War in Ancient India*, Dacca: University of Dacca.

Chandra, Suresh, 1984, *Approach to the Study of the Arthaśāstra of Kauṭilya,* Delhi: Department of History, University of Delhi.

Chatterjee, H.L., 1958, *International Law and Interstate Relations in Ancient India*, Calcutta: Banchharam Akrur Lane.

Chaturvedi, Badrinath, 2006, *The Mahabharata: An Inquiry in the Human Condition*, New Delhi: Orient Longman.

Chaturvedi, D.C., 1974, *Indian Government and Politics*, Meerut: Meenakshi Prakashan.

Chaudhari, B.B., 1984, *Indian Government and Politics*, Delhi: Sri Mahavira Book Depot Publishers, 3rd edn.

Chaudhari, R., 1949, "A Short Note on the Principles of Taxation in Ancient India", *Journal of Ganga Nath Jha Research Institute*, 7: 66-67.

Daftari, K.L., 1946, "The Date of Mahābhārata War", in *Proceedings and Transactions of All-India Oriental Conference, Twelfth Session*, vol. II, Banares: Banaras Hindu University, pp. 481-89.

Das, Bhagvan, 1959, *The Science of Social Organisation*, Madras: The Theosophist Office.

Dasgupta, S.N., 1932, *Indian Philosophy*, vol. 2, Cambridge: Cambridge University Press.

Dass, A.K., 1944, *The Economic History of Ancient India*, New Delhi: Vohra Publishers and Distributors.

Date, G.T., 1929, *The War in Ancient India*, London: Oxford University Press.

Datta, R.C., 1889, *A History of Civilisation in Ancient India*, 3 vols, London: Trübner and Co.; Calcutta: Thacker Spink and Co.

———, 1910, *The Rāmāyaṇa and the Mahābhārata*, London: J.M. Dent and Sons.

Dhar, Somnath, 1981, *Kauṭilya and the Arthaśāstra,* New Delhi: Marwah Publications.

Dharma, P.C., 1941, *The Rāmāyaṇa Polity*, Madras: The Madras Law Journal

Press.

Dikshitar, V.R.R., 1929, *Hindu Administrative Institutions*, Madras: University of Madras.

———, 1940, "Society and State in Ancient India", *The Aryan Path*, 9: 82-88.

———, 1948, *War in Ancient India*, London: Macmillan and Co.

——— 1951, *Purāṇa Index*, 3 vols, Madras: University of Madras.

Dillion, Conley H., 1958, *Introduction to Political Science*, Princeton, NJ: D. van Nostrand Company.

Divanji, P.C., 1947, "Authorship and Date of the Bhārata Epic and Bhagavad-Gītā", *Journal of Ganga Nath Jha Research Institute*, IV: 113-24.

Dreakmeter, C., 1956, *Kingship and Community in Early India*, Bombay: Oxford University Press.

Dougles, P.H., 1953, *Ethics in Government*, Bombay: Howard University Press.

Dowson, John, 1961, *A Classical Dictionary of Hindu Mythology and Religion, Geography, History and Literature*, London: Routledge and Kegan Paul.

Dunning, William Archibald, 1970, *A History of Political Theories: Ancient and Medieval*, New York: Macmillan.

Dutt, R.C., 1910, *The Rāmāyaṇa and Mahābhārata* (*Condensed into English Verse*), London: J.M. Dent.

Dutta, B.N., 1944, *Studies in Indian Social Polity*, Calcutta: Purabi Publishers.

Dunham, John, 1991, "Manuscripts Used in the Critical Edition of the Mahābhārata: A Survey and Discussion", in *Essays in Mahābhārata*, ed. Arvind Sharma, Leiden: E.J. Brill.

Ebenstein, W., 1974, *Modern Political Thought*, New Delhi: Oxford & IBH Publishing Co.

Émile, Benveniste, 1969, *Indo-European Language and Society*, tr. Elizabeth Palmer, London: Faber and Faber.

Finer, Herman, 1932, Theory and Practice of Modern Government, New York: Dial Press.

Fleet, J.F., 1888, *Corpus Inscriptionum Indicarum,* vol. III: *Inscriptions of the Early Gupta Kings and Their Successors,* Calcutta: Supernindent of Govt Printing.

Foster, Michael B., 1941, *Masters of Political Thought*, vol. I, Boston: Houghton and Mufflin.

Gamble, Andrew, 1981, *An Introduction to Modern Social and Political Thought*, London: Macmillan.

Ganguly, J.N.C., 1926, "Philosophy of Dharma (Law)", *Indian Historical Quarterly*, II: 575-86.

———, 1944, "Kingship in Ṛgveda", *Indian Historical Quarterly*, XX(1): 43-52.

———, 1948, "On the Hindu Theories of Social Contract and Divine Right", *Indian Historical Quarterly*, XXIV: 68-71.

———, 1955, "On Some Recent Interpretations on Mahābhārata, Theory of Kingship", *Indian Historical Quarterly*, XXXI(3).

Garner, J.W., 1910, *Introduction to Political Science*, New York: American Book Company.

———, 1928, *Political Science and Government*, New York: American Book Company.

Geldren, R.H., 1942, "Conception of State and Kingship in South East Asia", *The Far Eastern Quarterly*, 2N: 14-30.

Gettell, Raymond G., 1910, *Introduction to Political Science*, Boston: Ginn Co.

———, 1949, *Political Science*, 2nd edn, Boston: Ginn and Company.

Ghosh , N.N., 1925, "The Rāmāyaṇa and the Mahābhārata: A Sociological Study", *Asutosh Mukherjee Silver Jubilee Volumes*, Pt II, pp. 361-406.

Ghosh, Prasanta Kumar, 1972, *Studies in Contemporary Political Theory*, Calcutta: Minerva Associates.

Ghoshal, U.N., 1923a, *A History of Hindu Political Theories*, London: Oxford University Press.

———, 1923b, *History of Public Life in Ancient India*, vol. I, Calcutta.

———, 1929, *Contributions to the History of the Hindu Revenue System*, Calcutta: University of Calcutta.

———, 1957, *Studies in Indian History and Culture*, Bombay: Orient Longmans.

Gilchrist, R.N., 1921, *Principles of Political Science*, London and New York: Longmans, Green and Co.

Gode, P.K., 1949, "Notes on the Use of Fire-appliances in Ancient India, Greece and Rome", *Journal of Ganga Nath Jha Research Institute*, VI: 221-29.

———, 1953, *Studies in Indian Literary History*, vol. I, Bombay: Shri Bahadur Singh Singhi Memoirs, vol. 5.

Gokhale, B.G., 1952, *Ancient India: History and Culture*, Bombay: Asia Publishing House.

Grimes, A.P., 1956, "The Pragmatic Course of Liberalism", *Western Political Quarterly*, IX(3): 633-44.

Gupta, J.N., 1911, *Life and Works of Ramesh Chandra Dutt,* London: J.M. Dent & Sons.

Gupta, S.P. and K.S. Ramachandran (eds), 1976, *Mahabharata: Myth and Reality*, New Delhi: Agam Kala Prakashan.

Hacker, A., 1961, *Political Theory*, New York: Macmillan.

Hall, William Edward, 1880, *International Law,* Oxford: Clarendon Press.

Hallappa, G.S., 1996, *Dilemmas of Democratic Politics in India*, Bombay: Manaktala and Sons.

Harmon, M.J., 1964, *Political Thought: From Plato to the Present*, New York: McGraw-Hill.

Harsh, D.D., 1989, *Mahābhārata kā Artha*, Bikaner: Vāgdevi Prakashan.

Held, G.J., 1935, *The Mahābhārata: An Ethnological Study*, London: Kegan Paul.

Hermann, Grette, 1947, *Politics and Ethics*, Bombay: The National Information and Publication.

Hiltebeitel, Alf, 1990, *The Ritual of Battle, Krishna in Mahabharata*, New York: SUNY Press.

Hobbes, Thomas, 1651, *Leviathan*, part I, London: Andrew Crooke.

Hopkins, E.W., 1899, "The Social and Military Positions of the Ruling Caste in Ancient India as Represented by the Sanskrit Epic", *Journal of the American Oriental Society*, XIII: 57-376.

———, 1901, *The Great Epic of India: Its Character and Origin*, New York: Scribner's Sons.

———, 1915, *Epic Mythology*, Strassburg: Verlag von Karl J. Trübner.

———, 1924, *Ethics of India*, New Haven: Yale University.

———, 1969, *The Great Epic of India*, Calcutta: Punthi Pusthak.

———, 1989, *The Social Military Positions of the Ruling Caste*, Meerut: Bharat Bharati.

Hopkins, R.V. Basin, 1989, *Mahabharata*, Columbia: University of South Carolina Press.

Jain, Ramchandra, 1979, *Jaya: The Original Nucleus of Mahābhārata*, Delhi: Agam Kala Prakashan.

Jauhari, Manorama, 1968, *Politics and Ethics in Ancient India: A Study Based on The Mahabharata*, Bombay: Bharatiya Vidya Bhavan.

Jayaswal, K.P., 1967, *Hindu Polity*, Bangalore: Bangalore Printing and Publishers.

Jhaveri, K.M., 1940, "Ethical Discourses of Bhīṣma", *Bhāratīya Vidyā*, VI: 36-43.

Johnson, W.J., 1998, *The Sauptikaparvan of Mahābhārata*, Oxford: Oxford University Press.

Jowett, Benjamin (tr.), 1823, *The Laws of Plato*, New York: Dover Publications.

Kane, P.V., 1941, *History of Dharmaśāstra*, vols. 1 and 2, Poona: Bhandarkar Oriental Research Institute.

———, 1942-43, "The Rājyaśāstra of Bṛhaspati, Uśanas, Bhāradvāja and Viśālākṣa", *Journal of the University of Bombay*, XI(2): 73-83.

———, 1965, *History of Dharmaśāstra*, vol. III, Poona: Bhandarkar Oriental Research Institute.

Kapoor, Y.N., 1958, *Dharma Nirpekṣa Prācīna Bhārata kī Prajātantrātmaka Paramparāyeṅ*, Agra.

Kapur, A.C., 1950, *Principles of Political Science*, New Delhi: S. Chand & Co.

Karindikar, J.S., 1943, *The Month and the Date of the Mahābhārata War,* England.

Karunakaran, K.P., 1964, *Continuity and Change in Indian Politics*, New Delhi: People's Publishing House.

Katre, S.M., 1943, "Dharmopaniṣada in Mahābhārata", *Journal of Ganganath Jha Research Institute*, 1: 118-22.

Katz, Ruth Cecily, 1989, *Arjuna in the Mahabharata*, Columbia: University of South Carolina Press.

Kaveeshwar, C.W., 1972, *Chronological Secrets of Mahābhārata War*, Indore: Author.

Kaveeswar, G.V., 1985, *Mahābhārata Yuddha ke Kālagaṇanātmaka Rahasya*, 1st edn, Ujjain: Vikram Viswavidyalaya.

Kaviraj, Sudipta, 1997, *Politics in India*, New Delhi: Oxford University Press.

Konow, James, 2003, "Which Is the Fairest One of All?: A Positive Analysis of Justice Theories", *Journal of Economic Literature*, 41(4): 1188.

Kothari, R., 1970, *Politics in India,* Canada: Little Brown and Company.

Kurtakoti, "The Influence of Mahābhārata over the People of India", *Annals of Bhandarkar Oriental Research Institute*, 19: 1-7.

Laski, H.J., 1925, *A Grammar of Politics*, New Haven, CT: Yale University Press.

———, 1935, *The State in Theory and Practice,* London: George Allen and Unwin.

———, 1936, *The Rise of European Liberalism: An Essay in Interpretation*, London: Ams Press.

———, 1940, *The Danger of Being a Gentleman*, New York: The Viking Press and London: George Allen and Unwin.

———, 1961, *An Introduction to Politics*, London: George Allen and Unwin.

Law, B.C., 1984, "The Chain of Justice", *Indian Culture* (Patna), VII: 85-88.

Law, Narendra Nath, 1914, *Studies in Ancient Hindu Polity*, vol. I, London: Longmans Green & Co.

———, 1920, *Interstate Relations in Ancient India*, London: Luzac and Co.

———, 1925, "Technical Hindu Constitutions", *Indian Historical Quarterly*, 1(1): 394.

———, 1960, *Aspects of Ancient Indian Polity*, Oxford: Clarendon Press.

———, 1934, The Six Guṇas in Kauṭilya, in *K.B. Pathak Commemmorative Volume*, Poona.

Leacock, Stephen, 1912, *Elements of Political Science*, Boston: Houghton Mifflin.

Levi, Sylvain, 1933, *Sanskrit Texts from Bali Issue no. 67*, Baroda: Oriental Institute.

Locke, John and Carpenter William Seal, 1924, *Of Civil Government* (two treatises), London and Torranto: J.M. Dent & Sons.

Lucas, J.R., 1996, *The Principles of Politics*, Oxford: Clarendon Press.

Macdonnell, A.A., 1927, *India's Past: A Survey of Her Literatures, Religions,* Languages and Antiquities, Oxford: Clarendon Press.

———, 1928, *A History of Sanskrit Literature*, London: William Heinemann.

Macdonell, A.A. and A.B. Keith, 2007, *Vedic Index*, Delhi: Motilal Banarsidass.

MacIver, R.M., 1926, *The Modern State*, Oxford: Oxford University Press.

———, 1946, *The Web of Government*, New York: The Macmillan Company.

Majumdar, B.B., 1944, *Principles of Political Science and Government*, 5th edn, Calcutta.

Majumdar, R.C., 1951, *The History and Culture of the Indian People*, vol. II: *The Age of Imperial Unity*, Bombay: Bharatiya Vidya Bhavan.

Majumdar, Ramesh Chandra, 1994, *Corporate Life in Ancient India*, Delhi: Cosmo Publication.

Matilal, B.K., 1989, *Moral Dilemmas in the Mahābhārata*, Shimla: Indian Institute of Advanced Study in association with Motilal Banarsidass, Delhi.

McCrindle, J.W., 1896, *The Invasion of India by Alexander the Great*, Westminister: Archibald Constable and Co.

Mcllwain, C.H., 1932, The Growth of Political Thought in the West: From the Greeks to the End of the Middle Ages, London: Macmillan.

Mees, G.H., 1935, Dharma and Society, London: Luzac & Co.

Mehta, V.R., 1992, *Foundations of Indian Political Thought: An Interpretation*, Delhi: Manohar.

Mishra, K.C., 1987, *Tribals in Mahābhārata*, Delhi: National Publishing House.

Mishra, Kameshwar Nath, 1972, *Mahābhārata mein Lokakalyāṇa kī Rājakīya Yojanāyeṅ*, Varanasi: A.A. Bharat Manisha.

Mishra, Suresh Chandra, 1984, *Approach to the Study of the Arthaśāstra of Kauṭilya*.

Mohanty, D.K., 1997, *Indian Political Tradition from Manu to Ambedkar*, New Delhi: Anmol Publications.

Montesquieu, 2002, *The Spirit of the Laws*, tr. and ed. Anne M. Cohler, Basia C. Miller and Harold S. Stone, New York: Cambridge University Press.

Mookerjee, Girija, 1973, *Diplomacy: Theory and History,* vol. I, New Delhi: Trimurti Publications.

Morris, Christopher, 1967, *Western Political Thought*, London: Longmans Green & Co.

Mukherjee, R.K., 1931, *Hindu Civilisation*, 2 vols, Bombay: Bhartiya Vidya Bhavan.

Müller, Max, 1860, *History of Ancient Sanskrit Literature*, London: Williams & Norgak, 2nd rev. edn.

Murray, Rev. R.H., 1946, *The Individual and the State*, London: Hutchinson and Co.

Narang, S.P., 1995, *Modern Evaluation of Mahabharata*, Delhi: Nag Publishers.

Narang, A.S., 1998, *Bhāratīya Śāsana aur Rājanīti*, New Delhi: Gitanjali Publishing House.

Narayana, Ikbal, 1962, *Rājnīti-Śāstra ke Mūla Siddhānta*, Agra: Ratan Prakashan Mandir.

———, 2001, *Modern Political Thoughts*, Granth Vikas.

Oldenberg, H., 1922, *Das Mahabharata*, Göttingen: Vandenhoek & Ruprecht.

Padhi, A.P., J.K. Baral and S.C. Hazary, 2000, *Political Theory: Concepts, Issues and Ideologies*, 5th edn, Cuttack: Vidyapuri.

Pandey, R.B., 1957, *Purāṇa Index (Political)*, vol. 1, Banaras: Banaras Hindu University.

Pandey, S.L., vs 2012, *Bhīma kā Rājadharma*, Arya Nagar, Lucknow.

———, *Manu kā Rājadharma*, Arya Nagar, Lucknow.

———, vs 2007, *Jantantravāda: Rāmāyaṇa aur Mahābhārata Kālīna*, Lucknow: Avadh Publishing House.

———, *Śukra kī Rājanīti*, Arya Nagar, Lucknow.

Pantulu, J.R., 1929, "Judicial Procedure in Ancient India, *Journal of Andhra Hist. Res. Society*, 4(1-2): 33-45.

Paramavitana, S. (ed.),1955, "Some Aspects of Divinity of Kings in Ancient India", *Proceedings and Transactions of Sixteenth All-India Oriental Conference.*

———, 2007, *The Econimic History of India,* New Delhi: Vohra Publishers and Distributors.

Pargiter, F.E., 1922, *Ancient Indian Historical Tradition*, London: Oxford University Press.

Pollock, Frederick, 1895, *An Introduction to History of Science of Politics*, London: Macmillan.

Prabhu, P.N., 1954, *Hindu Social Organization*, Bombay: Popular Book Depot.

Prasad, Beni, 1927, *The Theory of Government in Ancient India*, Allahabad: The Indian Press.

———, 1928, *State in Ancient India,* Allahabad: The Indian Press.

Pusalkar, A.D., 1955, *Studies in the Epics and Purāṇas*, Bombay: Bhartiya Vidya Bhavan.

Radhakrishnan, S., 1931, *Indian Philosophy*, vol. 1, London: Luzac & Co.

Raghavan, V., 1940, "Notes on Some Mahābhārata Commentaries", *Kane*

Commemoration Volume, pp. 351-55.

———, 1958, *The Indian Heritage: An Anthology of Sanskrit Literature*, Chennai: Dr V. Raghavan Centre for Performing Arts.

Rajagopalachari, C., 2012, *Mahabharata*, Bombay: Bharatiya Vidya Bhavan.

Rao, M.R., 1945, "The Purāṇic Date of the Mahābhārata", *Journal of Ganganath Jha Research Institute*, 2: 124-43.

Rao, N. Jagannatha, 1931/1976, *The Age of Mahābhārata War*, Varanasi: Bharata Bharati Prakashan.

Rice, E.P., 1934, *The Mahābhārata: Analysis and Index*, Humphrey Milford: Oxford University Press.

Rousseau, Jean-Jacques, 1762, *The Social Contract* I & II, Published by Penguin classics, 2003.

Roy, P.C. (tr.), 1890, *The Mahabharata, Sānti Parva*, Calcutta: Bharata Press.

Roy, S.B., 1976, *Date of Mahabharata Battle*, Gurgaon: The Academic Press.

Rukmani, T.S., 2005, *The Mahābhārata: What Is Not Here Is Nowhere Else*, Delhi: Munshiram Manoharlal Publishers.

Saletore, B.A., 1963, *Ancient Indian Political Thought and Institutions*, New York: Asia Publishing House.

Saletore, B.N., 1958, *India's Diplomatic Relation with the West*, Bombay: The Popular Book Depot.

Sankar, K.G., 1930-31, "Some Problems of Indian Chronology", *ABORI*, XII: 301-61.

Sarkar, B.K., 1922, *The Political Institutions and Theories of the Hindus: A Study of Comparative Politics*, Leipzig: Von Market and Petters.

Sartori, G., 1965, *Democratic Theory*, Calcutta: Oxford and IBH Publishing.

Saxena, R.N., 1981, *Indian Social Thought*, New Delhi: Minaksi.

Sen, Amartya, 2006, *The Argumentative Indian: Writings on Indian History, Culture and Identity*, New York: Picador.

Sen, Ajit Kumar, 1926, *Studies in Hindu Political Thought*, Calcutta Chatterjee & Co.

Shamasastry, R., 1920, *Evolution of Indian Polity*, Calcutta: University of Calcutta.

Sharan, P., 1984, *Government and Politics in India*, New Delhi: Metropolitan Book Co.

Sharma, D.S., 1944, *Studies in the Renaissance of Hinduism in the Nineteenth and Twentieth Centuries*, Banaras: Banaras Hindu University.

Sharma, M.M., 1978, *Inscription of Ancient Assam*, Guwahati: Gauhati University.

Sharma, Ram Sharan, 1959, *Aspects of Political Ideas and Institutions in Ancient India*, Delhi: Motilal Banarsidass.

———, 1985, *Material Culture and Social Formation in Ancient India*, London: Macmillan.

Sharma, Urmila and S.K. Sharma, 2007, *Principles and Theory in Political Science*, vol. I, New Delhi: Attlantic Publishers and Distributors.

Shashtri, Ajay Mitra, 2004, *Mahābhārata: The End of an Era*, Shimla: Indian Institute of Advanced Study and New Delhi: Aryan Books International.

Shukla, L.R., 1949, *Nītiśāstra*, Banaras: Sanmarg Press.

Siddhanta, N.K., 1929, *The Heroic Age of India: A Comparative Study*, London: Kegan Paul & Trench Trübner.

Singh, Suryavanshi Bhagvan, 1986, *Geography of the Mahābhārata*, Delhi: Ramanand Vidya Bhavan.

Singh, G.P., 1993, *Political Thought in Ancient India*, New Delhi: D.K. Printworld.

Sinha, A.K., 1985, *Śānti Parva Meiṁ Viśleṣita Naitika Vicāra*, Allahabad.

Sinha, N.K.P., 1976, *Political Ideas and Ideals in the Mahābhārata: A Study of the First Two Parvans*, New Delhi: Oriental Publishers and Distributors.

Sinha, H.N., 1938, *Sovereignty in Ancient Indian Polity: A Study in the Evolution of Early Indian State*, London: Luzac & Co.

Sorensen, S., 1925, *An Index to the Names in the Mahābhārata: With Short Explanations and Concordance to the Bombay and Calcutta Editions,* tr. P.C. Ray, Part I, London: Williams and Norgate.

Spellman, J.W., 1964, *Political Theory in Ancient India*, Oxford: Clarendon Press.

Skinner, Quentin, 1978, *The Foundation of Modern Political Thought*, Cambridge: Cambridge University Press.

Sukthankar, V.S., 1957, *On the Meaning of Mahābhārata*, Bombay: The Asiatic Society of Bombay.

Sutton, Nicholas, 2000, *Religious Doctrines in Mahābhārata*, New Delhi: Motilal Banarsidass.

Swami, P.J., 1976, *Warfare in Ancient India*, 1st edn, Madras: G.A. Natesan & Co.

——— et al. (eds) 1971-76, *The Mahābhārata Text as Constituted in Its Critical Edition*, vols 1-5, Poona: Bhandarkar Oriental Research Institute.

Tandon, Kiran, 1994, *Bhāratīya Saṁsakṛti*, Delhi: Eastern Book Linkers.

Thadani, N.V., 2007, *The Mystery of Mahābhārata*, Delhi: Bhartiya Kala Prakashan.

Thakur, Anantlal, 1995, *Elements of Political Science in Mahābhārata*, Delhi: Delhi Dharma Hinduja International Centre of Indic Research.

Tilak, Bal Gangadhar, 1965, *Śrīmad Bhagavadgītā Rahasya or Karma Yoga Śāstra,* tr. Alohandra Sitarama, Poona: Tilak Brothers.

Tripathi, Harinath, *Prācīna Bhārata Meiṅ Rājya Aur Nyāyapālikā*, Delhi: Motilal Banarsidass.

Upadhyaya, Baldev, 2001, *Saṁskṛta Sāhitya kā Itihāsa*, Varanasi: Sharda Niketan.

Vaidya, C.V., 1904, *Mahābhārata: A Criticism*, Bombay: The Bombay Book Depot.

———, 1907, *Epic India: Or, India as Described in Mahabharata and the Ramayana*, Bombay: R.A. Sagoon.

———, vs 1917, *Mahābhārata Mīmāṁsā*, Poona: Indian Press.

Vaidya, P.L., 1937, *The Mahbhārata, Its History and Character*, *The Cultural Heritage of India*, vol. II, Calcutta: The Ramkrisna Mission, Institute of Culture.

Vaidya, R.V., 1967, *A Study of Mahabharata: A Research*, Poona: A.V.G. Prakashan.

Vajpai, A.P., vs 1998, *Hindū Rājyaśāstra*, Prayāg: Hindi Sahitya Sammelan.

Vandyopadhyaya, N.C., 1926, *Development of Hindu Polity and Political Thought*, Calcutta.

Varma, Vishwanath Prasad, 1954, *Studies in Hindu Political Thought*, Delhi: Motilal Banarsidass.

Varma, K.I., 1958, *Pācātya Rājanītika Vicāroṅ kā Itihāsa*, Banaras: Nandkishor and Bross.

Varma, V.P., 1959, *Studies in Hindu Political Thought and Its Metaphysical Foundations*, Delhi: Motilal Banarsidass.

Verma, Prativa, 1988, *Social Philosophy of the Mahābhārata and The Manusmṛti*, New Delhi: Classical Publishing Company.

Vidyālaṁkāra, Sumedhā, 1984, *Mahābhārata meiṅ Śānti Parva kā Ālocanātmaka Adhyayana*, Delhi: Eastern Book Linkers.

Vidyālaṁkāra, Satyaketu, 1999, *Prācīna Bhārata Kī Śāsana Saṁsathāyeiṅ, aur Rājanītika Vicāra*, 6th edn, New Delhi: Sri Saraswatī Sadan.

Vidyalankar, P.P., vs 1978, "Rāṣṭra ke Lakṣaṇa tathā Vicāra", *Nāgarī Pracāriṇī Patrikā*, part 2.

Vishwanatha, S.V., 1925, *International Law in Ancient India*, London: Longmans Green & Co.

Vora, Dhairyabala P., 1959, *Evolution of Morals in the Epics* (*Mahābhārata and Rāmāyaṇa*), Bombay: Popular Book Depot.

Whitney, F.L., 1960, *The Elements of Research,* 3rd edn, NewYork: Prentice Hall.

Wilimbe, Y.S., 1990, *Political and Moral Conceptions in the Śāntiparvan of Mahābhārata*, Delhi: Ajanta Publications.

William, P., 1910, *The Principles of Moral and Political Philosophy*, Dublin: M.H. Gill.

Willoughby, W.W., 1898, *An Examination of the Nature of the State*, New York: Macmillan.

———, 1924, *The Fundamental Concepts of Public Law*, New York: Macmillan.

Winternitz, M., 1927/1953, *A History of Indian Literature*, English tr. 2 vols, Calcutta: University of Calcutta.

Zakaria, Fareed, 2007, *The Future of Freedom: Illiberal Democracy at House and Abroad* (revised edn), W.W. Norton and Company Inc.

Thesis and Dissertation

Anjana (Kumari), 2001, "Dharma in Mahābhārata", New Delhi Centre of Historical Studies, JNU, New Delhi.

Aneja, Harbanslal, 1982, "Critical Study of Ethical Values in Śānti-Parva of Mahābhārata", Kurukṣetra.

Datta, Kusuma, 1989, "WMahābhārata ke Śānti-Parva meiṅ Dharma kā Svarūpa evaṁ Vivecanā", Kurukṣetra.

Deopurkar, 1952, "Philosophical Trend in Śānti-Parva of Mahābhārata", Ramchandra Trimak, Bombay.

Kumar, Deo, 1979, "Philosophy of Āpaddharma in Śānti-Parva of Mahābhārata", Aligarh.

Mani, Diwakar, 2008, "Online Indexing of Ādi-Parva of Mahābhārata", Special Centre for Sanskrit Studies, JNU, New Delhi.

Singh, Balraj, 1999, "Rājadharma as Described in Mahābhārata", Rohtak.

Singh, Rajamani, 1984, "Rājadharma in Mahābhārata", Avadh.

Dictionaries and Encyclopaedia

SANSKRIT

Amarakośa, Amarasingh, Bombay: Nirṇaya Sāgara Press, 1961.

Bhāratīya Darśana Paribhāṣā Kośa, Dīnānātha Śuklā, Delhi: Pratibha Prakashana, 1993.

Śabdakalpadruma (5 vols), Radhākāntadeva, Delhi: Chaukhamba Samskrta Granthamala, T.N.73, 1967.

Mahābhāratakośaḥ, Ramkumar Roy, Delhi: Chaukhamba Samskrta Samsthana.

Vācaspatyam (6 vols), Vāraṇasī: Chaukhamba Samskrta Granthamala, T.N.94, 1961.

ENGLISH

A Dictionary of Philosophy, A.R. Lacey, London: Routlege & Kegan Paul, 1976.

A Dictionary of Hinduism, Margret and James Statly, New Delhi, 1986.

Encyclopedia of Indian Philosophies, ed. Karl H. Potter, Delhi: Motilal Banarsidass, 1995.

Encyclopedia of Religion, New York: F. Vergilious, 1945.

Encyclopaedia of Religion and Ethics, vols V and VIII, Edinburgh: T.&T. Clark 1912, 1915.

English-Sanskrit Dictionary, Monier-Williams, Delhi: Munshiram Manoharlal, 1976.

Practical Sanskrit-English Dictionary, V.S. Apte, Delhi: Motilal Banarsidass, Vikrami Samvat, 2022.

The Student's Sanskrit-English Dictionary .V.S. Apte, Delhi: Motilal Banarsidass, 2015.

Internet Sources

http://www.wikipaedia.com

http://www.britanica.com

http://www.hindunet.com

http://mahabharata-resources.org

http://www.indopedia.org/Mahabharata.html

http://www.experiencefestival.com/mahabharata

http://www.mahabharata-resources.org-commentaries

http://www.rogerdarlington.co.uk/Indianpoliticalsystem.html

http://www.tradechakra.com/india-political-system.html

http://www.en.wikipedia.org/wiki/Politics

http://www.en.wikipedia.org/wiki/Politics_of_India

http://www.en.wikipedia.org/wiki/Political_science

http://www.en.wikipedia.org/wiki/Krishna_in_the_Mahabharata

http://www.en.wikipedia.org/wiki/Mahabharata

http://www.newworldencyclopedia.org/entry/Mahabharata

http://www.mahabharata-resources.org/mbh_comm.html

http://www.mahabharata-resources.org/

http://www.rogerdarlington.co.uk/Indianpoliticalsystem.html

http://en.wikipedia.org/wiki/Nicomachean_Ethics

http://en.wikipedia.org/wiki/Politics_(Aristotle)

Index